TEACHING OF
LIFE SCIENCES

TEACHING OF LIFE SCIENCES

Mrs. K. YADAV
M.Sc., M.Ed.

ANMOL PUBLICATIONS PVT. LTD.
NEW DELHI - 110 002 (INDIA)

ANMOL PUBLICATIONS PVT. LTD.
Regd. Office: 4360/4, Ansari Road, Daryaganj,
New Delhi-110002 (India)
Tel.: 23278000, 23261597, 23286875, 23255577
Fax: 91-11-23280289
Email: anmolpub@gmail.com
Visit us at: www.anmolpublications.com

Branch Office: No. 1015, Ist Main Road, BSK IIIrd Stag
IIIrd Phase, IIIrd Block, Bengaluru-560 085 (India)
Tel.: 080-41723429 • Fax: 080-26723604
Email: anmolpublicationsbangalore@gmail.com

Teaching of Life Sciences

First Edition, 1993

Reprint, 1996, 1997, 1998, 2001, 2003, 2004, 2005

Reprint, 2006, 2007, 2008, 2011, 2014

PRINTED IN INDIA

Printed at Balaji Offset Press, Delhi

Preface

'Teaching of Life Sciences' deals with the latest in the field of life sciences education world wide. It takes into consideration the recent changes in content and methodology in the teaching of life sciences. The quality of education depends on the quality of teachers imparting education. The quality of teachers can be improved to some extent by providing them in-service training in addition to pre-service training. These aspects of education have been given due consideration in the text.

The basic purpose of writing this book is to provide a comprehensive matter of contents and methods of teaching life sciences for the students of B.Ed. classes in Indian Universities. Most of the topics dealt with in the book primarily deal with the conditions prevailing in India.

The material from reports of various education commissions and committees have been included at appropriate places to support and emphasise a point. Works of many other authors have been consulted during the preparation of the book. The author expresses his deep sense of gratitude to all such persons.

Author also places on record his thanks to a number of colleagues and friends for their invaluable suggestions for improvement of the book.

My thanks are also due to Mr. J.L. Kumar of M/s Anmol Publications for publishing this book.

Suggestions for the further improvement of the book shall be thankfully accepted.

Author

Contents

Chapter 1

Introduction

1.1 WHAT IS BIOLOGY?

Biology refers to the life sciences, comprising two major disciplines Zoology and Botany. It is included in general science and forms an important part of the syllabus of general science.

It is also a part of nature study which is an essential part of the curriculum of primary school child. The object of nature study is to develop the childs' sensitiveness and to make him feel at home with nature.

Biology defies classification as one particular form of knowledge as it must necessary deal with all kinds of discipline. Biologists must therefore prepare themselves to admit ignorance.

1.2 PLACE OF BIOLOGY IN SCHOOL CURRICULUM

In primary schools biology forms a part of general science course or it is taught as *environmental science* or as *natural history*. Even when biology exists as a separate subject, there is increasing awareness of its relative importance with consequent increase in time allotted to it. More time has to be allotted to biology because it is a time consuming subject. Animals and plants are unpredictable; growth and seasonal factors have to be considered; experimental work is rarely clear cut and field studies are time consuming.

In most countries, biology, in some form, is compulsory at primary school stage and sometimes even upto high school stage. In higher classes biology is given about 6 periods a week. In school system where biology is available as an elective subject about 80% students opt for it. It is the most popular of the sciences and continues to grow in popularity relative to other subjects in the curriculum.

Place of Life Science Education in India

Jawahar Lal Nehru, the first Prime Minister of India strongly advocated the science education. In any science education programme life science has its own important place and it has a direct bearing on the welfare of the society.

The importance of science education was also stressed in its report by Kothari Commission. According to the report of Kothari Commission, "There is of course, one thing about which we feel no doubt or hesitation. Education science based and in coherence with Indian culture and values can alone provide the foundation as also the instrument for nations progress, security and welfare". It further says, "Science education should be an integral part of school education and ultimately become a part of all courses at university stage".

No doubt, science based education is acquiring its prominent place in Indian schools due to sustained efforts of the educational authorities. Life science is developing as a compulsory subject in the science education scheme in our schools. The quality of science education would depend upon the facilities available and the quality of teachers of this subject.

1.3 BRANCHES OF LIFE SCIENCE

Life science or biology can be broadly divided into the following main sub-divisions:

(*i*) Botany
(*ii*) Zoology
(*iii*) Visology

However the disciplines of biology are of the following type.

1. Applied disciplines
2. Pure or fundamental.

Some important branches of biological sciences are as under:

1. **Agriculture.** It is the branch of biology that deals with the science of crops, plants, soil management, fertilizers etc.
2. **Organic Evolution.** It is the branch of biology that deals with the origin of newer type of organisms from the previous type by modification.

3. **Physiology.** It is the branch of biology which deals with the study of all types of body functions.
4. **Paleontology.** It is the branch of biology that deals with forests or remains of plants and animals in rocks of different ages.
5. **Embryology.** It is the branch of biology that deals with the study of early development of living beings from fertilized egg.
6. **External Morphology.** It is the branch of biology that deals with the study of external structure and relative positions of various body organs.
7. **Genetics.** It is the branch of biology dealing with heredity or inheritence of characters including variation of parents with off-springs.
8. **Forestry.** It is the branch of biology that deals with the study and management of forests, trees and forest products.
9. **Histology**. It deals with the study of tissues or details of internal structure by means of a microscope.
10. **Space Biology.** It refers to the study of effects of space conditions on various types of organisms and creation of self-regulated atmosphere on other planets, space-platforms etc.
11. **Cytology.** It refers to the study of the cell including its various aspects such as its form, structure, functions etc.
12. **Eugenics.** It deals with the improvement of human race.
13. **Ecology.** It deals with the study of living organism in relation to their living beings, from fertilised eggs.
14. **Internal Morphology.** It deals with the internal structure. It is further sub-divided into Anatomy, Cytology, Histology etc.
15. **Morphology.** It is the branch of biology dealing with the study of form and structure of living beings. It is furthur divided into internal morphology and external morphology.
16. **Microbiology.** It is the study of microscope organism particularly those connected with human welfare.

17. **Animal Husbandry.** It deals with the care and improvement of domestic animals.
18. **Anatomy.** It is the study of gross internal structure that can be seen with the naked eye after dissection. In case of plants Anatomy is equivalent to Histology.
19. **Taxonomy.** It is the branch of biology that deals with the nomenclature and classification or arrangement of organism into groups.
20. **Pathology.** It deals with the study of different kinds of plants and animal diseases including their causes and cures.
21. **Parasitology.** It refers to the study of parasitic forms.
22. **Radiation Biology.** It is the branch of biology that deals with the study of effects of radiations on organism. It includes the effects due to X-rays, β-rays, γ-rays etc. It deals with the study of good as well as ill effects of these radiations.

1.4 EDUCATIONAL ROLE OF BIOLOGY

The relative popularity of biology reflect a changing emphasis in the philosophy of curriculum. In past more stress was given to the descriptive and taxonomic subject matters in teaching of biology but now-a-days more emphasis is laid on the concept of evolution and the history of life on earth. Since evolution now is considered more of a law than a theory, more emphasis is laid on teaching of mechanism of evolution than that on the details of structure and taxonomy.

The outdated and imbalanced content has been replaced by modern discoveries in the fields of cell biology, basic genetics, bioengineering and biotechnology. For example, knowledge of details of the reproductive system of the earth worm or the life cycle of the slime mould are replaced by an understanding of the principles of reproduction and of general concepts of life cycles. Newer areas such as ecology, demography and population genetics give meaning to studies of diversity and evolution.

In place of giving training to students to prematurely become specialists in narrow fields the knowledge is imparted in general understanding of the principles and broad values of biology. Stress is now placed on application of, big ideas of biology, in community affairs. So instead of merely describing the ecology of rain forest, consideration is given to the issue of whether or not rain forests should be logged for timber, cleared for crop growing or flooded by hydro-electric schemes. Questions of environmental and biological management and the resolution of such conflicts in society are increasingly seen to be a central concern of the biology programme. School biology is seen as performing a social role. In some countries emphasis is on overcoming alcoholism, drug abuse, obesity, occultism, pseudo-religious mysticism and other counter-productive social trends. It also helps in programmes of family planning, health and nutrition, agricultural policies and the utilisation of natural resources.

1.5 SCOPE OF TEACHING LIFE SCIENCES

Most young children come to school eager to learn. They are alive with curiosity, on edge to explore among other things the wonderland of nature, animate and inanimate. Nature study should thus be an essential part of the curriculum at the primary school stage.

The object of nature study is to develop the child's sensitiveness and to make him feel at home with nature. For this the teacher should create the proper atmosphere and stimulate the interest in normal child by birds, butterflies, fishes and flowers. For this the teacher should himself be interested in nature. He should develop his powers of observation and should cultivate a love for animal and bird life along with a scientific understanding.

Nature study is the study of nature at first-hand in all its branches – plant, animal and physical; it is not a superficial or simple course of botany in which a few common flowers, plants and trees are studied in relation to seasons. It is an inquisitive, appreciative, and intelligent outlook on natural phenomena. It is not designed to produce naturalists it aims to deepen the interest of the child in the world around him and to train him in the habit of careful observation and clear thinking.

The subject is important because of the following reasons:

1. It makes later work in biology and other sciences.
2. It has practical utility in its relation to gardening and health.

3. It trains children to be observant, develops their reasoning power, educates hand and eye, and produces respect for life and a humane consideration for everything living.

"The aim of the course is to teach the children to make observations, to talk and write about what they observe, to acquaint them with the wonder and beauty of nature and with certain simple natural phenomena and processes, and to give them through this knowledge an appreciative love of nature and her ways".[1]

Nature study should not be taught by object lessons. The child should be made to observe and handle each specimen, and encouraged under the guidance of the teacher to use his own reasoning powers about the subject of study.

The teacher should use heuristic method – asking questions and stimulating questions.

The subject of study should be vitalized, so that it appeals to children.

Outdoor excursions should form a premier feature even if they have to be confined to parks and open spaces, and when material is used in the classroom it should preferably be living material. Living insects and small animals may be kept in school for certain periods under conditions of food and environment as near as possible to those in which they are found.

A seasonal method of treatment will be useful. Natural phenomena appropriate to each period can be thus dealt with. The relations between the weather, the condition of the ground, vegetable and animal life should be clearly impressed, so also the interdependence of all living things – plants, animals, and man.

Visits to the zoo, the museum and the local nursery should be encouraged.

Experimental work will be possible in a school garden or even a small outdoor plot. Besides, pupils will get opportunities to make rockeries, pools and sundials. If a garden does not exist, plants should be grown in flowerpots and, if possible, botanical specimens should be displayed. Plants grown in flower-pots offer good opportunities for

[1] Brown, John, *Teaching Science in Schools* (University of London Press), p. 76.

simple experimental work indoors—the effect of light on growth of plants, conditions favourable for germination, respiration and transpiration.

The collective instinct of pupils should be used in encouraging them to make collections of leaves, flowers and other specimens. These collections will lead to the growth of a school museum.

In the life science course for pupils in the middle stage, *i.e.*, between the ages of 10 or 11 and 13 or 14, should provide for some instruction in the elementary principles of hygiene.

The course will naturally be simple and treated in a general, non-technical way. Lessons in the form of talks and discussions are recommended. The pupils should be made to feel the whole time that the subject under discussion is of great importance to them. Simple experiments on respiration, the purification of water, etc., may be performed by the students as also by the teacher.

For topics to be included, the following be considered as sufficient:

Water—Sources; properties; purification for domestic purposes; uses.

Air—Two chief constituents; properties of oxygen; importance of nitrogen in the atmosphere; impurities in air; ventilation; carbon dioxide; respiration and circulation; uses of green plants.

Food and Drink—Uses; importance of healthy food; chewing of food; digestion; temperance.

Diseases—A few common infectious diseases; disinfection; malaria, plague, etc.

Personal Hygiene—Cleanliness of eyes, ears, teeth, etc.; clothing; exercise; sleep.

At the high school stage, this subject stands as a separate one in a group of elective optionals.

A few points for the guidance of the teacher of this subject are given below:

1. In addition to teaching the prescribed course, certain interesting thing of common interest be also referred to on suitable occasions. For example, muscular and tissue

repair after injury should be mentioned during a lesson on the muscular system, and the process of nerve regeneration during a lesson on the nervous system.

2. Pupils should learn that the human body is a combined physical, chemical and biological laboratory, and they should never lose an opportunity of finding applications of these sciences to bodily health.
3. General talks on social applications of modern hygiene and on village sanitation and public health should form part of the course.
4. An account of greater workers—Jenner, Pasteur, Lister, Ross—who laboured to reduce the suffering of humanity must be included.
5. The story of man's endeavours to combat disease may be correlated with history and geography—leprosy and plague in the East, scurvy on long sea-voyages, healthy and unhealthy parts of the world, tropical diseases, malaria and the Panama Canal.

Teaching of Biology

Biology forms an important part of the syllabus of life science. It is a compulsory subject for the Higher Secondary School Examination. While the basic principles of teaching science apply equally well to the teaching of biology, there are certain special points which the teacher of biology must keep in view.

1. The subject should not be taught merely by object lessons instead living materials should be used in the classroom to the maximum possible extent. Nature should be shown as a complete whole. Natural relationship and interdependence of life must be maintained.
2. Pupils should handle each specimen so as to observe things for themselves. They should be encouraged to think, to reason and to draw inferences from what they observe. For proper teaching of this subject schools should possess a small aquarium, a vivarium and a garden plot. Pot-plants, caged birds, insects and botanical specimens are quite

helpful for schools situated in big cities where it may not be possible to acquire a plot for the school garden.

3. The teacher should illustrate lessons with experiments and encourage pupils to perform simple experiments themselves. They can, for example, grow some plants and study for themselves the conditions favourable for germination etc.
4. Excursions to the countryside, local gardens, parks, nursery, natural history museums, and the zoo must be encouraged to provide students an opportunity for getting first-hand information.
5. While on an excursion, students be asked to collect flowers, leaves and other natural history specimens. These can later be placed in the school science museum.
6. Outdoor work must be supplemented by class demonstrations to stress important points. Students be asked to write out accounts of what their observations and be encouraged to draw diagrams.
7. Biology may be considered as a science in action in day to day life. It is, therefore, essential that lessons in this subject should be closely connected with the daily life of pupils and with their environments and surroundings.
8. Life science should not be treated as a collection of topics from different sciences but should be taken as a whole. Biology should not, therefore, be taught in isolation from other branches of science but in correlation and coordination with them.

1.6 IMPORTANCE OF LIFE SCIENCE

The study of life science is becoming important because of the following:

(*i*) Population education can be arrested by proper teaching of life science.

(*ii*) Life science teaching helps in use of national resources systematically.

(*iii*) It encourages and helps to develop healthy living conditions.

(*iv*) It helps to produce good breed of animals and healthy crops.

(*v*) It is a must for career planning.

(*vi*) Its study is good for student's curiosity.

(*vii*) Its study helps in modern living.

(*viii*) It improves scientific understanding and develops human thinking and love.

(*ix*) It helps in the control of diseases.

It has been truly said that as science and technology progress it encourages the study of some subjects. Most of the effort in science teaching is directed, these days, to improve conditions of life and in tackling the new problems that arise. Therefore the importance of life science teaching in schools is increasing. The study of life sciences is quite helpful in eradication of certain problems. With the fast changing times more and more emphasis is put on the health of country man. India shall need specialists in the fields of medicine, health, agriculture, animal husbandary etc. The talent in these fields shall come from the life science. It is for these reasons that the subject has become so popular in our secondary schools and is taught as a compulsory subject in secondary schools. It has now been realised that life science has a great role to play and so it be given its proper place in school curriculum.

Chapter 2

Aims and Objectives of Teaching Life Sciences

2.1 INTRODUCTION

Teaching of any subject become much effective and more systematic only when the teacher is fully aware of the aims and values of teaching of life sciences. Because, the basic principle of teaching is "know what you do and only do what you know". Hence, we have to understand the aims and values of teaching life sciences.

2.2 AIMS OF TEACHING LIFE SCIENCES

The following criterion is used to select the aims and objectives of teaching life science.

(*i*) This knowledge should help the pupil in his daily life.

(*ii*) It should be related to the materials with which the pupil is familiar and should not be based on obsolete devices and ideas.

(*iii*) It should make the pupil fit for society.

(*iv*) It must provide him some practical experiences which form a part of his learning process.

(*v*) It should train the student in methods of life sciences.

(*vi*) It should develop scientific attitude and science – related values among students.

2.3 OBJECTIVES OF TEACHING LIFE SCIENCES

According to the Dictionary of Education, objective is "the end toward which a school sponsored activity is directed". Effecting tangible changes in pupil's behaviour is the end of schooling. Such goal is known as objective.

The objectives of a topic in life sciences help in realising some general aim of teaching life sciences. The characteristics of a good objective are as under:

(*i*) It should be specific and precise.

(*ii*) It should be attainable.

Instructional Objectives

A set of more specific objectives suitable to the subjects and the pupils and such specific objectives which bring about perceptible behavioural changes in pupils when subjected to instructions are known as "Instructional objectives". They are stated in terms of the learner's behaviour.

Major Instructional Objectives

The major Instructional objectives are as under:

(*i*) The pupil acquiring the knowledge of a subject *i.e.* Physics Chemistry Botany or Zoology.

(*ii*) Understanding the subject.

(*iii*) Application of acquired knowledge of a specific subject.

(*iv*) Developing skills in a specific science.

(*v*) Appreciation of a subject.

Hierarchial Order of the Instructional Objectives

The hierarchial order of the instructional objectives are as under:

(*i*) Knowledge

(*ii*) Understanding

(*iii*) Application

(*iv*) Skill knowledge is the basis for understanding. Understanding leads to Application. Application develops skill.

Benjamin Bloom has mentioned three domains of objectives. They are

(*i*) Cognitive domain

(*ii*) Affective domain

(*iii*) Psychomotor domain.

The objectives dealing with recall and recognition of knowledge and development of intellectual skills were brought under cognitive domain.

Objectives relating to interests, attitudes, value appreciation and adjustment were included under the affective domain. The psychomotor or motor skill domain has not yet been classified into objectives.

Cognitive Domain Objectives

The Cognitive domain includes six educational objectives. They are as under:

(*i*) knowledge of functional facts, terms concept etc.

(*ii*) comprehension involving translation, interpretation and extrapolation.

(*iii*) application involving steps in problem solving.

(*iv*) analysis splitting the whole into its component parts.

(*v*) synthesis involving assembling of parts.

(*vi*) evaluation involving appropriate judgement based on evidence.

Affective Domain Objectives

The objectives in this domain are not precisely developed. Yet Benjamin Bloom proposed an order of objectives. They are as under:

(*i*) receiving which includes individual's awareness of different sources of information.

(*ii*) responding involving further activity.

(*iii*) valuing involving attitude and inter nationalisation of ideas.

(*iv*) organisation involving analysis, synthesis, resolution and establishing relationship.

(*v*) characterisation by a value or value set, the highest level of the Affective domain involving characterisation of a persons behaviours.

A brief discussion of these objectives is given below:

1. Knowledge. To impart knowledge in the basic aim of education and so it naturally is the basic aim of teaching of any subject including life science. By imparting knowledge of life science to the student it is expected that he acquires the knowledge of:

(*i*) natural phenomenon.
(*ii*) scientific terminology.
(*iii*) scientific concepts and formulae.
(*iv*) modern inventions of science.
(*v*) importance of animal life and plant life to man.
(*vi*) manipulation of nature by man.
(*vii*) correlation and inter-dependence of various branches of life-science.
(*viii*) environment.

Knowledge objective is considered to have been achieved if the student is able to recall and recognise scientific terms, facts, symbols, concepts etc.

2. Understanding. This objective considered to have been achieved if the student is able to:

(*i*) interpret charts, graphs, data, concept etc., correctly.
(*ii*) illustrate scientific terms, concepts, facts, phenomenons etc.
(*iii*) explain scientific facts, concepts, principles etc.
(*iv*) discriminate between different facts, concepts etc. that are closely related to each other.
(*v*) identify relationships between various facts, concepts, phenomenon etc.
(*vi*) change tables, symbols, terms etc. from any given form to some other desired form.
(*vii*) find faults, if any, in statements concepts etc.

3. Applications. This objective seems to be the most neglected one in our educational system. The common observation that supports it is that a science graduate fails to insert even a fuse wire in the electric circuit of his house. This objective is considered to have been achieved to a great extent if the pupil can:

(*i*) analyse a given data.
(*ii*) explain giving reasons various scientific phenomenon.
(*iii*) formulate hypothesis from his observations.
(*iv*) confirm or reject a hypothesis.

(*v*) correctly infer the observed facts.
(*vi*) find cause and effect relationship.
(*vii*) give new illustrations.
(*viii*) predict new happenings.
(*ix*) find relationships that exist between various facts, concepts, phenomenon learnt by him.

4. Skills. This objective can be considered to have been achieved if a pupil learns

(*i*) handling piece of apparatus,
(*ii*) assembling pieces of apparatus for experiment,
(*iii*) drawing diagrams and illustrations,
(*iv*) constructing things, and
(*v*) carrying our repairs of apparatus and appliances.

Thus here we aim to develop three types of skill in the pupil. These are (*a*) Drawing skill, (*b*) manipulative skill and (*c*) observational and recording skill.

The drawing skill is considered to have been achieved if pupil is able to draw labelled sketches and diagrams quickly.

The manipulative skill is considered to have been achieved if pupil is able to

(*i*) keep and handle the apparatus or specimen properly.
(*ii*) improvise models and experiments.
(*iii*) observe various precautions while handling apparatus and doing experiments.

The observational and recording skill is considered to have been achieved if the pupil can

(*i*) read correctly the instrument or apparatus
(*ii*) record observations faithfully
(*iii*) make calculations correctly and
(*iv*) draw inferences correctly.

5. Interests. To achieve this objective the pupil is provided with scientific hobbies and other leisure time activities. By providing such activities our aim is to inculcate, among pupils, a living and substaining interest in environment in which he lives.

This aim is considered to have been achieved if the pupil becomes curious and develops such an interest in life science that he is always eager and is on look out to:

(*i*) take to some interesting scientific hobby.
(*ii*) visit places of scientific interest.
(*iii*) undertake some science projects.
(*iv*) meet and interact some reputed person of science.
(*v*) read scientific literature.
(*vi*) collect specimen, scientific photographs, scientific biographics etc.
(*vii*) participate in science fair, science exhibition, science club etc.
(*viii*) actively participate in scientific debates, declamation contests, quiz etc.

6. Attitudes. Development of scientific attitude is one of the major objectives of teaching life science. The development of scientific attitude makes pupil open minded, helps him to make critical observations, develops in him intellectual honesty, curiosity, unbiased and impartial thinking etc.

This objective is considered to have been achieved if a pupil:

(*i*) becomes free of superstitions and prejudices
(*ii*) depends for his judgement only on verified facts and not on opinion
(*iii*) is readily willing to reconsider his own judgement when some more facts are brought to his notice
(*iv*) has an objective approach and
(*v*) is honest in recording and collecting scientific data.

7. Abilities. By the teaching of life science we expect to develop the following abilities in the pupil:

(*i*) ability to use scientific method
(*ii*) ability to use problem solving method
(*iii*) ability to process information
(*iv*) ability to report things in a technical language
(*v*) ability to collect scientific data from suitable source and to interpret it correctly
(*vi*) ability to organise science fair, science exhibition, science club etc.

8. Appreciation. To achieve this objective the teaching of life science has to be done in an evolutionary way. For this the curriculum should include such topics where it is possible to reveal stirring biographical anecdotes, some scientific stories having some incidents of adventure, charm and romance. It is possible to achieve this objective by teaching history of science including life stories of some scientists. This objectives can also be achieved by telling the impact of modern science on life.

This objective of teaching science may be considered to have been achieved if the pupil:

(*i*) appreciates the contribution of various scientists to human progress.

(*ii*) appreciates the history of scientific development.

(*iii*) realises the importance of science in modern civilisation.

(*iv*) takes pleasure in understanding the progress made by science.

9. Providing Vocational Career. In the modern world majority of Career Courses depend to a large extent on the basic knowledge of science. Some Vocational Courses can be taken up only by students of science, *e.g.* Engineering, medicines, Agriculture etc. For various courses offered by I.T.I's the knowledge of science is the basic requirement. Thus life science opens a vast field of opportunities for taking up any vocational course and choose a career. Not only this the knowledge of life science develops in a pupil the manipulative skills and he can easily improvise apparatus and experiments and can use his knowledge and skill to make many a common things like ink, soap, candle, chalk, cosmetics, boot polish, nail polish etc. All these provide the pupil with a profitable leisure time work.

2.4 VIEWS OF SOME COMMITTEES ABOUT OBJECTIVES OF TEACHING SCIENCE

These very objectives of teaching science have been emphasised by various commissions. A brief summary of some of these is given here.

Taradevi Report

The important seminar on an all India basis was held at Taradevi (H.P) in 1956. The following is the summary of aims and objectives of teaching science as recommended at this seminar.

The aims and objectives of teaching science at primary, middle and secondary level are as under:

(*i*) *Primary Level*. The main aims of teaching of science at primary level are:

(*i*) to arouse and maintain interest in nature and physical environment.

(*ii*) to arouse love for nature and the habit of conserving nature and natural resources.

(*iii*) to inculcate habit of observation, exploration, classification and a systematic way of thinking.

(*iv*) to develop manipulative powers and creative and inventive faculties.

(*v*) to inculcate habits of healthful living.

(*ii*) *Middle School Level.* At middle school level, teaching of life science aims at the following in addition to the aims given above:

(*i*) it aims at acquisition of a lot of information about nature and science.

(*ii*) it aims at developing ability of make generalisations and use them for solving problems in every day life.

(*iii*) it aims at understanding the impact of science on our way of life.

(*iv*) it aims to develop an interest in various scientific hobbies and

(*v*) inspire pupils by telling them stories of some great scientists and their discoveries.

(*iii*) *High and Higher Secondary Level*. At this stage the aims of teaching life science are:

(*i*) to familiarise the student with his surroundings and to make him understand the impact of science on society and thus enable him to adjust himself with his environment.

(*ii*) to familiarise him with 'scientific method' and thus to help him to develop the scientific attitude

(*iii*) to make him understand the evolution of science in the historical perspective.

Kothari Commission (1964-66)

An education commission was constituted under the chairmanship of Dr. D.S. Kothari and it made the following recommendations in its report.

(*i*) The teaching science in primary schools should aim at developing proper understanding of main facts, concepts, principles and processes in physical and biological environments.

(*ii*) The science education be imparted making use of both deductive and inductive approaches, however more emphasis be given to deductive approach.

Following recommendations were made by Kothari Commission (1964-1966) for different school stages:

1. *Lower Primary Stage*

(*i*) At this stage emphasis be put on the child's environment – social, physical and biological.

(*ii*) In classes (I) and (II) more attention be paid to cleanliness, formation of healthy habits and development of power of observation.

(*iii*) In classes (III) and (IV) more emphasis be given on personal hygiene and sanitation.

(*iv*) In class (IV) Roman alphabets be taught to the students as these are the internationally accepted symbols for units of scientific measurements. Moreover the symbols of elements and compounds are also make use of Roman alphabets.

(*v*) At this stage an effort be made to develop proper understanding of important facts, concepts, principles etc. that we come across in physical and biological sciences.

2. *Higher Primary Stage:* The teaching of science at this stage should emphasize on the acquisition of knowledge alongwith the ability of logical thinking and drawing conclusions for taking decisions at a higher level. At this stage a disciplinary approach of teaching science is favoured instead of an integrated science teaching. The teaching of physics, chemistry, botany, etc. is likely to develop more effective scientific base.

3. *Secondary Stage*

(*i*) At this stage science be taught as a discipline of mind and a preparation of higher education.

(*ii*) In lower secondary classes (class IX and X) the subjects of physics, chemistry, biology and earth sciences be made compulsory.

(*iii*) At higher secondary stage diversification of courses and provision for specialisation be allowed.

The Patel Committee (1977)

The following objectives were listed by Patel Committee for the first ten years of schooling.

(*i*) Promoting an understanding and appreciation of our cultural heritage and at the same time stimulating desirable changes in our traditional culture-pattern.

(*ii*) Making an ideal citizen as visualised in Indian constitution.

(*iii*) Releasing learning of most of its bookishness and elitist character and bring it more closer to society by introducing socially productive manual work.

(*iv*) Encouraging rationalism and scientific attitude.

(*v*) To lay more emphasis on qualities such as simplicity, integrity, tolerance and cooperation in all aspects of life.

(*vi*) Providing education to all irrespective of caste, creed, sex, age, religion, place of birth, economic position etc.

(*vii*) To provide education in such a way that it is possible to combine working and learning.

Recommendations of N.C.E.R.T.

The objectives of teaching science according to various recommendations of N.C.E.R.T. may be summarised as under:

(*i*) To explore immediate environment of the pupil.

(*ii*) To observe, record, report accurately in oral, written and graphic form.

(*iii*) To formulate precise questions about various things in environment.

(*iv*) To collect information from various sources and use it in a given situation.

(*v*) To classify objects, events, phenomenon.

(*vi*) To arrange objects and data in a sequence so as to assertain a pattern.

(*vii*) To analyse data and make inference.

(*viii*) To find some cause – effect relationship from the data available.

(*ix*) To make predictions.

(*x*) To design simple experiments.

(*xi*) To solve problems.

(*xii*) To develop an objective attitude towards experimental evidences and to make decisions on the basis of facts and data.

(*xiii*) To understand the role of Indian scientists in the development of science.

(*xiv*) To make a judicious use of national resources after their proper identification.

(*xv*) To be careful to avoid any wastage of natural resources and to take necessary steps for prevention of pollution.

(*xvi*) To correlate the knowledge of science and technology to economic and social development of the community.

(*xvii*) To place due emphasis on scientific knowledge in everyday life.

(*xviii*) To make proper use of scientific knowledge for development of desired social and moral values.

(*xix*) To develop instrumental, communicational and problem solving skills.

(*xx*) To develop scientific attitude, spirit of cooperation, scientific temper and scientific approach.

Objectives of Biology Teaching as Recommended by Central Board of Secondary Education

The following objectives were outlines by Biology Committee for biology instruction for Class IX and X:

(*i*) Development of awareness of, interest in and inquisitiveness towards the environment so that the student acquires knowledge of the essential biological facts, concepts, principles, processes, terms, etc. based on the elementary knowledge of living organisms.

(*ii*) To make student understand and appreciate the unity rather than the diversity in the structure, organs, existence and development of living organisms and to recognise the relationship between structure and function.

(*iii*) To put more stress on the relevant and important aspects like environmental conservation, pollution, position of man in biosphere and his impact on it.

(*iv*) To provide a balanced view of biology so that the student may develop a modern outlook of the subject.

(*v*) To enable the student to recognise the social and economic implications of biology and relate it to the needs of mankind in the widest sense.

(*vi*) To develop the skills in observation and experimentation.

(*vii*) To encourage in the student creativity, innovation and improvisation.

(*viii*) To enable the student to carefully assess and interpret simple biological phenomena from daily life.

(*ix*) To help students to acquire a working knowledge of those portions of physics, chemistry and mathematics which are necessary for proper understanding of biology.

The Biology books for secondary classes were prepared keeping the above objectives in view.

2.5 SCIENTIFIC ATTITUDE

One of the major aims of teaching life sciences is the development of *scientific attitude* in the pupil. Following are some of the various aspects included in the scientific attitude:

(*i*) Making pupils open minded.

(*ii*) Helping pupils make critical observations.

(*iii*) Developing intellectual honesty among pupils.

(*iv*) Developing curiosity among pupils.

(*v*) Developing unbiased and impartial thinking.

(*vi*) Developing reflective thinking.

NSSE (National Society of the Study of Education) has defined scientific attitudes as "open mindedness, a desire for accurate knowledge, confidence in procedures for seeking knowledge and the expectation that the solution of the problem will come through the use of verified knowledge".

The views regarding scientific attitude expressed at a work shop conducted by the National Council of Educational Research and Training (NCERT) at Chandigarh in 1971 can be summarised as follows. A pupil who has developed scientific attitude.

(*i*) is clear and precise in his activities and makes clear and precise statements.

(*ii*) always bases his judgement on verified facts and not on opinions.

(*iii*) prefers to suspend his judgement if sufficient data is not available.

(*iv*) is objective in his approach and behaviour.

(*v*) is free from superstitions.

(*vi*) is honest and truthful in recording and collecting scientific data.

(*vii*) after finishing his work takes care to arrange the apparatus, equipments etc. at their proper places.

(*viii*) shows a favourable reaction towards efforts of using science for human welfare.

2.6 TECHNIQUES FOR DEVELOPING SCIENTIFIC ATTITUDES

In the previous pages an effort was made to define the term '*scientific attitude*'. By developing scientific attitude in a person certain mind-sets are created in a particular direction. Such mind-sets may be developed either by direct teaching in schools or by out of school experiences gained by the pupil. Though out of school experiences contribute to a large extent yet according to *Curtis* direct teaching does modify the attitude of young pupil.

Tyler also made some suggestions for planning learning experiences in order to inculcate scientific attitude in the pupil. These are summarised below:

(*i*) The increase in the degree of consistency of the environment helps in developing and inculcating scientific attitude in the pupil.

(*ii*) The scientific attitude can be inculcated in a pupil by providing him more opportunities for making satisfying adjustments to attitude situations.

(*iii*) The scientific attitude can also be developed in the pupil by providing him opportunity for the analysis of problem or situation so that a pupil may understand and then rest intellectually in desirable attitude.

Role of Science Teacher

The major role can be played by the science teacher in developing scientific attitudes among his students and this he can do by manipulating various situations that infuse among the pupils certain characteristics of scientific attitudes. He can also help in developing a scientific attitude among his students if he possesses and practices various elements of these attitudes. The practical examples given by the teacher leaves an indelible mark on the personality of his students.

Teacher can use one or more of the ways for developing scientific attitude among his pupils.

(*i*) *Making use of Planned Exercises*: A large number of exercises for development of certain scientific attitudes are reported by various journals and magazines. Teacher can frequently use such exercises for developing certain scientific attitudes among the pupils. He can also make use of cuttings from newspapers and science magazines and can display such materials on bulletin board so that it is used again and again for direct teaching.

Exercises which are always included in good text books can also be used by the teacher for developing scientific attitude among his pupils.

(*ii*) *Wide Reading*: On the basis of a study conducted by him, *Curtis* reported, that those pupil who engage themselves in wide reading in science, develop scientific attitudes more than those who study only one textbook. Thus a teacher should encourage his students to read library books and supplementary books on science. For this it is essential that each school at least has a science corner in its library. The teacher himself must be in habit of making proper use of science library so that his students get encouragement for use of science library. The teacher himself be familiar with the latest new titles in his subject and he willing to share his joys of new readings with his pupils. He should refer some suitable books to his students.

Writing about teachers, Dr. Rabinder Nath Tagore has observed, "A teacher can never truly teach unless he is still learning himself. A lamp can never light another unless it continues to burn its own flame. The teacher who has come to the end of his subject, who has no living traffic with his knowledge, but merely repeats his lessons to his students, can only load their minds. He cannot quicken them".

(*iii*) *Proper use of Practicals Period:* A student of science gets many an opportunities for learning scientific attitudes during his practical periods. It is for the teacher to properly use such opportunities for developing scientific attitudes amongst his pupils. Teacher should take extra care to state the problem of the experiment and should present hypotheses on solution. He should practice the proper method of testing the hypothesis. He should actively participate in discussion and interpretation of results after the experiment. He must inculcate in his students the habit to postpone judgements in the absence of sufficient evidence to support a hypothesis.

(*iv*) *Personal Example of the Teacher:* Personal example of the teacher is perhaps the single greatest force that is helpful in inculcating the scientific attitudes amongst his pupils. Psychologists have found a great tendency amongst the students to copy their teachers. In this regard some have stated, "As is the teacher, so is the student". It is therefore essential that science teacher is free from bias and prejudices while dealing with his pupils. He should have an open mind and be critical in thought and action in his everyday dealings. He should be totally free from superstitions and unfounded beliefs and should be objective and impartial in his approach to his everyday problems. He should be truthful and should have faith in cause and effect relationship.

(*v*) *Study of Superstitions:* There are different types of superstitions that still prevail in Indian society. Simply talking of these superstitions and calling them bad and out of date, will not leave a lasting impression on the minds of the pupils. It will be more useful if the teacher can encourage at least a few of his students to carry out practicals on some popular superstitions such as that the presence of a broken mirror in any home leads to disharmony in that home or that if a cat crosses your way when you are going out for some work, then your work will not be done on that day etc. etc.

Such beliefs can easily be discarded by a student if he keeps a broken mirror at his home and finds to his satisfaction that it has not created any type of disharmony in his home. Similarly other superstitions and misbeliefs can be tested and easily discarded by a student of science. Various researches carried out in the field have drawn the same conclusion *i.e.* by practical survey and study of such common beliefs, students have developed permanent mind-sets or attitudes towards such superstitions.

(*vi*) *Co-curriculum Activities in Science*: Various co-curricular activities such as organising science club, hobbies club, science society, photographic club, organising scientific tours and excursions etc. can be taken up by science teacher. Such activities should be properly organised by science teacher under his direct supervision but students be given enough freedom to plan their activities. It will help inculcate in students some desirable scientific attitudes. Co-curricular activities may include making of scientific charts and models, making of improvised science apparatus etc.

(*vii*) *Atmosphere of the Class:* A proper atmosphere in the class room provided a desirable atmosphere for inculcating of certain scientific attitudes in the pupils. By a proper class atmosphere we mean that the room is properly arranged and suitably decorated in such a manner that it provides an incentive to the pupil to inculcate the habit of cleanliness and orderliness. In addition to such a congenial physical atmosphere of the class room, the teacher's behaviour also contributes to the development of proper class room atmosphere. For inculcating the scientific attitudes amongst his pupils teacher should encourage them in their various activities. He should also take care to see that his lessons contain are such as to encourage the students to ask a large number of intelligent questions. He should feel pleasure in answering and explaining such questions and must not snub his pupils for asking so many questions.

2.7 SCIENTIFIC METHOD

It has already been pointed out that two basic aims of teaching science and (*i*) development of scientific attitude and (*ii*) training in scientific methods.

In previous section we have discussed same ways for developing scientific attitude and in this section our aim is to concentrate mainly on training in scientific methods.

A 'scientific method' is 'a method which is used for solving a problem scientifically'. It is also referred to as 'the method of science' or 'the method of a scientist. Sometimes it is called as 'problem solving method'. So far it has not been possible to arrive at any commonly agreed definition of scientific method.

The scientific method of teaching science is based upon the process of finding out results by attacking a problem in definite steps, therefore there cannot be any one 'particular method' but such methods have certain common characteristics.

According to Fitzpatrick, "Science is a cumulative and endless series of emperical observations which result in the formation of concepts and theories, with both concepts and theories being subject to modification in the light of furtheir empirical observation. Science is both the study of knowledge and the process of acquiring and refining knowledge". From this it because quite clear that student of science be exposed to the scientific method of finding out. Scientific method helps to develop in a student the power of reasoning, critical thinking and application of scientific knowledge. It also helps in developing positive attitudes amongst the pupils. A list of such traits as given by Woodburn and Oburn is as under:

(*i*) A scientist must have an unsatiable curiosity, inquisitiveness and a spirit of adventure.

(*ii*) He should be capable of independent thinking and be ready to abandon the disproved.

(*iii*) He should be knowledgeable, enlightened and informed.

(*iv*) He should possess a power of sound judgement and prudent foresight.

(*v*) He should possess a high degree of perseverance.

Steps of Scientific Method

Since we don't have any single well defined scientific method so we cannot have any well defined fixed steps for a scientific method. However in general the scientific method of teaching science proceeds in the following steps:

(i) Problem in an area of science learning is identified and well stated.

(ii) Relevant data is collected.

(iii) Certain hypothesis are proposed for testing.

(iv) Experiments are set and done to test the proposed hypothesis.

(v) Prediction of other observable phenomenon are deduced from the hypothesis.

(vi) Occurence or non-occurence of predicted phenomenon is observed.

(vii) From observations, the conclusions are drawn to accept, reject or modify the proposed hypothesis.

Thus the scientific method is a sequenced and structured way of finding out the results through experiments. Various steps of scientific method are discussed here.

(i) *Statement of the Problem*: A student comes across so many things which arouse his curiosity and he has a large number of questions to ask. A good science teacher always encourages his students to ask questions and tries to answer them in a simple and understandable manner. However in answering a particular question the teacher brings to fore many new problems and it has rightly been said that, "when we double the known, we quadruple the unknown".

Most of the question asked are about 'what?', 'why?' or 'how?' type and these can be conveniently classified as under.

(i) 'what' type of questions are *predictive*

(ii) 'why' type of questions are *explanatory*

(iii) 'how' type of questions are *inventory*

The most important thing in a scientific method is a simple and well defined statement of the problem. The statement of the problem be such that it clearly defines the scope of the problem as also its limitations.

(ii) *Data Collection:* When the problem has been stated in cleai terms an effort be made to collect the data from as many differen source as is possible. Such data may be available in books in science library which are an important source for data collection. Data may b collected by use of certain instruments etc. and observations. In dat collection an effort be made to minimise the errors that are likely to be caused due to apparatus and instruments used *(mechanical errors)* and those which are likely to be caused due to personal bias *(personal errors)*.

(*iii*) *Proposing a Hypotheses:* On the basis of collected data a tentative hypothesis is proposed for testing. A hypothesis is in fact a certain tentative solution to the problem. The hypothesis should be proposed only after an objective analysis of the available data because any number of hypothesis can be proposed for a problem. For an objective analysis the student be given a training so that he is free from all his bias towards the problem.

(*iv*) *Conducting Experiments:* After a hypothesis has been proposed suitable experiments are designed to test the validity of the hypothesis. From the observations of such experiments the validity of the hypothesis is tested. The experiments will show the occurence or non-occurence of the expected phenomenon and from this we will be able to accept or reject or modify the hypothesis.

Advantages of Scientific Method

Some of the advantages of scientific method are:

(*i*) Students learn science by their own experiences and the teacher is just a guide who provides them an opportunity and proper environment for learning science.

(*ii*) It trains the students to identify and formulate scientific problems.

(*iii*) It gives enough training to students in techniques of information processing.

(*iv*) It develops in students the power of logical thinking as he is required to interpret data in a logical way.

(*v*) It helps to develop an intellectual honesty in the student because he is required to accept or reject the hypothesis on the basis of evidences available.

(*vi*) It helps the students to learn to see relationships and patterns amongst things and variables.

(*vii*) It provides the students a training in the methods and skills of discovering new knowledge.

Disadvantages of Scientific Method

Some important disadvantages of scientific methods are as under:

(*i*) It is a long drawn out and time consuming process.

(*ii*) It can never be a full fledged method of learning science.

(*iii*) Majority of science teachers cannot implement it successfully because of their back of exposure to such a method.

(*iv*) It is not suitable for all students as it suits only bright and creative students.

Chapter 3

Life Science Curriculum

3.1 INTRODUCTION

In this chapter an attempt has been made to undertake an analysis of the present state of biology in schools the world wide. Material has been taken from the survey undertaken by the Commission for Biology Education of the International Union of Biological Sciences (IUBS – CBE).

On the whole, biology is one of the popular subject in school and college. Over the past few decades biology has firmly established as a main stream subject or as part of integrated or general science. Biology is generally the most popular and appreciated elements of the total curriculum. It is taught almost universally at all levels in the formal education system and is rapidly spreading within the non-formal and informal sectors.

3.2 CURRICULUM

Curriculum is a gist of lessons and topics which are expected to the covered in a specified period of time in any class. However this traditional concept of curriculum has undergone a change in modern times. Now curriculum refers to the totality of experiences that a child receives through various class room activities as also from activities in library, laboratory, workshop, assembly hall, play fields etc. Thus according to modern concept curriculum includes the whole life of the school. Thus those activities which were previously referred to as co-curricular or extra-curricular activities have now become curricular activities.

According to this concept the science curriculum can be considered to include the subject matter in science, various co-curricular activities in science etc.

Curriculum is derived from Latin word "currere" meaning "to run". Thus curriculum in the medium to realise the goals and objectives of teaching a particular course of study.

According to the *Secondary Education Commission of 1952-54, curriculum* does not mean academic subjects traditionally taught alone. It includes variety of experiences that pupils acquire from the school, classroom, library, laboratory, workshop, play ground etc. It includes numerous information obtained from contacts between teachers and pupils. In short curriculum includes the whole life of school which touches the life of students at all levels and helps in promoting a balanced personality.

Science Curriculum

Before venturing to form a curriculum in science for being taught in our schools we have to take into consideration the kind of school population and other requirements. We shall also have to keep in mind the aim of teaching science in our schools. It is our endeavour to include in the science curriculum various natural phenomenon, physical laws and some simple applications of science that we come across in our every day life. More over since knowledge of science in the basis of various vocational courses (*e.g.* medicines and engineering etc.) so the curriculum in science must also such topics as are required for success in such a vocational course.

For formation of curriculum in science we can easily classify the school population in two classes as under:

(*i*) Those students who complete their education at the primary or middle stage, and

(*ii*) Those who continue in high/higher secondary schools.

Only a small fraction of the students who continue their education in high/higher secondary school offer for science courses.

The curriculum in science should be different for the above two classes of school population. For those students who are not likely to continue with education after middle stage we should offer a general science course that may be of use to them as a part of sound liberal education. For those students who are likely to continue with science subjects at high/higher secondary stage we should offer a course that provides specialised knowledge of one or more branches of science.

If we look at the existing science curriculum we find it to be defective as it is a hotch-potch mixture of various branches of science. It appears that it has no definite goals to achieve and so it defeats the very purpose of teaching science. It burdens the students mind with dead information and does not provide him any encouragement for taking up creative and useful activities.

The Secondary Education Commission (1953) refers to the criticism of the existing curriculum as under:

(*i*) It is a narrowly conceived curriculum.

(*ii*) It is theoretical and bookish.

(*iii*) It is over crowded.

(*iv*) It does not provide rich and significant subject matter.

(*v*) In it there is inadequate provision for practical work.

(*vi*) It fails to develop a balanced personality.

(*vii*) It fails to cater to the various needs and capacities of adolescents.

(*viii*) It is an examination dominated curriculum.

The Kothari Commission (1966) also considered it and according to it the dissatisfaction with science curriculum in our schools may be due to the following two factors.

(*i*) The tremendous explosion in knowledge, in various branches of science, that has occurred in recent years. This explosion in knowledge has led to reformulation of some of the basic concepts in physical sciences, biological sciences and social sciences. This advancement in knowledge of science has intended the already existing gulf between the school and the university in major academic disciplines.

(*ii*) There is a rethinking in the duration of education that is imparted in ordinary schools. There is a unanimity in the views of educationist all of whom now favour the increase in the period of general education thereby postponing the entry into specialised courses of study. This has necessitated the introduction of some more significant topics in an already over packed school curriculum. For this we have to discard some topics from the existing curriculum.

3.3 PRINCIPLES OF CURRICULUM FORMATION

There are certain basic principles of curriculum planning which should form the basis for the formation of a good science curriculum. These are:

1. *The principle of child centredness*: The curriculum should be based on the present needs and circumstances of the child.
2. *Curriculum should provide a fulness of experience for children.*
3. *The curriculum should be dynamic and not static.*
4. *It should be related to every day life.*
5. *It must take into account the economic aspect of life of the people to whom an educational institution belongs.*
6. *The curriculum should be realistic and rationalistic.*
7. *While forming the curriculum a balance be struck between the education of nature and education of man.*
8. *It should lay emphasis on learning to live rather than on living to learn.*
9. *In curriculum such activities must be included, which help in preserving and transmitting the traditions knowledge and standards of conduct on which our civilisation depends.*
10. *It should be elastic and flexible.*
11. *It should be well integrated.*
12. *It should provide both for uniformity and variety.*
13. *It should be able to serve the needs of community.*

As far as science curriculum is concerned it should be elastic and variable, child-centred, community centred, activity centred. It should be such as to be use for adjustment in life and helps to integrate the activities of the child with his environment. It should be helpful to conserve and transmit the traditions, culture and civilisation. It must help in arousing the creative faculties of the children.

Objectives of Present Day Curriculum

The present day science curriculum has the following objectives: (*i*) providing a continuous and sequential experiences to pupils; (*ii*) Approaching science conceptually; rather than factually; (*iii*) introducing different methods of instruction with the nature of scientific enterprise and with various process of science; (*iv*) providing deeper insights into the philosophy, history and methods of inquiry of science; (*v*) providing effectively for 'individual differences' abilities, needs and interests; (*vi*) optimising use of local skills and resources; and (*vii*) providing for built in mechanism providing continuous and critical revaluation.

3.4 APPROACHES TO CURRICULUM PLANNING

There are a number of approaches to curriculum planning in science. The extremes of such approaches are given below (Table 3.1).

TABLE 3.1
The Extreme of Curriculum Formation

One extreme	*Other extreme*
Integrated	Disciplinary
Child-centred	Teacher-centred
Flexible	Structured
Process-based	Content-based
Conceptual	Factual

Actually no single way of curriculum planning exclusively based on one approach can fulfil the curricular needs of pupils. It is always better to combine different approaches to plan an effective curriculum in science.

3.5 CURRICULUM STYLES

Curriculum can be classified as:

(*i*) Instrumental curriculum.
(*ii*) Interactive curriculum.
(*iii*) Individualistic curriculum.

Instrumental Curriculum

In this type of curriculum more emphasis is placed on the utility value or vocational value of science. It makes learning an intense competition among students.

The basic approach in such a curriculum is disciplinary and emphasises the acquisition of knowledge or information. The role of teacher is that of a dominant teacher in such a curriculum.

Interactive Curriculum

This type of curriculum is society oriented and lays more emphasis on the social development of child. In this type of curriculum class room instructions becomes an interactive or a cooperative process. The approach is interdisciplinary and the curriculum is loosely structured and consists of learning packages.

Individualistic Curriculum

In this type of curriculum more emphasis is placed on the personal development of the individual and it is based on interdisciplinary approach. It helps to develop creativity in the individual. This type of curriculum is based on self-calculation by the student.

3.6 CURRICULUM IN GENERAL SCIENCE CONTENT

Keeping in view that the major aim of teaching life science is to acquaint the students with himself and his environment (*i.e.* things around him), it is desirable if the student is imparted a working knowledge of almost all the main branches of science. To achieve this the general science course should include topics from the following branches of science:

(*i*) Physics
(*ii*) Chemistry
(*iii*) Botany
(*iv*) Zoology
(*v*) Geography
(*vi*) Physiology
(*vii*) Astronomy
(*viii*) Geology and
(*ix*) Home Science (for girls).

For selecting different topics, from various branches of science, for inclusion in such a general science curriculum the following points be given due consideration.

(*i*) Content should be selected in terms of broad concepts and principles of science.
(*ii*) Content should be related to the different age-groups and daily life.

(*iii*) It should be able to serve the needs of the community.

(*iv*) It should be very closely associated with the environment.

(*v*) It should be such as could be dealt within the available time under existing conditions of staff, equipment etc.

Arrangement of Material

In case of general science curriculum the best arrangement is the one based on 'topics' or 'units' because such an arrangement provides a natural method of learning. In such an arrangement the 'units' should be such as are of immediate interest to the student and are related to the local environment and community. 'Topics' should arise out of environment and experiences of the pupil and the study material should be arranged around these topics in such a fashion that it brings about a closer integration between various branches of science. It should also bring about a greater correlation with life situations and every day experiences of the child.

The general science course for elementary schools can be organised around the following main units:

(*i*) Living things, (*ii*) Earth and universe, and (*iii*) Matter and Energy.

Alternatively it can be organised around the following main units:

(*i*) Our surroundings.

(*ii*) Nature of things.

(*iii*) Energy and work.

(*iv*) Life.

(*v*) Human machine.

The curriculum must include some experiments for the children in addition to subject matter. It should also indicate various related activities for different topics. Example illustrates it (See Next page).

All India Seminar on Science Teaching has suggested the following for bringing about a closer cooperation between various branches of science. The units be

(*i*) Environment centred

(*ii*) Life centred

(*iii*) Environment and life centred

Content	*Demonstration*	*Experiment*	*Activities*
Unit *Our surroundings*			
(*i*) The earth, rocks and soil, different kinds of rocks and minerals	(*i*) Three classes of rocks (*ii*) Identification of minerals (*iii*) Making artificial rocks	(*i*) Study of some rocks (*ii*) Making a model of volcano	Visit to hilly and arid areas and collecting rocks and minerals

Units based on Environment-centred Topics

Unit I	The atmosphere
Unit II	Water, Elixir of life
Unit III	The earth
Unit IV	Heat
Unit V	Light
Unit VI	Metals and Non-metals
Unit VII	Work and energy
Unit VIII	Means of transport and communication
Unit IX	Plant and animal life
Unit X	The study of the Body Machine.

Units based on Life-centred Topics

Unit I	Importance of science in our life
Unit II	The air
Unit III	The water
Unit IV	The food
Unit V	The clothes
Unit VI	The homes
Unit VII	The machines
Unit VIII	Power and Energy
Unit IX	Protection from disease
Unit X	Biological resources
Unit XI	Mineral resources

Unit XII Means of transport
Unit XIII Means of communication
Unit XIV Our universe
Unit XV Story of life.

Units based on Environment and Life Centred Topics

Unit I Importance of science
Unit II Human body, the machine and its working
Unit III Our health
Unit IV Our biological resources and their use for better living
Unit V Our mineral resources and their use for better living
Unit VI Energy and machines
Unit VII Time, measurement and mass production
Unit VIII The weather
Unit IX The solar system, stars and other universes
Unit X Science in daily life
(*a*) Heating our homes
(*b*) Lighting our homes
(*c*) Electronics in our homes
(*d*) Sound in homes.

3.7 CURRICULUM IN SCIENCE FOR DIFFERENT STAGES

1. Primary Stage

The students at primary stage are in the age group 5-10 and so they are quite immature thus they be given only a formal education in science. At this stage it is desirable to develop the subject matter under the following heads:

(*i*) Living things
(*ii*) Universe
(*iii*) Matter and Energy.

The curriculum must provide for some students activity in addition to the subject matter. Of the estimated 100 hours allotted to teaching of science in a class about 20 hours be spent on excussions and visits, about 50 hours on projects and other activities and the remaining 30 hours be given to class room teaching.

Kothari Commission (1966) recommended as under:

(*i*) In lower primary classes, the focus should be on the child's environment – social, physical and biological

(*ii*) In classes I and II accent should be on (*a*) cleanliness (*b*) Formation of healthy habits (*c*) development of lower of observation.

(*iii*) In addition to emphasising the above qualities in class III and IV the information be provided about (*a*) Personal hygiene (*b*) Sanitation (*c*) Plants and animals in surroundings of the child (*d*) Air (*e*) Water (*f*) Weather (*g*) Earth (*h*) Simple Machines (*i*) Care of body (*j*) Heavenly Bodies.

(*iv*) To provide direct and valuable experiences of natural phenomenon it is recommended that school gardening be encouraged.

2. Middle Stage

At this stage it is desirable to place more emphasis to the acquisition of knowledge and the ability to think logically. It should also be the aim at this stage that a student in encouraged to draw conclusion and take decisions. It would be desirable if science at this stage is taught as physics, chemistry and biology etc. At this stage this disciplinary approach will be more effective.

Keeping in view the above recommendations of Kothari Commission (1966) science is taught as physics, chemistry and Biology in our schools.

However now NCERT has framed a syllabus for integrated science course from class VI, VII and VIII and the outlines of this newly framed curriculum are given below:

Integrated Science Curriculum

Objectives:

1. To put emphasise on the relevance of science to daily life.
2. To develop scientific attitudes.
3. To create an environment that is conducive to more reliance on the use of principles and practices of science.

4. To familiarise the students with different natural phenomena.
5. To emphasise the experimental nature of science.
6. To emphasise the unity of methods of various disciplines of science.

Nature of the Course. In this we have tried to integrate science with the environment of the child rather than making an artificial integration of various disciplines of science. The students with the back ground of general science at primary level, would find this course as a continuation of their earlier knowledge. They will also be mentally prepared to offer science courses at secondary level. NCERT have developed Composite Integrated Science Kit alongwith text-books for classes VI, VII and VIII.

3. High School Stage

The recommendations of Kothari Commission (1966) are as under:

(*i*) In classes IX and X it would be desirable to introduce newer concepts of Physics, Chemistry and Biology. Moreover the experimental approach to learning of science be emphasised at this stage.

(*ii*) It was also recommended that provisions be made for advanced courses in science subjects for talented students in some selected secondary schools. Such schools be provided with necessary facilities of staff and laboratories.

(*iii*) As far as possible science teaching in rural areas be linked to agriculture and in urban areas to technology.

The content of specialized science courses in physics, chemistry and biology should be such as to useful for further vocational studies in the respective fields. An effort be made to present the subject matter as a synthetic whole and not merely as collection of few principles and facts. Various examples and illustrations be given from daily life of students and from their local environment. For this purpose the subject matter be arranged around broad based units.

National Policy on Education as given by Government of India states as under.

"With a view to the growth of the national economy, science education and research should receive high priority. Science and mathematics should form an integral part of general education till the end of school stage".

With the above policy statements in view new Integrated Science Curriculum were prepared by NCERT. Outlines of these are given below:

3.8 NEW INTEGRATED SCIENCE CURRICULUM OF NCERT

Class VI

1. Measurement
2. Materials around us
3. Separation of substances
4. Changes around us
5. Motion, force and pressure
6. Simple machines
7. The universe
8. The living world
9. Study of structures and functions in plants and animals
10. Food and health
11. Man's dependence on plants and animals and the balance of nature
12. Environment
13. Water
14. Energy.

Class VII

1. Motion, mass and friction
2. Pressure and buoyancy
3. Heat
4. Light
5. Sound
6. Current Electricity
7. Static Electricity

8. Magnetism
9. Nature and composition of substances
10. Air
11. Water
12. Acids, bases and salts
13. Preservation of self
14. Population Explosion
15. Pollution.

Class VIII

1. Light
2. Electricity
3. Electrical energy
4. Electrical magnetism
5. Structure of atom
6. Nuclear energy
7. Carbon
8. Our living world
9. Cell and tissue
10. Reproduction
11. Growth and development
12. Heredity and variation
13. Organic evolution
14. Materials
15. Agricultural practices and implements
16. Our crops
17. Improvement of crop production
18. Some useful plants and animals
19. Animal husbandry
20. Conservation of natural resources
21. Science in human welfare.

3.8 LIFE SCIENCE SYLLABUS IN OUR SCHOOLS

Step by step, during the development of science, life science has acquired a position of honour. Before 1977, life science was an elective subject upto higher secondary stage and only an elementary knowledge was given in life sciences as a part of general science.

In the new pattern of education (10+2+3) that has been adopted almost all over India life sciences, which are mainly following, have been included as compulsory subject upto Class X.

1. Animal husbandry
2. Agriculture
3. Biology
4. Botany
5. Zoology
6. Home Science etc.

Among all the above branches of life sciences, biology plays the major role.

The **New syllabus** of life sciences as laid down by NCERT in collaboration with CBSE is on the following lines.

Unit I

1. Nature and scope of biology
2. Characters of living being

Unit II

1. Structural levels of organisations of life.
2. Cell structure and functions.
3. Plant and animal tissues.
4. Biosphere.
5. Organ, Organ systems and organism.
6. Population.
7. Community.
8. Eco-system.

Unit III

1. Maintenance of Equilibrium in nature.
2. Conservation of Natural resources.
3. National and Internal efforts for conservation of nature.

Unit IV

1. Reproduction.
2. Nutrition.
3. Photosynthesis.
4. Respiration.
5. Internal transport.
6. Excretion.

Unit V

1. Heredity and variation.
2. Nature of gene.
3. Human Genetics.
4. Population Genetics.
5. Origin of Life.
6. Evidences of Organic Evolution.
7. Evolution of Man.

Unit VI

1. Crop production.
2. Agriculture practices in India.
3. Manures and Fertilizers and their importance.
4. Crop diseases, pests and their control.
5. Improvement of crops, soil.
6. Elements of Animal husbandry.

Unit VII

1. Food, function and nutrients for living world.
2. Nutrient requirements and balanced diet.
3. Nutrition deficiency. Diseases in India.
4. Storage and preservation of food.
5. Food adulteration.
6. Population Education.

The purpose of this syllabus is the general upliftment of the country men. Science is making various contributions for betterment of civilisation. Rapid developments have occurred in the field of agriculture and animal husbandry. Many a changes have been brought about by hybridisation, induced variations and genetic engineering. Much advance has taken place in the field of control of diseases. There is a spread of family planning and population education all over the world. Every country is making its contribution towards development of life sciences.

3.9 DEFECTS IN PRESENT DAY BIOLOGY TEACHING

The defects in our present biology have been realised by professors, college teachers, school teachers and other specialists of Biological sciences. The major defects pointed out by them are as under:

(*i*) Inclusion of dead topics in the curriculum;

(*ii*) Less emphasis is made on practical work;

(*iii*) The relationship between biological science and physical science is not realised and recognised;

(*iv*) There is more emphasis on morphological work and no integrated approach;

(*v*) The psychological work is not given emphasis then and there;

(*vi*) Biology teaching is meant for specialisation only. It is not made general education for all.

3.10 REFORMS IN BIOLOGICAL SCIENCE CURRICULUM

The Biological science curriculum study (BCBS) expounded reforms relating to biological science curriculum.

The Biological science curriculum study was organised in 1959 by the Education committee of the American Institute of Biological Sciences at the University of Colorado U.S.A. The organisation of BSCS was necessitated by the inadequaties and defects found in the conventional biological science teaching. The conventional treatment of biology was defective as:

(*i*) It included dead topic is syllabi;

(*ii*) Practical work was less stressed;

(*iii*) Neglected the relationship between Biological sciences with physical sciences;

(*iv*) Neglected integrated approach; and

(*v*) Laid stress on morphological work rather than psychological work.

Hence the BSCS was organised. The BSCS, by recognising the relationship between biological sciences and the physical sciences, has opened up new vistas for the science of Biology. It further recognised and established that biology teaching was not only for specialisation but also for general education and for all people.

The treatment of Biology by BSCS differs from the conventional treatment of Biology in three major aspects. They are as under:

(*i*) BSCS materials have significant unified threads;

(*ii*) The conventional treatment laid emphasis on the study of tissue and organ. Where as the treatment of BSCS placed emphasis on molecular, physiological and other aspects of Biological sciences and

(*iii*) BSCS laid more emphasis on practical or laboratory work where as the traditional treatment emphasised learning and understanding of facts.

The unified thread of BSCS materials have a nine phase they are as under:

(*i*) Evolution;

(*ii*) Discovery of the type and unity of pattern of living things;

(*iii*) Genetic continuity of life;

(*iv*) Complementarity of structure and function;

(*v*) Biological roots of behaviour;

(*vi*) Complementarity of organism and function;

(*vii*) Regulation and Homeostasis;

(*viii*) Science as inquiry;

(*ix*) Intellectual history of biological concepts.

These nine phases must be reflected in three versions namely the Green, Yellow and Blue. The approach to these versions must be integral. These three courses are differ slightly in approach. The Green version is developed from the ecological point of view. The yellow version is developed from the genetic point of view. The Blue version is developed from the linear or functional approach. These versions are suitable for average and above average students. A fourth version for low ability students is yet to be developed.

The most important study materials of the BSCS are as under:

(*i*) A text book;
(*ii*) Laboratory manual;
(*iii*) Teacher's handbook and guide;
(*iv*) A series of laboratory block units;
(*v*) Investigation booklets;
(*vi*) Bulletin series on biological education;
(*vii*) Films on laboratory techniques;
(*viii*) Information media; etc.

The BSCS approach attempts to place biological knowledge in its modern perspective. The controversy on selection of a particular version from the three versions suggested by BSCS still continues. It is increasingly difficult to choose a particular version for particular age group and for a particular environment. However the decision should be left to the teacher concerned. Yet the students shall acquire an intellectual and asethetic appreciation of living things and the inter relationship with physical environment with the help of BSCS materials.

Differences in BSCS from the conventional treatment of Biology

The BSCS differs from the conventional treatment of biology in following three major aspects.

(*i*) The BSCS materials have significant unified threads;
(*ii*) In the conventional treatment much emphasis was made on the study of organ tissue. But the BSCS curriculum emphasises molecular and psychological aspects of biological sciences; and
(*iii*) The BSCS lays more emphasis on practical or laboratory work where as the conventional treatment lays emphasis on understanding of facts.

Different phases of the unified thread of BSCS materials

The BSCS materials have significant unified threads. These unified threads have the following phases:

(*i*) Evolution;

(*ii*) Diversity of the type and unity of patterns;
(*iii*) Genetic continuity of life;
(*iv*) Complementarity of structure and function;
(*v*) Biological roots of behaviour;
(*vi*) Regulation; and homeostasis;
(*vii*) Science as inquiry; and
(*viii*) Intellectual history of biological concepts.

Study Materials of BSCS

The study materials of BSCS are made up of:

(*i*) A text book;
(*ii*) Laboratory mannual;
(*iii*) Teacher's hand book;
(*iv*) Teacher's guide;
(*v*) A series of laboratory block units;
(*vi*) Investigation booklets;
(*vii*) Bulletin series on biological education;
(*viii*) Films on laboratory techniques;
(*ix*) Information media including film;
(*x*) News Letter; and
(*xi*) International News Note Services.

3.11 NUFFIELD FOUNDATION SCIENCE TEACHING PROJECT

The Primary and Secondary Aims of Nuffield Foundation Science Teaching Project (NFSTP)

The Primary aim of the Nuffield Foundation Science Teaching Project is to provide and a sound introduction to modern biology who will leave school at the age of sixteen with no more formal science teaching. The secondary aims of NFSTP is to provide a suitable background for more advanced specialist work in the sixth form leading to G.C.E. at advanced level. It also aims at providing a basis for additional courses of science at sixth form level suitable for those not pursuing science as a specialist subject.

Nuffield Foundation Science Teaching Project

The Nuffield Foundation Science Teaching Project was organised in England in April 1962. It attempted to develop suitable courses in "Sciences for all". The courses in sciences for all meant for meeting the requirements of both citizens and specialists. This task is performed by the practising teachers. In the Nuffield project—Biology project at O. Level link has been maintained between Biology and Chemistry and Physics. For example respiration in biology be taught only after teaching oxidation in chemistry.

Aims of Nuffield Project Course

The course designed by the Nuffield project aims as under:

(*i*) Providing a sound introduction of modern biology to those who leave school at the age of 16 with no more formal sciences teaching;

(*ii*) Providing a suitable background for specialised work in the sixth from leading G.C.E. and

(*iii*) Providing a basis for additional courses of science at sixth form level for those who do not study science as a special subject.

3.12 CHALLENGES OF THE FUTURE

Biotechnology is likely to have a more prominent place in future biology curricula, particularly in its applications to transferring wastes, medicines, agriculture and the synthesis of natural products. Biology while retaining the qualities and characteristics of science in likely to be taught so as to give students' deeper insights into the human condition and human behaviour. The courses in biology are likely to contribute to *improved quality* of life and encourage *positive social and personal development.* They are likely to thread together elements which are biological, technological, social and personal foci.

In future more emphasis is likely to be placed on *problem solving* and improvement of *skills* of *decision-making.* The skills of interpreting and applying facts for making decisions and predicting societal outcomes are likely to be a central concern for any future biology programme.

One of the aims of biology teaching at school will be concerned with increasing sensitivity to and understanding and tolerance of others and the combating of prejudices, bias and unreasoned dogmatism in the rapidly changing world. The future biology courses will be such as to lead to understanding of herbal medicines, acupuncture, low energy cooking methods, methods of effective grain storage etc.

3.13 ROLE OF COMPUTERS

Computers are likely to play a major role in teaching of biology as in other science subjects. Schools will be required to use *computer-based information networks* established in their country as also internationally. The advent of international data banks, the development of computer networks, a reduction in cost of hardwork and the rapid growth of suitable computer programmes for both teaching and administration will make it possible for all school systems to respond rapidly to changes in the content of biology and to changing emphasis in pedagogy.

Another important role that has to be played by biology in future is to combat directly irrational forces in society which include *anti-science* and *pseudo-science* movements. Teachers of science shall have to work hard to show how the positive achievements of science and technology can be applied to overcome negative aspects. The growth of irrational views of the world like scientism, astrology, creationism, belief in variations from outer space, pyramidology etc. have to be exposed either as illogical or false.

In future biology courses stress shall have to be placed on those conditions and situation which are favourable to future cultural evolution of our species and which will foster an improved quality of life.

Chapter 4

Methods of Teaching Life Sciences

4.1 INTRODUCTION

There is no way of teaching biology, just as there is no definition of the factual content covered by the term.

Over the past decade there have been significant advances in biological knowledge and clear search trends have emerged. At the same time there has been a series of changes in education, particularly in regard to its perceived role in society and its aims and objectives. These two factors have together caused major changes in the methodology of teaching biology at all levels.

4.2 CHANGES IN CONTENT

As already pointed out in chapter on curriculum, most aspects of biotechnology are included in school programmes in various countries particularly in U.S.A., Japan etc. The emergence of an emphasis on human biology in school programme is another major development. Studies of the frog or the rabbit have been replaced by a study of human body, illustrated of course by animal dissections.

The environmental movement of the 1960's and 1970's has had a considerable impact on the teaching of school biology. In most of school courses units on ecology and field work have been included. Units on pollution and the general impact of development on the natural environment are also included in most of the syllable.

4.3 CHANGES IN EDUCATION

There has been a lot of change in last 20-30 years in education which have a bearing on teaching of biology. These changes include changes in aims and more emphasis on enquiry and problem-solving, a trend towards integration of subject matter, a growth of non-formal education, a trend towards participatory learning and a growth of information technology.

Because of these changes biology class rooms are now more open, flexible, student-oriented, and participatory. Practical work is universally accepted as of major importance. There is a trend towards considering socially relevant issues rather than the academic principles of biology.

4.4 METHODS OF TEACHING LIFE SCIENCES

Any one or more of the following methods can be applied to the teaching of life sciences.

1. The Project method.
2. The Heuristic method.
3. Concentric method.
4. The topical method for specific areas in life science subjects.
5. Problem-solving method.
6. Scientific method.
7. Discussion method.
8. Activity method.
9. Assignment method.
10. Lecture method.
11. Historical method.
12. Lecture-cum-Demonstration method.
13. Learning by Doing method.
14. Object teaching method.
15. Programmed learning method.
16. Individualised Instruction method.

1. Lecture Method

Lecture method is the most commonly used method of teaching science. This method is most commonly followed in colleges and in schools in big classes. This method is not quite suitable to realise the real aim of teaching science. In lecture method only the teacher talks and students are passive listners. Since the students do not actively participate in this method of teaching so this method is a teacher controlled and information centred and in this method teacher works as a sole resource in class room instructions. Due to lack of participation students get bored and some of them some times may go to sleep. In this method students is provided with readymade knowledge by the teacher and due to this spoon feeding the students loses interest and his powers of reasoning and observation get no stimulus.

In this method the teacher goes ahead with the subject matter at his own speed. The teacher may make use of black board at times and may also dictate notes. This teacher oriented method in its extreme from does not expect any question or response from the students.

Advantages of Lecture Method

It has the following advantages:

(*i*) It is quite economical method. It is possible to handle a large number of students at a time and no laboratory, equipment, aids, materials are required.

(*ii*) Using this method the knowledge can be imparted to the students quickly and the prescribed syllabus can be covered in a short time.

(*iii*) It is quite attractive and easy to follow. Using this method teacher feels secure and satisfied.

(*iv*) It simplifies the task of the teacher as he dominates the lesson for 70-85% of the lesson time and students just listen to him.

(*v*) Using this method it is quite easy to impart factual information and historical anecdotes.

(*vi*) By following this method teacher can develop his own style of teaching and exposition.

(*vii*) In this method teacher can easily maintain the logical sequence of the subject by planning his lectures in advance. It minimises the chances of any gaps or overlappings.

(*viii*) Some good lectures delivered by the teacher may motivate, instigate, inspire a student for some creative thinking.

Disadvantages of Lecture Method

The disadvantages of lecture method can be as under:

(*i*) In this method the students participation is negligible and students become passive recipients of information.

(*ii*) In this method we are never sure if the students are concentrating and understanding the subject matter being taught to them by the teacher.

(*iii*) In this method knowledge is imparted so rapidly that weak students develop a hatred for learning.

(*iv*) It does not allow all the faculties of the student to develop.

(*v*) In this method there is no place of 'learning by doing' and thus teaching by this method strikes at the very root of science.

(*vi*) It does not take into account the previous knowledge of the student.

(*vii*) It does not provide for corrective feed back and remedial help to slow learners.

(*viii*) It does not cater to the individual needs and differences of students

(*ix*) It does not help to inculcate scientific attitudes and training in scientific method among the pupils.

(*x*) It is an undemocratic and authoritarian method in which students depend only as the authority of the teacher. They cannot challange or question the verdict of the teacher. This checks the development of power of critical thinking and proper reasoning in the student.

Conclusion

After considering various merits and demerits of method it may be concluded that this method may be suitable for teaching in higher classes (XI, XII) where we aim to cover the prescribed syllabus quickly. In these classes this method can be used successfully for imparting factual knowledge, introducing some new and difficult topics, make generalisation from the facts already known to the students, revision of lessons already learnt etc.

Teaching by this method these students of classes XI and XII will also help those students who intend to join college so that they can prepare themselves for college where lecture method of teaching is a dominant method of imparting instruction.

This method of teaching can be made more beneficial if the teacher encourages his students to take notes during the lesson. After the lesson teacher can give his students some time for asking questions and answer their queries without any hesitation. While delivering his lesson the teacher may see that the lesson is delivered in good tone, loudly and clearly. He should use only simple and understandable words for delivering his lesson. If a teacher can introduce some humour in his lesson it would keep students interested in his lesson.

2. Lecture Demonstration Method

This method of teaching is sometimes also referred to as *Lecture-cum Demonstration Method*. This is considered to be a superior method of teaching in comparison to lecture method. In lecture method the teacher speaks and students listen so it is a one way traffic of flow of ideas and students are only passive listeners. This one sidedness is the major drawback of lecture method. A teaching method is considered better if both teacher and taught are active participants in the process of teaching. This particular aspect is taken care of in demonstration method.

This lecture-demonstration method is used by good science teachers for imparting science education in class room. By using this method it is possible to easily impart concrete experiences to students during the course of a lesson when the teacher wants to explain some abstract points. This method combines the instructional strategy of 'information imparting' and 'showing how'. This method combines the advantages of both the lecture method and the demonstration method.

In this method of teaching the teacher performs experiment before the class and simultaneously explains what he is doing. He also asks relevant questions from the class and students are compelled to observe carefully because they have to describe each and every step of the experiment accurately and draw inferences. After thorough questioning and cross-questioning the inferences drawn by the students are discussed in the class. In this way the students remain active participants in the process of teaching. The teacher also relates the outcomes of his experiment to the content of the on-going lesson. Thus while in lecture method teacher merely talks in demonstration method he really teaches.

Principle

This method is based on the principle: *Truth is that which works*.

Requirements for a Good Demonstration

For success of any demonstration following points be always kept in mind:

(*i*) It should be planned and rehearsed by the teacher before hand.

(*ii*) The apparatus used for demonstration should be big enough to be seen by the whole class. It would be much better if a large mirror is placed at a suitable angle above the teachers table which will enable the pupils to have a view of everything that the teacher is doing while performing the experiment.

Alternately, if the class is well disciplined the teacher may allow the students to sit on the stools placed on the benches to enable them to have a better view.

(*iii*) Adequate lighting arrangements be made on demonstration table and a proper back ground be provided.

(*iv*) All the pieces of apparatus be placed in order before starting the demonstration. The apparatus likely to be used should be placed on the left hand side of the table and it should be arranged in the same order in which it is likely to be used. After an apparatus is used it should be transferred to right hand side. Only things relevant to the lesson be placed on demonstration table.

(*v*) Before actually starting the demonstration, a clear statement about the purpose of demonstration be made to the students.

(*vi*) The teacher must make sure that the demonstration-cum-lecture method leads to active participation of the students in the process of learning. This he can achieve by putting well structured questions.

(*vii*) The demonstration should be quick and slick and should not appear to linger on unnecessarily.

(*viii*) The demonstration should be interesting so that it captures the attention of the students.

(*ix*) The teacher must be sure of success of the experiment to be demonstrated and for this he should rehears the experiment under the conditions prevailing in the class room. However even after all the necessary precaution the experiment fails in the class room due to one reason or the other, the teacher should not get nervous instead he should make an effort to find the reasons for the failure of the experiment. Sometimes in this process a good teacher may draw very useful conclusions.

(*x*) No complaints about inadequate and faulty apparatus he made by the teacher. In such a situation a good teacher finds an opportunity to show his skill.

(*xi*) It would be much better if the teacher demonstrates those experiments which are connected with common things which are seen and handled by students in their every day life.

(*xii*) There should be a correlation between the demonstrations and the sequence of experiments performed by the students in their practical classes.

(*xiii*) For active participation of students, the teacher may call individual student, in turn, to help him in demonstration work.

(*xiv*) During lecture-cum-demonstration session, teacher must act like a 'showman' and a 'performer'. He should know different ways of arresting the attention of the students.

(*xv*) He should write, a summary of the principles arrived at because of demonstration, on the black board. The black board can also be used for drawing necessary diagrams.

How to Conduct a Demonstration Lesson

We commonly find science teachers making use of demonstration method for teaching of science. The conduct of a demonstration lesson is very difficult and here we will try to discuss some of the essential steps that should be followed in a demonstration lesson.

1. *Planning and Preparation*

A great care be taken by the teacher while planning and preparing his demonstration lesson. He should keep the following points in mind while preparing his lesson:

(*a*) subject matter,

(*b*) questions to be asked;

(*c*) apparatus required for the experiment

To achieve the above stated objective the teacher should thoroughly go through the pages of the text book, relevant to the lesson. After this he should prepare his lesson plan in which he should essentially include the principles to be explained, a list of experiments to be demonstrated and the type of questions to be asked from the students. These questions be arranged in a systematic order that has to be followed in the class. Before actually demonstrating the experiment to a class the experiment be rehearsed under the conditions prevailing in the class room. Inspite of this, some thing may go wrong at the actual lesson, so reserve apparatus is often useful. The apparatus should be arranged in a systematic order on the demonstration table. Thus for the success of demonstration method a teacher has to prepare himself as thoroughly as a bride prepares herself for the marriage.

2. *Introduction of the Lesson*

As in every other subject so also in case of science the lesson should start with proper motivation of the students. It is always considered more useful to introduce the lesson in a problematic way which would make students realise the importance of the topic. The usual ways in which a teachers could easily introduce his lesson is by telling some personal experience or incident a simple and interesting experiment, a familiar anecdote or by telling a story.

A good experiment when carefully demonstrated is likely to leave an everlasting impression on the young mind of the pupil and it would set his pupils talking in school and out of it, about the interesting experiment that had been demonstrated to them in the science class. This should be kept in mind not only to start the lesson but be used, on every suitable occasion, during the lesson.

It is not possible to give an exhaustive list of such interesting experiments but as an illustration we can consider the opening of soda water bottle in the class room, by the teacher, following by a direct question to his pupil, have they seen any gas coming out of the bottle? At this stage the teacher can introduce the topic of carbon dioxide. Similarly a lesson on magnet and magnetism may be introduced by telling the story of the shephered boy and his crook. The simple way to introduce a lesson about human heart is to prick in the finger of one of the students which will result in blood coming out. The teacher can now introduce the lesson by asking the question, from where has this blood come?

3. *Presentation*

The method of presenting the subject matter is very important. A good teacher should present his lesson in an interesting manner and not in a boring way. To make the lesson interesting the teacher may not be very rigid to remain within the prescribed course rather he should make the lesson as much broad based as is possible. For widening of his lesson the teacher may think of various useful applications of the principle taught by him. He is also at liberty to take examples and illustrations from other allied branches of science to make his lesson interesting. The life history and some interesting facts from the life of the great scientist whose name is associated with the topic under discussion can also be cited to make the lesson interesting. Thus every effort be made to present the matter in a lively and interesting manner and a lesson should never be presented as 'dry bones' of an academic course. Thus in a lesson dealing with Archimedes principle the teacher should not feel satisfied just by stating the principle and then demonstrating it with one or two experiments rather he should discuss its applications in daily life such as ships, floating bodies, diving and rising of submarines, the use of balloons and air ships etc. It is also advisable to make use of pictures, posters, diagrams, slides, films etc. in addition to experiments to illustrate the topic in hand.

Constant questions and answers should from part of every demonstration lesson. Questions and cross questions are essential for properly illuminating the principle being discussed. Questions be arranged in such a way that their answers from a complete teaching unit. Though an effort be made to encourage the students to answer a large number of questions but if students fails to answer some questions teacher should provide the answers to such questions. It is unwise to expect all the answers from the pupil and a teacher should feel satisfied if he has been able to create a desire in a student to know what he does not know.

The lesson the presented in a clear voice and the teacher should speak slowly and with correct pronunciation. He should avoid the use of any bombastic and ambiguous terms. The continuous talk is likely to monotony and to avoid it experiments be well spaced throughout the lesson.

4. *Performance of Experiments*

A good observer has been described as a person who has learned to use his senses of touch, sight, smell and hearing in an intelligent and alert manner. We want children to observe what happens in experiments and to have ample opportunities to state their observations carefully. We also want them to try to explain what happens in reference to their problem, but we want to make certain. There is separation between observations and generalization and conclusions. We will be violating the true spirit of science if we allow children to generalise from one experiment or observation.

The following steps are generally accepted as valuable in developing and concluding science experiments with the children:

1. Write the problems to be solved in simple words so that every one understands.
2. Make a list of activities that will be used to solve problems.
3. Gather material for conducting experiments.
4. Work out a format of the steps in the order of procedure so that every one knows what is to be done.
5. The teacher should always try the experiment himself to become acquainted with the equipment and procedure.
6. Record the findings in ways commensurate with the maturity level and purposes of the student.
7. Assist students in making generalisations from conclusions only after sufficient evidence and experiences.

The demonstration experiment be presented by the teacher in a model way. He should work in a tidy, clean and orderly manner while demonstrating an experiment. Some of the important points to be kept in mind while demonstrating an experiment are as under:

(*i*) Experiments should be simple and speedy

(*ii*) The experiments must work and their results should be clear and striking.

(*iii*) Experiments be properly spaced throughout the lesson.

(*iv*) Keep some reserve apparatus on the demonstration table.

(*v*) Keep the demonstration apparatus in tact till it has to be used again.

5. *Black Board Summary*

A summary of important results and principles be written on the black board. Use of black board should also be frequently made for drawing necessary sketches and diagrams. The black board summary should be written in neat, clean and legible way. Since black board summary is an index to a teacher's ability he should keep the following points in mind while writing on black board.

(*i*) Proper space be left between different letters and words.

(*ii*) Always start writing from left hand corner of the black board.

(*iii*) Start a new line only when the first one has extended across the black board.

(*iv*) Take care not to divide the words at the end of a time.

(*v*) Make all efforts to keep all the paragraphs and similar signs in calculations under one another.

(*vi*) While drawing sketches and diagrams preferably use 'single lined' diagrams.

(*vii*) All the diagrams drawn on the board be properly labelled.

6. *Supervision*

Students be asked to take the complete notes of the black board summary including the sketches and diagrams drawn. Such a record will be quite helpful to the student for learning his lesson. Such a summary will prove beneficial only if it has been copied correctly from the black board and to make sure that students are copying the black board summary properly the teacher should check it by frequently going to the seats of the students.

Common Errors in a Demonstration Lesson

A summary of common errors committed while delivering a demonstration lesson is given below:

(*i*) The apparatus may not be ready for use

(*ii*) There may not be an apparent relation between the demonstration experiment and the topic under discussion.

(*iii*) Black board summary is not upto the mark.

(*iv*) Teacher may be in a hurry to arrive at generalisation without allowing sufficient time to arrive at these generalisation from facts.

(*v*) Teacher may some times fail to ask right type of questions.

(*vi*) Teacher some times may use a difficult language.

(*vii*) Teacher some times takes to talking more which may mar the enthusiasm of the students.

(*viii*) Teacher may not have allowed sufficient time for recording data etc.

(*ix*) Teacher has not given proper attention to supervision.

Merits of Demonstration Method

Following are the merits of this method

(*i*) It is an economical method as compared to purely student centred approaches.

(*ii*) It is a psychological method and students take active interest in teaching learning process.

(*iii*) It leads students from concrete to abstract situations and thus is more psychological.

(*iv*) It is a suitable method if the apparatus to be handled is costly and sensitive. Such an apparatus is likely to damaged if handled by students.

(*v*) This method can be more safe if the experiments to be demonstrated are dangerous.

(*vi*) In comparison to Heuristic method, project etc., it is time saving but lecture method is too speedy.

(*vii*) It can be used successfully for all types of students.

(*viii*) In this method such experiments which are difficult for students can be included.

(*ix*) This method can be used to impart manual and manipulative skills to students.

Disadvantages of Demonstration Method

Some of the disadvantages of this method are as under:

(*i*) It provides no scope for 'learning by doing' for students as students just observe what the teacher is performing. Thus students fail to relish the joys of direct personal experience.

(*ii*) Since the teacher performs the experiment in his own pace, many students cannot comprehend the concept being clarified.

(*iii*) Since the method is not child centred so it makes no provision for individual differences. All types of students including slow learners and genius have to proceed with the same speed.

(*iv*) It fails to develop laboratory skills in the students. It can not work as a substitute for laboratory work by students in which they are required to handle the apparatus themselves.

(*v*) It fails to impart training in scientific attitude.

(*vi*) In this method students many a times fail to observe many finer details of the apparatus used because they observe it from a distance.

Conclusion

It is thoroughly accepted that success is greater with experiments in elementary schools if they start with a real purpose, are simply done with uncomplicated apparatus, are done by children under careful direction of the teacher, and help the children think and draw valid, tentative conclusion.

This is considered as one of the best methods of teaching science to secondary classes. An effort be made to involve a larger number of students by calling them in batches to the demonstration table.

Science teachers should encourage more direct experimentation by children in order to help children broaden their range of fact finding skills beyond three T's – teacher, textbook, television.

3. Heuristic Method

Heuristic method is a pure discovery method of learning science independent of teacher. The writings and teachings of H.E. Armstrong, Professor of Chemistry at the City and Guilds Institute, London, have had much influence in promoting since teaching in schools. He was a strong advocate of a special type of laboratory training – heuristic training ('heuristic' is derived from the Greek word meaning 'to discover'). In Heuristic method, the student be put in the place of an independent discoverer. Thus no help or guidance is provided by the teacher in this method. In this method the teacher sets a problem for the students and then stands aside while they discover the answer.

In words of Professor Armstrong, "Heuristic methods of teaching are methods which involve our placing students as far as possible in the attitude of the discoverer – methods which involve their finding out instead of being merely told about things".

The method requires the student to solve a number of problems experimentally. To almost every one – especially children – experiments and science are synonymous. Once an idea occurs to a scientist he immediately thinks in terms of ways of trying out his ideas to see if he is correct. Trying to confirm or disprove some thing, or simply to test an idea, is the backbone of the experiment. Experiments start with questions in order to find answers, solve problems, clarify ideas or just to see what happens. Experimenting should be part of the elementary school science programme as an aid to helping children find solutions to science problems as well as for helping them to develop appreciation for one of the basic tools of science.

Procedure of the Method

The method requires the students to solve a number of problems experimentally. Each student is required to discover everything for himself and is to be told nothing. The students are led to discover facts with the help of experiments, apparatus and books. In this method the child behaves like a research scholar.

In the stage managed heuristic method, a problem sheet with minimum instructions is given to the student and he is required to perform the experiments concerning the problem in hand. He must follow the instructions, and enter in his notebook an account of what he has done and results arrived at. He must also put down his conclusion as to the bearing which the result has on the problem in hand. In this way he is led to reason from observation.

Essentially therefore, the heuristic method is intended to provide a training in method. Knowledge is a secondary consideration altogether. The method is formative rather than informational.

The procedures and skills in science problem solving can only be developed in class rooms where searching is encouraged, creative thinking is respected, and where it is safe to investigate, try out ideas, and even make mistakes.

Teachers Attitudes

One of the most important aspects of the problem solving approach to children's development in scientific thinking is the teachers attitude. His approach should be teaching science with a question mark instead of with an exclamation point. The acceptance of and the quest for unique solutions for the problem that the class is investigating should be a guiding principle in the teacher's approach to his programme of science. Teachers must develop sensitiveness to children and to the meanings of their behaviour. Teachers should be ready to accept any suggestion for the solution of problems regardless of how irrelevant it may seem to him, for this is really the true spirit of scientific problem solving. By testing various ideas it can be shown to the child that perhaps his suggestion was not in accord with the information available. It can then be shown that this failure gets us much closer to the correct solution by eliminating one possibility from many offered by the problem.

In this method teacher should avoid the temptation to tell the right answer to save time. The teacher should be convinced that road to scientific thinking takes time. Children should never be exposed to ridicule for their suggestions of possible answers otherwise they will show a strong tendency to stop suggestions.

For success of this method a teacher should act like a guide and should provide only that much guidance as is rightly needed by the student. He should be sympathetic and courteous and should be capable enough to plan and devise problems for investigation by pupils. He should be capable of good supervision and be able to train the pupils in a way that he himself becomes dispensable.

Merits of Heuristic Method

This method of teaching science has the following merits:

(*i*) It develops the habit of enquiry and investigation among students.

(*ii*) It develops habit of self learning and self direction.

(*iii*) It develops scientific attitudes among students by making them truthful and honest for they learn how to arrive at decisions by actual experimentations.

(*iv*) It is psychologically sound system of learning as it is based on the maximum, "learning by doing".

(*v*) It develops in the student a habit of diligency.

(*vi*) In this method most of the work is done in school and so the teacher has no worry to assign on check home task.

(*vii*) It provides scope for individual attention to be paid by the teacher and for closer contacts. These contacts help in establishing cordial relations between the teacher and the taught.

Limitations of Heuristic Method

Main limitations of this method are as under:

(*i*) It is a long and time consuming method and so it becomes difficult to cover the prescribed syllabus in time.

(*ii*) It pre-supposes a very small class and a gifted teacher and the method is too technical and scientific to be handled by an average teacher. The method expects of the teacher a great efficiency and hard work, experience and training.

(*iii*) There is a tendency on the part of the teacher to emphasize those branches and parts of the subject which lend themselves to heuristic treatment and to ignore important branches of the subject which do not involve measurement and quantitative work and are therefore not so suitable.

(*iv*) It is not suitable for beginners. In the early stages, the students needs enough guidance which if not given, may greatly disappoint them and it is possible that the child may develop a distaste for studies.

(*v*) In this method too much stress is placed on practical work which may lead a student to form a wrong idea of the nature of science as a whole. They grow up in the belief that science is some thing to be done in the laboratory, forgetting that laboratories were made for science and not science for laboratories.

(*vi*) The gradation of problems is a difficult task which requires sufficient skill and training. The succession of exercises is rarely planned to fit into a general scheme for building up the subject completely.

(*vii*) Some times experiments are performed merely for sake of doing them.

(*viii*) Learning by this method, pupils leave school with little or no scientific appreciation of their physical environment. The romance of modern scientific discovery and invention remains out of picture for them and the humanizing influence of the subject has been kept away from them.

(*ix*) Evaluation of learning through heuristic method can be quite tedious.

(*x*) Presently enough teachers are not available for implementing learning by heuristic method.

Conclusion

This method cannot be successfully applied in primary classes but this method can be given a trial in secondary classes particularly in higher secondary classes. However, in the absence of gifted teachers, well equipped laboratories and libraries and other limitations this method has not been given a trial in our schools. Even if these limitations are removed this method may not prove much useful under the existing circumstances and prevailing rules and regulations. Though not recommending the use of heuristic method for teaching of science it may be suggested that at least a heuristic approach prevails for teaching of science in our schools. By heuristic approach we mean that students be not spoon fed or be given a dictation rather they be given opportunities to investigate, to think and work independently alongwith traditional way of teaching.

4. Assignment Method

The heuristic method is based exclusively on laboratory work where as the lecture method and demonstration method do not give any opportunity for laboratory work. For teaching of science, assignment method is best suited because it involves a harmonious combination of training at the demonstration table and individual laboratory work. In this method of teaching science, the given syllabus is split into well planned assignments with a set of instructions about solving the assignments. It is also possible to plan assignments based on the individual needs of the students.

Procedure

The whole of the prescribed course is divided into so many connected weekly portion or assignments. One topic is taken and a set of instructions regarding the study is drawn up. The printed page containing instructions or the assignment is handed to the pupil a week in advance of their practical work. They are then required to read the pages of the text book referred to in the assignment and write answers to a few (generally not more than three or four) questions in a note-book. The students then hand over these answers to the teacher a day before the practicals. The teacher corrects the answers. If there are a lot of mistakes in the assignments then the teacher sets the remedial and corrective assignments.

The second part of every assignment consists of laboratory work. Full instructions about laboratory work *i.e.* fitting up of apparatus, recording of results, precautions to be taken etc. On the day of the practical work the students are returned their note-books and those students whose preparatory work is found satisfactory by the teacher are allowed to proceed with the practical work.

Teaching by this method demands a lot of careful planning by the teacher and generally two out of six periods allotted to science in time-table are reserved for demonstration work and remaining four for practical work. During periods reserved for demonstration work teacher gives a demonstration on a topic that is considered to be a difficult one by the pupils. These period can also be utilized by the teacher to clarify some facts which are not very clear to the pupils. For the success of assignment method the teacher should prepare a list of experiments to be demonstrated by him and another list of experiments which are to be done by the students. The success of this method mainly depends on properly drawn assignments. If the teacher keeps a progress chart he can easily distinguish between a good and an average or dull student. He can then prepare special assignments according to the needs of the student. An assignment chart may be of the following type on the next page.

Aims

Aims of assignment method are as follows:

(*i*) To provide a synthesis of various methods of learning.
(*ii*) To provide students a training in information processing.
(*iii*) To develop a habit of self study among the students.
(*iv*) To develop scientific attitude and a habit of critical thinking among students.
(*v*) To expose students to various resources of learning.

To achieve these aims the following points be kept in mind while drawing up an assignment.

(*i*) The assignment must be based on one textbook.
(*ii*) The assignment should clearly state what portion of textbook are to be read.
(*iii*) It should draw attention to particular points and give explanation of difficult points.
(*iv*) It should also indicate those portions of matter which can be omitted by the students.
(*v*) Questions are an essential part of the assignment and the questions be so designed that
 (*a*) they test whether the student has read and understood the portion assigned.
 (*b*) their answers are short.
 (*c*) their answers require diagrams to be drawn
 (*d*) they ask for a list of apparatus for coming laboratory work
(*vi*) In each assignment the teacher should indicate portion of book dealing with the same or allied topics.
(*vii*) The assignment should include detailed instructions about the experiment. This portion of instructions should include.

Assignment Method
Specimen of Progress Chart

School ______ Class ______ From ______ To ______

No.	*Name of Student*	*Class Test Result*					*Assignments*					*Term Exam. Results*			*Remarks*
		1	*2*	*3*	*4*	*......*	*1*	*2*	*3*	*4*	*......*	*I*	*II*	*III*	

(*a*) the procedure of the experiment.
(*b*) the method of recording results.
(*c*) the precautions to be observed.
(*d*) a diagram illustrating the set up of the apparatus.

Features of a Good Assignment

(*i*) It should be related to subject matter under study.
(*ii*) It should be concise and balanced which can be finished by student easily and quickly.
(*iii*) Its purpose should be clear and its objective be made known to the students.
(*iv*) It should be so worded that it fosters thinking and independent learning.
(*v*) It should be such so as to suit to the age, aptitudes and interest of the student.
(*vi*) It should be able to combine various methods of teaching.

Teacher's Role

The teacher has to do the following for the success of assignment method of teaching.

(*i*) He should split up the prescribed course in science into successive and progressive assignments.
(*ii*) He should list down the objectives for each assignment which students must achieve.
(*iii*) He should prepare a progress chart for each student.
(*iv*) He must prepare and provide a list of reference material required for each assignment.
(*v*) To cover up the learning gaps he should prepare remedial assignments.
(*vi*) He should also prepare activity sheets for laboratory work and experiments.

Merits of Assignment Method

This method of teaching has the following advantages

(*i*) It provides the students an opportunity for self study.

(*ii*) It synthesizes various methods of teaching of science and makes the learning process very effective.

(*iii*) It provides an opportunity to the student to learn at his own pace and thus the progress of the brighter students is not hindered by weaker students.

(*iv*) In this system teacher gets the central role of contingency manager and facilitator of learning. The teacher acts as a guide and interferes least in the student's work.

(*v*) It places more emphasis on practical work and provides students a training in skill of information processing.

(*vi*) It provides a feel for the scientific methods to students.

(*vii*) In this process the learning process can be individualized to a great extent by having differential assignment.

(*viii*) It provides for corrective feed back and remediation.

(*ix*) The progress chart with the teacher shows the progress of each student at a glance which gives the teacher an idea of a gifted and weaker students.

(*x*) In this process the student learns to work himself because in laboratory he is not provided with any laboratory attendant.

(*xi*) Habit of extra study is developed because a number of books for extra study are recommended by the teacher. Such a study helps in widening the outlook of the pupil.

(*xii*) Since the burden of work lies on pupil so he learns to take responsibility.

(*xiii*) Since the students perform experiments at their own speed so owing to their different speeds they do not perform the same experiment at the same time. Thus a large quantity of same kind of apparatus is not required.

Disadvantages of Assignment Method

Some of the disadvantages of assignment methods are as follows:

(*i*) It burdens the teacher with a lot of planning and thus increases his work load to a large extent. It requires the teacher to prepare a well thought out scheme for the year before starting the method.

(*ii*) No source material is available in the market for assignments preparation of assignments for different students becomes an uphill task for the teacher. For teaching science beginner is advised to use the book "Assignments in Practical Elementary Science" by Dr. Whitehouse. However, if a book other than "Experimental Science" by Gregory and Hodges is being used as a textbook then the above book of assignments should only be used after making necessary/alteration in connection with references.

(*iii*) The success of method depends on the availability of rich library and laboratory facilities. It makes the method very expensive.

(*iv*) Before starting with this method teacher must satisfy himself that the apparatus and chemicals required for practical work are available in the laboratory. He should also satisfy himself about the availability of text books, laboratory manual, note book etc. and see that each student possesses them.

(*v*) Teacher should also be vigilant to see that weak students do not get a chance to copy the answers from the note books of brighter students.

(*vi*) Weaker students need a lot of help and guidance at individual level and it becomes an unnecessary drain on the teacher's energies.

(*vii*) This method is suitable only for a small graph of students.

Conclusion

Though the method has some limitations but can be used successfully if following points are given due consideration.

(*i*) The teacher should prepare a well thought out plan for the year.

(*ii*) He should find some good resource book and use the same after necessary changes.

(*iii*) He should be very particular to check copying by weaker students. As remedial measures the teacher should clearly explain difficult topics and principles to the students during demonstration class and set only a limited number of questions in his assignment.

(*iv*) The availability of apparatus and chemicals needed for experiment be confirmed before hand.

(*v*) Only those students who have text book, laboratory mannual and note book whose preparatory work has been found to be satisfactory be allowed to do the practical work.

(*vi*) A new experiment be allowed to a student when he has completed his previous experiment and has shown it to the teacher.

(*vii*) Students be asked to record all their observations directly in the fair note book. They should be asked to complete their practical note book in the class itself.

(*viii*) Teacher can provide necessary help to needy students and for this he should move from one table to another when the students are performing the experiment.

5. Project Method

This method was given by Dewey – the American philosopher, psychologist and practical teacher. The project method is a direct outcome of his philosophy. According to Dr. Kilpatrick "A project is a unit of whole hearted purposeful activity carried on preferably, in its natural setting". According to Stevenson "A project is a problematic act carried to its completion in its natural setting". According to Ballard, "A project is a bit of real life that has been incorporated into the school".

The project method is not totally new. Project equivalents are advocated for the adolescent period by Rousseau in Emile (BK-III). A project plan is a modified form of an old method called "concentration-of-studies". The main features of "concentration-of-studies plan" is that some subject is taken as the core or centre and all other school subjects as they arise are studied in connection with it.

Project method is based on the following principles:

(*i*) Learning by doing.

(*ii*) Learning by living.

(*iii*) Children learn better through association, cooperation and activity.

What is an Educational Project?

Various definitión of project has already been considered. A modified definition of project is given by Tomas and Long. They define it as "a voluntary undertaking which involves constructive effort or thought and eventuates into objective results".

Considering various definitions of project we may consider it as a kind of life experience which is an outcome of a craving or desire of the pupils. This is a method of spontaneous and incidental teaching. "Learning by living" may be a better meaning of project method, because life is full of projects and individuals carry out these projects in their every day life.

The projects may broadly be classified as

(*i*) Individual projects, and

(*ii*) Social projects

Individual projects are to be carried out by individuals where as social projects are carried out by a grant of individuals.

Steps in a Project

For completing a project we have five stages in actual practice. These are

(*i*) Providing a situation

(*ii*) Choosing and proposing.

(*iii*) Planning of the project.

(*iv*) Executing the project.

(*v*) Judging the project.

Recording the project is also essential.

(*i*) *Providing a Situation*

A project should arise out of a need felt by pupils and it should never be forced on them. It should be purposeful and significant. It should look important and must be interesting. For this the teacher should always be on the look out to find situation that arise and discuss them with students to discover their interests. Situations may be provided by different methods. Some such methods may include talking to students on the topics of common interest *e.g.* how did they spend their holidays, what did they see in Delhi etc.

(ii) Choosing and Proposing

From various definition of an educational project we get the same underlying ideas (*a*) school tasks are to be as real and as purposeful as the tasks of wider life beyond the school wall (*b*) they are of such a nature that the pupil is genuinely eager to carry them out in order to achieve a desirable and clearly realised aim.

According to Kilpatrick, "the part of the pupil and the part of the teacher, in most of the school work, depends largely on who does the proposing". The teacher should refrain from proposing any project otherwise the whole purpose of the method would be defeated. Teacher should only tempt the students for a particular project by providing a situation but the proposal for the project should finally come from students. The teacher must exercise guidance in selection of the project and if the students make an unwise choice, the teacher should tactfully guide them for a better project. The essentially of a good project are:

(*i*) It should have evident worth for the individual or the graph that undertakes them.

(*ii*) The project must have a bearing on a great number of subjects and the knowledge acquired through it may be applicable in a variety of ways.

(*iii*) The project should be timely.

(*iv*) The project should be challenging.

(*v*) The project should be feasible.

It is for the teacher to see that the purpose of the project is clearly defined and understood.

(iii) Planning

The students be encouraged by the teacher to plan out the details of the project. In the process of planning teacher has to act only as a guide and he should give suggestions at times but actual planning be left to the students.

(iv) Execution

Once the project has been chosen and the details of the project have been planned, the teacher should help the students in executing the project according to the plan. Since execution of a project is the longest step in the project method so it need a lot a patience on the part of the students and the teacher. During this step the teacher should carefully supervise the pupils in manipulative skills to prevent waste of materials and to guard accidents. The teacher should assign work to different students in accordance with their tastes, interests, aptitudes and capabilities. Teacher should see that every member of the grasp gets a chance to do some thing. Teacher should constantly check up the relation between the chalked out plans and the developing project and as far as possible 'at the spot' changes and modification be avoided. However if such changes become unavoidable these should be noted and reasons explained for future guidance.

(v) Evaluation

The evaluation of the project should be done both by the pupils and the teacher. The pupils should estimate the qualities of what they have done before the teacher gives his evaluation. The evaluation of the project has to be done in the light of plans, difficulties in the execution and achieved results. Let the students have self criticism and look through their own failings and findings. This step is very useful because as a result of the project, the pupils can know the values of the information, interest, skills and attitudes that have been modified by the project.

(vi) Record

A complete record of the project be kept by the students. The record should include everything about the project. It should include the proposal, plan and its discussion, duties allotted to different students and how far were they carried out by them. It should also include the details of places visited and surveyed, maps etc. drawn, guidance for future and all other possible details.

Role of Teacher

(*i*) In project method of teaching the role of a teacher is that of a guide, friend and philosopher.

(*ii*) He helps the students in solving their problems just like an elder brother.

(*iii*) He encourages his students to work collectively, amicably in the graph.

(*iv*) He also helps his students to avoid mistakes.

(*v*) He makes it a point that each member of the group contributes some thing to the completion of the project and in this process helps the shy and weaker students to work along with their class mates.

(*vi*) If the students face failure during execution of some steps of the project the teacher should not execute any portion of the project but should only explain to his students the reasons of their failure and should suggest them some better methods or techniques that may be used by them next time for the success of the project.

(*vii*) During the execution step teacher also learns some thing.

(*viii*) Teacher should always remain alert and active during execution, step and see that the project goes to completion successfully.

(*ix*) During execution of the project teacher should maintain a democratic atmosphere.

(*x*) Teacher must be well read and well informed so that he can help the students to the successful completion of the project.

Merits of the Project Method

(*i*) It is a method of teaching based on psychological laws of learning. The education is related to child's life and he acquires it through meaningful activity.

(*ii*) It imbibes the spirit of cooperation as it is a cooperative venture. Teacher and students join in the project.

(*iii*) It stimulates interest in natural as also man made situations. More over the interest is spontaneous and not under any compulsions.

(*iv*) The method provides opportunities for pupils of different tastes and aptitudes with in the frame work of the same scheme.

(*v*) It upholds the dignity of labour.

(*vi*) It introduces democracy in education.

(*vii*) It brings about a close correlation between a particular activity and various subjects.

(*viii*) It is a problem solving method and places very less emphasis on cramming or memorising.

(*ix*) It helps to inculcate social discipline through joint activities of the teacher and the taught.

(*x*) A project can be used to arouse interest in a particular topic as it blends school life with outside world. It provides situations in which the students come in direct contact with their environment.

(*xi*) It develops self confidence and self discipline.

(*xii*) A project tends to illustrate the real nature of the subject.

(*xiii*) A project affords opportunity to develop keenness and accuracy of observation and produces a spirit of enquiry.

(*xiv*) It puts a challenge to the student and thus stimulates constructive and creative thinking.

(*xv*) It provides the students an opportunity for mutual exchange of ideas.

(*xvi*) This method helps the children to organise their knowledge.

Drawbacks of the Project Method

(*i*) Projects require a lot of time and this method can be used as a part of science work only.

(*ii*) Though the method provides the student superficial knowledge of so many things it provides insufficient knowledge of some fundamental principles.

(*iii*) In the project planning and execution of the project the teacher is required to put in much more work in comparison to other methods of teaching.

(*iv*) The teacher has been assumed as master of all subjects which is practically not possible.

(*v*) Good text books on these lines have not yet been produced.

(*vi*) It is an expensive method is it involves tours, excursions, purchase of apparatus and equipment etc.

(*vii*) The method of organising instructions is unsystematised and thus the regular time table of work will be upset.

(*viii*) The method may fit those who cannot listen but it is very questionable if it has the same value for those who can listen.

(*ix*) The method leaves a gap in pupils knowledge.

(*x*) It underestimates man's power of imagination which enables him to savour the full experience of another without the necessity of undergoing the experience himself.

(*xi*) Some times the projects may be too ambitious and beyond pupils capacity to accomplish.

(*xii*) Larger projects in hands of an unexperienced teacher lead to boredom.

(*xiii*) The education given by projects is likely to emphasise relationships in breadth than in depth.

Conclusion

The project method provides a practical approach to learning of both theoretical and practical problems. If it is difficult to follow this method of teaching it would be better at least not to ignore the spirit of this method.

This method has been found to be more suitable for primary and middle classes and is of restricted use for high and higher secondary classes. This method may be tried alongwith formal class room teaching without disturbing the school time-table. With this in view some projects may be undertaken by the students to be completed on certain fixed days of a week. Alternately first half of the day may be devoted to class room teaching and the project work be carried out in the remaining half day. To help solve the problem of fund's shortage such projects be choose which are self-supporting or the projects selected be such that their final products can be sold to partially support the funds. Some such projects are improvising science apparatus, growing a vegetable garden etc. Costly projects should be avoided. As it is not suitable for drill and continuous and systematic teaching, it is not very desirable to use it freely.

Some good life science projects are as under:

1. Plant parasites
2. Carnivorous plants
3. Study of rocks
4. Locomotion of animals
5. Spider and their ways
6. Bird migration
7. Butterflies and moths
8. Ways of preserving food
9. The Ecology of a bond
10. Maintaining an aquarium
11. A study of Nests and Nesting habits of birds
12. Cacti and succulents
13. Microscopic plants
14. Factors affecting germination of plants
15. Flower or fruit
16. How plants reproduce etc.

6. Concentric Method

This is a system of organising a course rather than a method of teaching. It is therefore better to call it *concentric system* or *approach*. It implies widening of knowledge just as concentric circles go on extending and widening. It is a system of arrangement of subject matter. In this method the study of the topic is spread over a number of years. It is based on the principle that subject cannot be given an exhaustive treatment at the first stage. To begin with, a simple presentation of the subject is given and further knowledge is imparted in following years. Thus beginning from a nucleus the circles of knowledge go on widening year after year and hence the name concentric method.

Procedure

A topic is divided into a number of portions which are then allotted to different classes. The criterion for allotment of a particular portion of the course to a particular class are the difficulty of portion and power of comprehension of students in that age group. Thus it is mainly concerned with year to year teaching but its influence can also be exercised in day-to-day teaching. Knowledge be given today should follow from knowledge given yesterday and should lead to teaching on following day.

Merits of Concentric Method

(*i*) This method of organisation of subject matter is decidely superior to that in which one topic is taken up in particular class and an effort is made to deal with all aspects of the topic in that particular class.

(*ii*) In provides a frame work from science course which is of real value to students.

(*iii*) The system is most successful when the teaching is in hands of one teacher because then he can preserve continuity in the teaching and keeps his expanding circle concentric.

(*iv*) It provides opportunity for revision of work already covered in a previous class and carrying out new work.

(*v*) It enables the teacher to cover a portion according to receptivity of learner.

(*vi*) Since the same topic is learnt over many years so its impressions are more lasting.

(*vii*) It does not allow teaching to become dull because every year a new interest can be given to the topic. Every year there are new problems to solve and new difficulties to overcome.

Drawbacks

For the success of this approach we require really capable teacher. If a teacher becomes over ambitious and exhausts all the possible interesting illustrations in the introductory year then the subject loses its power of freshness and appeal and nothing is left to create interest in the topic in subsequent years.

In case the topic is too short or too long then also the method is not found to be useful. A too long portion makes the topic dull and a two short portion fails to leave any permanent and lasting impression on the mind of the pupil.

Conclusion

It is a good method for being adopted for arranging the subject matter. It should be kept in mind, by the organisers, while organising the subject matter that no portion is too long or too short. It would also be much useful if the same teacher teaches the same class year after year so that he can reserve some illustrative examples for each year and thus can maintain the interest of the students in the topic.

7. Unit Method

It is one of the latest methods in the field of education. It involves pupils more actively in learning process.

Different authors define *unit* in a different way. Hanna, Hageman, Potter define it as, "a unit is a purposeful learning experience that is focussed on some socially significant understanding which will modify the behaviour of learner and adjust him to adjust to a life situation more effectively".

However all the definitions of *unit* imply that it possesses the following characteristics.

(*i*) It is an organisation of activities around a purpose.

(*ii*) It has significant content.

(*iii*) It involves students in learning process.

(*iv*) It modifies the students behaviour to such an extent that he can cope with new problems and situations more competently.

Types of Units

Mainly the units may be classified as

(*i*) Subject matter units.

(*ii*) Experience units.

(*iii*) Resource units.

The teaching of general science can be carried out in a better way and it is better understood and appreciated by the students if it is taught as units of immediate interest to the pupils. Such units may be (*i*) life centred (*ii*) environment centred (*iii*) life and environment centred.

For this The Tara Devi Seminar[1] (1956) recommended the following:

Life Centred Units

1. The world that science has built.
2. The air we breathe.
3. The water we use.
4. The food we eat.
5. How man gets his food.
6. The clothes we wear.
7. The homes we live in.
8. The machines we use.
9. The power we work with.
10. Protection from disease.
11. Our biological resources.
12. Our mineral resources.
13. Means of transport.
14. Means of communicate with the world.
15. The universe we live in.
16. Story of life.
17. How to be yourself.

Environment-centred Units

1. The atmosphere.
2. Water, a vital need of life.
3. The earth surface.
4. Fire and heat.
5. Effects on heating and cooling in air and water.
6. Study of light.
7. Civilization and the use of metals.
8. Work and energy (the occupations of man).
9. Problems of transport and communication.
10. Plants and animals in relation to life.

1. Report of All India Seminar on the Teaching of Science in Secondary Schools, held at Tara Devi (Simla Hills), 1956, Ministry of Education, New Delhi.

11. The study of the body-machine.
12. Understanding ourselves.
13. Science and philosophy of life.

Environment of Life-centred Units

1. The world that science has built.
2. Your body-machine and how it works.
3. Health to you.
4. Using biological resources for better living.
5. Using mineral resources for better living.
6. Energy and machines for the world of tomorrow.
7. Time, measurement and mass production.
8. The weather and what we can do about it.
9. Astronomy:
   (*a*) The solar system in which we live.
   (*b*) Billions of stars and other universes.
10. Science for our homes.

For teaching science the lessons are grouped round the various topics. For learning a unit entitled 'means of transport' we can group the lessons dealing with various means of transport such as bicycle, steam engine, internal combustion engine, electric motor, aeroplanes, ships etc. While dealing with these we can introduces many ideas *e.g.* while teaching about bicycle we can introduce the study of levers, use of levers for harnessing energy, gaining speed with the help of livers etc. Some new term as speed, velocity, acceleration, retardation, brake, friction, lubrication, mechanical advantage etc. may also be introduced. While dealing with electric motors we can tell the use of such motors in electric trains, generation and transmission of electricity. The terms volt, ohm, resistance, capacitance etc. can also be introduced.

Similarly for teaching of biology 'Farm', 'Garden', 'Pond' etc. can be used as a unit. From it we can introduce the student to the teaching of various kind of soils, insects, water, weather etc.

Similar interesting lessons can be developed on 'Air', 'Water' etc. These can be used for teaching of hydrogen, nitrogen, water, carbondioxide etc.

Essentials of a Good Unit

(*i*) It should deal with a sizeable topic.

(*ii*) It should emerge out of students past experiences and should lead to broader interests.

(*iii*) It should be of appropriate difficulty in terms of child's understanding, interest.

(*iv*) It should provide scope for using a variety of materials and activities like community resources, audiovisual materials etc.

(*v*) It should allow use of sufficient amount of books and other learning materials.

(*vi*) Units should be such as to draw materials from several fields so that children may develop richer insight into human relationships and processes.

(*vii*) It should be functional and should be in accordance with the maturity level of the learner.

Merits of Unit Method

This method of teaching has the following advantages:

(*i*) It brings about a closer integration between various branches of science.

(*ii*) It makes subject matter more interesting and realistic.

(*iii*) It provides a better understanding of the environment and life.

(*iv*) It focuses attention on significant facts and avoids confusion.

(*v*) The unit because of its flexibility provides facility in adopting instructions to individual's differences.

(*vi*) It is quite useful to teaching general science in elementary classes.

Limitations of Unit Method

(*i*) This method cannot be used if the teacher is required to complete some prescribed course in a specified time.

(*ii*) There are only a few teachers who are so widely read that they can introduce material and illustration from various branches of science while keeping before their students one central topic.

Unit method or *topic method* is a varied slightly in America. In American schools the teacher announces one topic and the students are asked to say what they already know about it. Then the topic is discussed in a question and answer session and those questions which no member of the class could answer are noted down for investigation. From this list of questions, such questions as are considered as too difficult for a particular class are eliminated by the teacher and the remaining questions are arranged in a planned manner for answers. These questions are then dealt within the class according to the plan. The great thing about such a course is that boys feel that it is their course and not some thing thrust upon them by authority.

In some American schools the teacher announces a topic and then hands over to the class a piece of mechanism, say electric bell, and asks them to discover everything about it. He adverse them to consult books, to ask questions and then come prepared, for discussion with his, after a week.

8. Historical Method

Some teachers prefer to develop a subject by following the stages through which the subject has passed during its course of development from its early beginnings. This type of teaching has a fascination which appeals to pupils. Various science subjects such as Chemistry, Physics, Bacteriology etc. which have an interesting historical background can be taught successfully by such a technique. It is possible to develop a topic starting from its early history and the various stages through which it developed before attaining the modern shape.

Chemistry, in particular, has a very interesting history and the works of Priestley, Lavoisier, Davy, Black and Dalton etc. can be given this type of treatment. The gradual development of atomic theory can be unfolded gradually by this method which will be quite interesting. Similarly the teacher can use stories from the history of science (*e.g.* Archimedes and his bath, Newton and the apple etc.) to arouse interest of the students in the topic under consideration.

While discussing the subject of Bacteriology the historical treatment can include invention and development of the microscope.

Through such a treatment may not be possible for all the topics but an occasional resort to such a treatment has its own uses.

9. Discussion Method

This method is found quite suitable for those topics in science which cannot be easily explained by demonstration or other such techniques. The discussion may be about a certain specimen or model or chart.

In this method the topics for discussion is announced to the students well in advance. The teacher gives a brief introduction about the contents of the topic and them suggests to his students various reference books, text books and other books. Students are then required to go through the relevant pages of these books and come prepared from a discussion of the topic on a specified day. During actual discussion period teachers poses a few problems and thus provides the necessary motivation. The students are then asked to answer the question one by one and when ever thinks fit advises some students not to go out of the scope of a particular question or topic under consideration. This check is essential otherwisc immature students may go out of the scope of the topic.

Following points if kept in view will help make the discussion successful.

(*i*) The topics for discussion should be of common interest of students.

(*ii*) Teacher should establish a favourable atmosphere in the class before starting the discussion.

(*iii*) Teacher should see that every one participates in the discussion. The whole essence of discussion is "Thinking together".

(*iv*) The teacher should talk to the bare minimum and also should not allow any one student to dominate the whole discussion.

(*v*) It is for teacher to see that the discussion remains a discussion and it does not change into a debate.

(*vi*) Teacher should keep a check on answers of the students and should not allow a student to go beyond the scope of a topic under discussion.

(*vii*) Teacher has to maintain discipline and he should see that only one student speaks at a time.

10. Scientific Method

This method of teaching of science is based upon the process of finding out the results by attacking a problem in a number of definite steps. It is possible to train the students in scientific method. In this method student is involved in finding out the answer to a given scientific problem and thus actually it is a type of discovery method.

Fitzpatrick defines science as, "science is a cumulative and endless series of empirical observations which result in the formation of concepts and theories, with both concepts and theories being subject to modification in the light of further empirical observation. Science is both a body of knowledge and the process of acquiring and refining knowledge".

Considering this definition of science it becomes imperative that the students be exposed to the scientific way of finding out. Scientific method of teaching helps to develop the power of reasoning, application of scientific knowledge, critical thinking and positive attitude, in the learner.

This method proceeds in the following steps:

(*i*) Problem in identified.

(*ii*) Some hypothesis are framed and these are proposed for testing.

(*iii*) Experiments are then devised to test the proposed hypothesis.

(*iv*) Data is collected from observations and the collected data is then interpreted.

(*v*) Finally conclusions are drawn to accept, reject or modify the proposed hypothesis.

Scientific method is therefore a well sequenced and structured method for finding the results through experiments.

Role of Teacher

For the success of scientific method the role of teacher is very important. He should act as a coinvestigator along with students and must also find sufficient and must also find sufficient time and have patience to attend to students' problems. Under the proper guidance of the teacher the science laboratory should become the hub for implementations of this method.

Merits

Scientific method has following advantages:

(*i*) Students learn science of their own and teacher works only as a guide.

(*ii*) It helps students to become real scientists as they learn to identify and formulate scientific problems.

(*iii*) It provides to students a training in techniques of information processing

(*iv*) It develops a habit of logical thinking in the students as they are required to interpret data and observations.

(*v*) It helps to develop intellectual honesty in students.

(*vi*) It helps the students to learn to see relationships and pattern among things and variables.

(*vii*) It provides the students a training in the methods and skills of discovering new knowledge in science.

Limitations

Some important limitations of the method are as under:

(*i*) It is a long, drawn out and time consuming method.

(*ii*) It can never become a full fledged method of learning science.

(*iii*) Due to lack of exposure to this method most of the science teachers fail to implement it successfully.

(*iv*) This method is suitable only for very bright and creative students.

11. Problem-Solving Method

'Problem-solving method' is one in which the problems are solved scientifically. It is a method which discipline the mind to approach all problems scientifically and in the same way. It is otherwise known as 'scientific method'.

In this method the existence of a problem in pre-supposed. A *problem* is an obstruction of some sort to the attainment of an objective, a sort of difficulty which does not enable the individual to reach the goal easily. The distinguishing thing about a problem is that it impresses the individual who meets it as a needing challange. These problems grow in complexity as the individual grows older and older. The solution of these gives him better hold on the environment, increases his store of knowledge and develops his intellectual powers.

Various Steps of Problem Solving Method

Following are the important steps in a problem solving method:

1. Locating and sensing the problem.
2. Defining the problem.
3. Analysing the problem.
4. Collecting the data.
5. Interpreting and analysing the data.
6. Formation of hypothesis.
7. Drawing conclusion and framing principles.

There may be a little deviation about the steps when students set the practical problem in the field.

(i) Locating and Sensing the problems. Problems are the Universal phenomena. They exist everywhere. But one must be capable of sensing specific problem, and isolating it from other problems. In the class room problems may be formed on the basis of the interaction of the pupil and teacher. The presentation of problem is thus a Co-operative venture. Problems may be developed through class room discussion, pupils' interest, their past experience, their future aspirations and their aptitudes.

Following points be given due consideration:

1. The problem should be suitable to maturity level of students.
2. The problem should be selected clearly and concisely.
3. The problem should not be too broad.
4. The problem should be properly delimited.
5. The problem selected should be such that it can be easily solved with the help of the material at hand.
6. The problem should be worth-while for the learner.

(ii) Defining the problem. The problem should be clearly and precisely defined. Pupils should be trained in this art. They should be trained to choose key words and phrases. They should analyse and interpret their problems. This will result in better understanding. A best way to defining the problem should be selected through discussion.

(iii) Analysing the problem. Analysing the problem helps in understanding it properly. It makes pupils understanding the real causes for observed events. Hence pupils should be capable of interpreting the problem. With the help of key words and phrases, they should analyse the problem from different views. Before stating the problem one should be aware of the constraints placed on him by his ability, equipment, and time.

(iv) Collection of Data. Data are available in different forms. They are collected from different sources. The most important of such sources are; (*i*) Experiments; (*ii*) Reference Books; (*iii*) Journals and Bulletins; (*iv*) Maps; (*v*) Field Trips; (*vi*) Observations; and (*vii*) Interviews.

However, before solving the problem, one should be capable of selecting a correct, relevant and reliable data from reliable sources. He should decide right type of data essential for solving the problem.

(v) Interpretation and Analysis of Data. Data are processed in order to form Hypothesis. Data are recorded and arranged in order. Important techniques such as: (*i*) Establishing causal relationship; (*ii*) Reasoning; (*iii*) Inferning; (*iv*) Identifying inconsistencies; (*v*) Generalising; (*vi*) Logical interpretation; (*vii*) with holding judgement for want of adequate data; (*viii*) Synthesising data; and (*ix*) Drawing conclusions are used in interpreting and analysing of data. The processed data must be read and understood. Students must learn to judge the reliability of data source. They must be able to construct a single theory from out of various observations. The judgements should be based on his ability to organise data into meaningful concept. He should look for additional sources of data.

(vi) Formation of Hypothesis. Hypothesis is a hunch or assumption. It is a variable fact based on logic and reasoning. It has a good chance of being correct. Hypothesis is related with assumption, conclusion and principle. However they differ among themselves Assumption is entirely, a crude logic. Hypothesis is based on logic and reasoning and it is likely to be true. Conclusion becomes theory after

experimental evidence. Principle is a fact established by experts after evaluation. The pupils should draw inferences after analysis and interpretation. The inferences should be synthesised into generalised hypothesis. This is the outcome of inductive reasoning.

From out of generalised hypothesis one should construct a single theory. More over the hypothesis should be tested with the help of experiments, observations and references. Until the correct or valid fact is attained testing should continue.

(vii) Drawing Conclusion and Framing Principles. This is the final step in attaining 'Scientific Method' or 'problems solving method'. Testing of hypothesis is followed by drawing conclusion. This conclusion is simply a solution to the problem concerned. The conclusion thus arrived at is stared in the form of a 'principle' using definite and precise wording with no substitute. The principle should be an underivable fact beyond all doubts. This principle can be experimented and it may have universal currency.

(viii) Applying Principles in New Situation. The application of the principle to new situations will help the individual to bride the gap between artificial class-room situation and real life situation. The pupil should be able to recognise the common and identical elements in the principles and a new life situation. He should be able to analyse and interpret new situations in the light of the conclusions arrived at.

Advantages of the Method

1. It is much easier to remember through this approach.
2. It develops in pupil good habits of planning, thinking and reasoning.
3. It encourages students to search, to enquire, to look for materials and to evaluate them critically.
4. It takes into account the individual differences.
5. It tends to increase the amount of experience.
6. It develops attitude of critical inquiry, independent thought and initiative.
7. It is a stimulating method.
8. It motivates the child to learn new things.
9. It helps the student to learn principles and to work honestly.

12. Inductive – Deductive Method

It is a combination of two methods. To be able to understand this combination it is necessary to understand them separately.

I. Inductive Method

In this method one is led from concrete to abstract, particular to general and from complex to general rule. In this method we prove a universal law by showing that if it is true in a particular case it is also true in other similar cases.

This method has been found to be quite suitable for teaching of science because most of the principles of science or the conclusions are results of induction. This process of arriving at generalisation can be illustrated as under.

Illustration. Take a piece of blue litmus paper and dip it in a test tube containing hydrochloric acid, observe the change in colour. (It turns red.)

Take another piece of blue litmus paper and dip it in a test-tube containing nitric acid. Observe the change in colour. (It turns red.)

Repeat the experiments with other acids in different test tubes (*e.g.* oxalic acid, acetic acid etc.). (In each case blue litmus turns red.)

From the above experiments we can make a generalisation that *acid turn blue litmus red*.

Following the same procedure the students may be asked to drop a piece of chalk, duster, books, pen, pencil etc. and observe him falling these on earth. From these observations it can then be easily generalised that *all substances are attracted by earth*.

Merits of the Inductive Method

(*i*) It helps understanding.

(*ii*) It is a scientific method.

(*iii*) It develops scientific attitude.

(*iv*) It is a logical method and develops critical thinking and habit of keen observations.

(*v*) It is a psychological method and provides ample scope for students activities.

(*vi*) It is based on actual observations, thinking and experimentation.

(*vii*) It keeps alive the students interest because they move from known to unknown.

(*viii*) It curbs the tendency to learn by rote and also reduces home work

(*ix*) It develops self-confidence.

(*x*) It develops the habit of intelligent hard work.

Drawbacks of Inductive Method

This method suffers from the following limitations

(*i*) It is limited in range and cannot be used in solving and understanding all the topics in science.

(*ii*) The generalisation obtained from a few observations are not the complete study of the topic. To fix the topic in the mind of the learner a lot of supplementary work and practice is needed.

(*iii*) Inductive reasoning is not absolutely conclusive. The generalisation has been done from the study of a few (three or four) cases. The process thus establishes certain degree of probability which can be increased by increasing the number of valid cases

(*iv*) This method needs a lot of time and energy and thus it is time consuming and laborious method.

(*v*) This method is not found to be suitable in higher classes because some of the unnecessary details and explanations may make teaching dull and boring.

(*vi*) The use of this method should be restricted and confined to understanding the rules in the early stages.

(*vii*) This method may be considered complete and perfect only if the generalisation arrived at by induction can be verified through deductive method.

II. Deductive Method

Deductive method is opposite of inductive method. In this method the learner proceeds from general to particular, from abstract to concrete. Thus in this method facts are deduced or analysed by the application of established formula or experimentation. In this case the formula is accepted by the learner as a duly established fact.

In this method teacher announces the topics of the day and he also gives the relevant formula/rule/law/principle etc. The law/ formula is also explained to the students with the help of certain examples which are solved on the black board. From these students get the idea of use or application of the concerned law/principle/ formula. Then the problems are given to the students who solve the problems following the same method as explained to them earlier by the teacher. Students also memorise the results for future application.

Following example illustrates the procedure.

Principle: Cooling is caused by evaporation.

Confirmation by Application: It can be confirmed by numerous application, such as, by wearing wet clothes, observing feeling after taking bath, by applying alcohol on your hand etc.

Merits of the Deductive Method

(*i*) It is short and time saving and so this method is liked by authors and teachers.

(*ii*) It is quite a suitable method for lower classes.

(*iii*) It glorifies memory because students are required to memorise a large number of laws, formulae etc.

(*iv*) For practice and revision of topic it is an adequate and advantageous method.

(*v*) It supplements inductive method and thus completes the process of inductive – deductive method.

(*vi*) It enhances speed and efficiency in solving problems.

Limitations

(*i*) It is not a scientific method because the approach of this method is confirmatory and not explanatory.

(*ii*) It encourages rote memory because pure deductive work requires some law; principle formula for every type of problem and it demands blind memorisation of large number of such laws/formulae etc.

(*iii*) Being an unscientific method it does not impart any training in scientific method.

(*iv*) It causes unnecessary and heavy burden on the brain which may some times result in brain fag.

(*v*) In this method memory becomes more important than understanding and intelligence which is educationally not sound.

(*vi*) It is an unpsychological method because the facts and principles are not found by the students themselves.

(*vii*) In this method students cannot become active learners.

(*viii*) It is not suitable for development of thinking, reasoning and discovery.

Conclusion

A careful consideration of merits and limitations of these two methods leads in to conclude that Inductive Method is the fore-runner of Deductive Method. For effective teaching of science, both inductive and deductive approaches should be used because no one is complete without the other. Induction leaves the learner at a point where he cannot stop and the after work has to be done and completed by deduction. Deduction is a process that is particularly suitable for final statement and induction is most suitable for exploration fields. Induction gives the lead and deduction follows. In science if we want to teach about *composition of water* then its composition is determined by a endiometer tube (inductive process) and confirmed by the process of electrolysis of water (deductive process).

4.5 CHOICE OF METHOD

The teacher is required to select the most suitable method according to his topic. He should exercise his wisdom in selecting the needed experiments in life science subjects.

As biology becomes more socially relevant, with its stress as such issues as bioethics, the critique of national science policies, the sociology of scientific community, questions of environ management, personal development, health, hygiene and vocational applications, so the methods of teaching has slowly changed. In the more responsive biology class room, a variety of teaching methods which were once considered to be suitable only for social science or for courses in personal development are now being applied. These include the following:

(*i*) Small group activities.

(*ii*) Group workshops.
(*iii*) Simulations
(*iv*) Dramatic and semi-dramatic methods.
(*v*) Work experience.
(*vi*) Independent learning.
(*vii*) Self-paced systems.
(*viii*) Individualized instructions.

As is suggested by this list, modern biology programmes are tending to stress social values and social applications. It is no longer considered as sufficient to rely on traditional methods of teaching. More and more techniques of social sciences are used in the biology class room. It should be stressed here that any teaching programme using a wide variety of teaching methods chosen to optimise the achievement of relevant objectives and to meet the individual needs of the learners. It is heartening to find that biology teachers world-wide are responding to this challange.

Chapter 5

Innovations in Teaching

5.1 INDIVIDUALISED INSTRUCTIONS: INTRODUCTION

Individualised instruction is not an independent study, auto-instruction or programmed instruction. Individualised instruction is a technique which makes learning self-initiated and self-directed. No two pupils agree, hence each pupil should assume the responsibility of learning. Because of individual differences of pupils, the class-room instructions need to be structured in such a way as to suit the individual needs of students. This method of instruction which caters to the needs of individual students is known as individualised instructions.

Various Approaches to Individualised Instruction

Some of the approaches to individualised instructions are as follows:

1. *Individually diagnosed and prescribed programmes.* These programmes have clearly specified behavioural objectives, with materials and methods of presentation matched to the objectives.

2. *Self-directed materials*. In this type of programme students and teachers cooperate to establish the outcome of learning. There is complete freedom to students to select the materials and methods for achieving the goals. This type of approach has been found quite useful for an above-average learner.

3. *Personalised Programme*. In this type of programme student in free to select his own objectives and then follow a directed programme with the help of specialised materials. This approach has been found to be more useful for high school students.

4. *Independent study*. In this type the child is free to select his own objectives as well as the topic. He is also at liberty to decide the

method of achieving the objectives. This approach is generally useful with above-average students.

5.2 MODULAR APPROACH: INSTRUCTIONAL MATERIALS

Individualised instruction uses several materials like printed materials, films, reports etc. These materials can be developed into small learning units. Such learning units are called 'modules'. A modular approach is involved in individualised instruction. Modular approach is one which allows the individual to learn on his own accord. The teacher acts as a guide. Each module involves a test. Self evaluation is made possible. Individual answers the questions of the module. He can verify his answers with the given module. Different steps are followed in preparing the module. They are, selecting the topics defining the objective, identifying activities, determining the level of mastery: preparing an outline, preparing instructions, trying out the module; and refining the module.

Advantages of Modular Approach

Modular approach has following advantages:

(*i*) Topics are organised in a proper sequence;

(*ii*) It motivates students to self directed activities;

(*iii*) It permits each child to progress at his own speed; and

(*iv*) It increases experience for investigating by each child.

Disadvantages of Modular Approach

(*i*) It has only limited application.

(*ii*) It can be used for average learner.

(*iii*) It can be used in a small class.

(*iv*) Materials for individualised instructions are not available.

(*v*) It needs more time for teacher to prepare and collect materials.

5.3 TEAM TEACHING

Team-Teaching emerged in American Education in 1954. It is relatively a new idea in the field of Education. Now it is widely used by almost all countries with slight modification. Team-Teaching, according to Shaplin, is a type of instructional organisation involving teaching personal and the students. Two or more teachers are given responsibility of working together for offering instruction to a group of students Team-Teaching includes the following components:

(*i*) A group of teachers;
(*ii*) Teaching being a joint responsibility;
(*iii*) Organisation of instructional materials; and
(*iv*) The size of the team depends on, the nature and objective of the course, size of the class and materials to be used.

Ways of Organising Team Teaching

The team teaching cannot be easily organised. It is really a tough task. Prof. Kenneth has suggested some ways of organising Team-Teaching. They are as under:

(*i*) At the secondary stage a number of specialist teachers can join together to teach a single subject;
(*ii*) Specialist teachers may restrict their efforts to a particular age group; and
(*iii*) We can have interdisciplinary approach in team teaching. Here experts from different field may join and work together.

Team teaching is feasible in colleges because experts in different fields are available. Its success depends upon team-leader and the components of the team. In this individual interest is sacrificed for common benefit. It promotes effective understanding. It is suitable for India in higher level teaching where there is a great deal of specialisation.

5.4 INDEPENDENT STUDY ASSIGNMENT

This is a popular technique in America where more devices like DAIRS are available. It places more importance on students. The students chooses his topic or course on his own accord and works himself. He works with the help of reference materials, taped lectures, programmed materials etc. The teacher may guide him in his activities. He may work either inside the school campus or outside the campus. Independent activities may take the form of, assigned reading, listening, viewing and writing, assignments, oral reports, projects and work experience and internship.

5.5 WORKSHOP TECHNIQUE

Workshop technique provides learning experiences to both students and teachers. The purposes of a good workshop are known, understood and accepted. The participants work, produce plans, collect resources, develop tests and solve problems of learning. Sufficient time is given to complete the task. Procedures can be modified. It involve follow-up activities. Experts help them but they do not lecture or direct. They help the participants drawing their inferences. All necessary physical resources should be made available. Time should not be wasted. Conflicting situations should be avoided.

The workshop technique is beneficial because of the following:

(*i*) It leaves much to the enthusiasm of the participants;

(*ii*) There is effective supervision by the consultants;

(*iii*) It develops thinking, and

(*iv*) It focusses attention on specific factors.

Yet it has some defects. For instance it is difficult to motivate students in the initial stage. Its success depends on the ability of the experts and consultants. It requires much physical and financial resources.

Steps to be followed in Organising a Workshop

In Organising a workshop the following steps to be followed:

(*i*) Selection of Problem area;

(*ii*) Pinpointing the specific problem;

(*iii*) Justifying the problem;

(*iv*) Defining the objectives of the problem;

(*v*) Organising groups dealing with different aspects;

(*vi*) Group delibration;

(*vii*) Group reporting;

(*viii*) Criticism, exchange of views and finalising conclusion;

(*ix*) Reporting of the conclusion;

(*x*) Follow up actions; and

(*xi*) Improving learning practices.

5.6 MICRO-TEACHING

Micro-Teaching is a scaled down sample of teaching. It was developed by Stanford University in 1963. It involves micro training for unproving teaching. It analyses teaching into several skills.

Skills Developed by Micro-Teaching

Micro-Teaching develops the following major skills:

(*a*) motivation skills;
(*b*) communication skills;
(*c*) questioning skills;
(*d*) skills of individual instructions;
(*e*) thinking, skills;
(*f*) evaluative skills; and
(*g*) skills of class room management and discipline.

Basic Assumptions of Micro-Teaching

Micro-Teaching is a scaled-down sample of teaching carried on under controlled conditions. It analyses teaching into various skills. Teaching skill involves teacher behaviour. This teacher behaviour can be isolated and made the focus of training. It further assumes that teacher behaviour can be defined and modified so as to suits a desired ideal.

However, Micro-Teaching is based on five important assumptions. They are as under:

(*i*) a practice setting where the class room instruction are reduced in relation to length and scope of the lesson, Students and class time;
(*ii*) increased control of practice;
(*iii*) expending the normal knowledge and feed back dimensions of teaching;
(*iv*) using video tape for optional feed back; and
(*v*) what is refined in micro situation is applicable to Micro-situations.

The Procedures to be followed in Micro-Teaching

The procedures followed in Micro teaching are as under:

(*i*) Defining and describing a teaching skill;
(*ii*) Recording the lesson in video tapes;
(*iii*) Reviewing the vedio and filling up the response sheet;
(*iv*) Discussing the lesson and improving it;
(*v*) Replanning and modifying the lesson;
(*vi*) Redoing in which the trainee teachers to a second group.

The skill approach is more analytical, specific and definite as compared to global approach. The skill developed in the micro-situation is transferred to the class room situation.

5.7 CONCLUSION

Thus the innovative teaching methods increase participation of students in the learning process. Application of innovative methods make teaching more effective interesting and dynamic. However some of these novel methods are far fetched and unrealistic under Indian conditions. A dynamic teacher should be open minded, willing to learn from others, and eagerly awaiting situations, for experimenting with novel teaching methods. It is the responsibility of the teacher to bring about reforms in the teaching methods.

5.8 OBJECTIVE-BASED INSTRUCTIONS

In ancient days class room instruction was based on Herbartian steps. Nowadays instructions are pupil centred. Importance is given to the learner and his learning experiences. Teacher plays a passive role in the modern class room instruction and prominence is given to the pupil. This is in short called the objective based instruction.

What is an Objective?

According to the Dictionary of Education, objective is "the end towards which a school sponsored activity is directed". Effecting tangible changes in pupil behaviour is the end of schooling. Such goal is called objective.

Instructional Objectives

A set of more specific objectives suitable to the subjects and the pupils and such specific objectives which bring about perceptible behavioural changes in pupils when subjected to instructions are called "Instructional objectives". They are stated in terms of the learner behaviour.

Major Instructional Objective

The major Instructional objectives are as under:

(*i*) The pupil acquiring the knowledge of a subject *i.e.* Physics Chemistry Botany or Zoology;

(*ii*) Understanding the subject;

(*iii*) Application of acquired knowledge of a specific subject;

(*iv*) Developing skills in a specific science; and

(*v*) Appreciation of a subject.

Hierarchial order of the Instructional Objectives

The hierarchial order of the instructional objectives are as under:

(*i*) Knowledge;

(*ii*) Understanding;

(*iii*) Application; and

(*iv*) Skill knowledge is the basis for understanding. Understanding leads to Application. Application develops skills.

The Lesson Plan under the Objective based Instruction

The lesson plan written under the objective based instruction contains four columns. There are

(*i*) Specification;

(*ii*) Content;

(*iii*) Learning experience; and

(*iv*) Evaluation.

The words mentioned in these four columns are highly interrelated and inter-dependent. Learning experiences depend on specifications. Content is given through appropriate learning experiences to realise the specification. Evaluation is meant for assessing the realisation of the specifications.

5.9 DOMAINS OF OBJECTIVES

Benjamin Bloom has mentioned three domains of objectives. They are as under:

(*i*) Cognitive domain;
(*ii*) Affective domain; and
(*iii*) Psychomotor domain.

5.10 SPECIFICATIONS

Instructional objectives which determine the difference between Entering behaviour and the Terminal behaviour of pupils can be reduced to more specific behavioural modifications. They are known as "specifications".

5.11 METHODS AND TOOLS FOR EFFECTIVE TEACHING

Teaching Method

Teaching is considered effective if it stimulate interest and participation and brings about desirable changes in pupils. Mere mastery over the subject is not enough. Learning experience is essential for producing desirable results. A teacher must be aware of a number of tools and methods. He must be also be capable of making proper use these tools and methods of teaching. A single identifiable teaching technique is known as '*a tool*'. A combination of such tools is known as '*teaching method*'. For example a lecture is a 'tool'. When a lecture is combined with a panel discussion or dramatisation it becomes a 'teaching method'.

The main aim of a teacher is to create interest in pupils and their participation in learning experience. The teacher aims at bringing about desirable changes in the thinking and attitude of pupils. He acts as a creator of learning experience. Nothing can be taught. But it has to be caught. A single method may not be used for teaching all topics. Different things are to be taught in different ways because a single method may not be enough to develop all skills and to bring about all desirable changes in pupils. For example a method which develops skills of knowledge may not be able to develop the skill of understanding. Hence no method can be used in isolation and a combination of methods should be used. For example a lecture method may be supplemented by the method of dramatisation. Thus the term teaching tool refers to a single identifiable technique say; a panel discussion. Teaching method refers to a combination of such teaching tools, say; a lecture supplemented by a group discussion. A teacher may use a specific tool to achieve a specific objective in a particular class. But generally he should use different tools as combination in order to make his teaching effective interesting and inspiring.

The most important conventional teaching tools and methods used by teachers for making teaching more effective are as under:

(*i*) Seminar,
(*ii*) Symposium;
(*iii*) Forum or panel;
(*iv*) Brain-Storming;
(*v*) The Lecture; and
(*vi*) The small group discussion.

A brief discussion of these methods is given in the pages to follow:

1. Seminar

Seminar is most common type of group discussion and is meant for the study and analysis of difficult problems over a period of time. The group consists of a chairman, resource persons and members ranging from 6 to 25. The effectiveness of group discussion depends on free exchange of ideas. Seminar is suited for specific situations. It is often used in isolation. When space and leadership are available it is used in combination with other tools. It is also called 'Staff Group'. Seminar provides a scope for free frank interchange of views on a particular problem. Large groups may be subdivided into smaller sub-groups and each subgroup may discuss in separate rooms.

Merits of Seminar

Some of the merits of seminar are:

(*i*) it facilitates high degree of participation;
(*ii*) it pursues the topic in depth;

(*iii*) it can work out its own rules and programme; and

(*iv*) it provides wide variety of ideas and experiences.

Demerits of Seminar

This suffers from following demerits:

(*i*) it requires more time, space and personal;

(*ii*) poor participation;

(*iii*) success depends on the ability of the group leader; and

(*iv*) if often degenerates into a question and answer session.

2. Symposium

In a symposium different Views on any specified problem are presented by two or more people which is then followed by either a small group discussion or question period. Symposium is superior over Lecture method because of the following:

(*i*) it introduces variety of experiences;

(*ii*) creates thrill among audience when the subject is controversial;

(*iii*) it is attractive and interesting; and

(*iv*) it involves audience.

Defects of Symposium

Symposium suffers from the following defects.

(*i*) it is less systematic; and

(*ii*) it may not cover the depth of the problem.

3. Panel Discussion or the Forum

The Forum or the Panel discussion is a speaker-audience technique. In panel discussion, two or more speakers present their controversial views on the same topic. Then their talk or opinions are considered by the audience. It is followed by a question to the particular speaker.

Organisation of Panel Discussion

In organising the panel discussion or Forum the following steps are followed:

(*i*) V shaped seating arrangements;
(*ii*) the chairman is to be seated at the point of the V;
(*iii*) placing the name card infront of each member; and
(*iv*) the leader has a perform several functions such as; introducing the members and the topic, raising inspiring questions, keeping talks on the main track; leading the audience in discussion; presenting the summary of the discussion etc.

Merits of Panel Discussion

The panel discussion commands following merits:

(*i*) an element of thrill;
(*ii*) develops the thinking power of audience;
(*iii*) covers broad topics;
(*iv*) it is interesting and attractive; is
(*v*) it is the speaker-audience technique which creates more interest and audience satisfaction.

Demerits of Panel Discussion

Some of the demerits of panel discussion are as under.

(*i*) presentation of topic is not systematic.
(*ii*) question are partially answered, and
(*iii*) it often becomes a presentation of opinion rather than of facts.

4. Brain-Storming

Brain-Storming is a technique in which each member of the group is allowed to express his opinion on the problem which is tough to be solved. It concentrates on ingenuity and creativeness to many minds on a single problem. The opinion offered by any member is not criticized. The process of giving opinion continues till a single usable solution to the problem is offered. The members should be much relaxed, familiar to each other and they must have mutual trust. The only unusual solutions will emerge. This method is often used for adult group but it can be effective with youngsters.

It is a technique suited for offering solutions to unsolved tough riddles.

Merits of Brain-Storming

This technique has following merits:

(*i*) It is more effective in eliciting unusual ideas;

(*ii*) It combines creative thought of individual and group situation;

(*iii*) It solves even unsolvable problems. However it is supposed to have the following.

Demerits of Brain-Stroming

This technique suffers from following demerits:

(*i*) requires group skill and climate;

(*ii*) people are relectant to enter into discussion; and

(*iii*) its success is unassured because the solutions offered are quite often ineffectual.

5. "Small Group Discussion"

The small groups discussion is the oldest technique in teaching. It divides large group into small ones. Small group discussion emerges spontaneously at the end of every interesting meeting. This is a natural teaching technique.

Advantages of Small Group Discussion

This technique has the following advantages:

(*i*) it is a satisfying tool from the view point of group members;

(*ii*) encourages active participation;

(*iii*) stimulate thinking;

(*iv*) it becomes every body's responsibility to think and offer solution;

(*v*) the answers given by group members are more meaningful;

(*vi*) it saves time;

(*vii*) it increases group unity;

(*viii*) each member functions with a teams spirit; and

(*ix*) creates confidence in members to handle problems effectively.

Chapter 6

Programmed Learning in Life Sciences

6.1 INTRODUCTION

One of the application of behavioural psychology in personalized instruction is 'programmed learning'. It considers learning as a behavioural change in the learner due to instructions. The important steps in such a learning are as under:

Presenting stimulus

↓

Providing clues

↓

Eliciting desired responses

↓

Reinforcing desired response immediately.

Fig 6.1 Steps in Behavioural learning.

Programmed learning is based on the "law of learning" explained by Thorndike. Programmed learning can be defined as "a process of arranging materials to be learnt in a series of small steps designed to lead a learner through self introduction from what be knows to the unknown of new and more complex knowledge and principles".

Various definition given by educators to the programmed learning are given below:

Programmed learning is a systematic step by step self instructional programme to ensure the learning of staked behaviour.

– Edgar Dale

Programmed instruction is a method of designing a reproducible sequence of instructional events to produce measurable and consistent effect on the behaviour of each and every acceptable student.

– S.M. Markle.

Programmed learning is a planned sequence of experiences, leading to the proficiency, in terms of stimulus-response relationships.

– Espick and Williams

Programmed instructions is a device which presents an exercise or a problem to a student, inducing him to respond, and revealing to him whether or not his response is correct.

– Kompfer.

A programme is a prearranged sequence of explanation and questions. A programme whether for a brief unit or for an entire course, is a carefully planned progression of ideas, beginning with elementary notions and working upto relatively complex theories or applications.

– Cronbach.

6.2 BASIC PRINCIPLES OF PROGRAMMING

The technique of programming is governed by five basic principles. They are as under:

(*i*) The content is divided into meaningful frames or segments.

(*ii*) Immediate checking of results or feed-back;

(*iii*) Learner oriented;

(*iv*) The learner is self-facing; and

(*v*) Pupils and teacher can evaluate themselves mutually.

The concept of programmed learning is based on the following premises:

1. Learning always takes place in a series of steps.
2. All human beings possess an urge for success.
3. Any success in a learning task motivates the learner to learn further.
4. Immediate reinforcement of correct response makes learning more lasting.

5. The next learning material should not be presented to a learner unless he shows mastery over his ongoing learning material.

6.3 VARIOUS TYPES OF PROGRAMMED LEARNING

Programmed learning is a device developed on the basis of Law of Effect or Laws of Learning explained by E.L. Thorndike. Programmed learning is a device in which materials are arranged to be learnt in a series of small steps. It helps the learner learning more complex knowledge and principles through self introduction. It is an auto instructional approach. It provides a scope for a great deal of feed back. Satisfying responses are reinforced.

Programmed learning is an important innovative teaching technique. It includes two types of programming namely (*i*) Linear Programming and (*ii*) Branched programming. We shall elaborate these two tools involved in programmed learning.

(i) Linear Programming

This type of programming was given by B.F. Skinner. It consists of a series of questions and answers, which a student masters step by step. The order of steps must be followed. This is also known as Skinnerian or Extrinsic type of programmed learning.

(ii) Branched Programming

S.L. Prassey and N.A. Crowder introducing this type of programming. In this type of programming there are branches and off shoot. The learner receives guidance from a sheet of information which gives every step of knowledge. N.A. Crowder used this technique of multiple choice items. The mistake of the student gives rise to a new learning as this matter is kept in view in this kind of programming. This is also known as Crowderian programming.

Distinction between linear and branched or Skinnerian and Crowderian programming

These two types of programmings may be compared on various consideration as under:

	Skinnerian Programming (Linear)	*Crowderian Programming (Branched)*
(*i*) Size	Small Size	Large Size
(*ii*) Steps	Lesser number	Larger number
(*iii*) Error Rate	5%	2%
(*iv*) Response	Immediately reinforced	Ultimately corrected
(*v*) Response type	Structured	Multiple choice
(*vi*) Area	Limited facts	Broad concepts
(*vii*) Cost	Cheap	Costly
(*viii*) Control	Controlled by Programmer	Controlled by Students
(*ix*) Level for use	Elementary level	From VI standard onwards
(*x*) Path	It follows a straight line	It need not be a straight line

6.4 STYLES OF PROGRAMMED INSTRUCTION

There are five main styles of programmed instructional material as follows:

1. Linear programming.
2. Branched programming.
3. Brainer programming.
4. Adjunct programming.
5. Mathetics.

These are briefly described below:

1. Linear Programming

The theory of operant conditioning was developed by B.F. Skinner of Harward University. Based on this theory he developed a teaching machine. It avoided all defects of pressey's machine. Skinners device is known as the Skinnerian programming or Linear programming. It is also called Extrinsic programming. Skinner's linear programming is a programmed material sequence wherein the students proceed in a straight line through a fixed set of items. Linear means proceeding on the straight line. Information is broken into small frames. All the learners follow the same path in a particular linear programme. But their paces differ; Programmer structures the path and controls the learner. Learner obeys the controller and strictly follow the path. The learner responds to all the frames and there is spontaneous feed back. Since the learner is controlled by programmer, an external force, this device is known as Extrinsic device. This method is costly, time consuming and it allows no freedom to learners.

Following figures illustrates the style of this type of programming.

Frame I → Frame II → Frame III → Frame IV.

2. Branched Programming

Norman, A. Crowder has developed this programming technique. Hence it is known as crowderian technique. Crowder's programme adopts to the needs of the students without the medium of extrinsic device as a computer. The learner here makes his own decision to suit his requirements. No external force controls his decision. Hence it is known as intrinsic programming'. In this type more options are allowed. A student has to respond to one out of many given options. Hence it is known as Branched programming. Each response to the question is keyed. In case of wrong response, the material will explain him why he is wrong. If he choose correct response it is reinforced. The learner can choose his own path and controls the sequence. The material presented to student is not in normal sequence. Hence it is known as 'Scrambled book'. This technique is also defective. Because answers could be guessed without reading the book. It is difficult to prepare different branches for different students and it is costlier than linear programming.

Following figure illustrates the style of this type of programming.

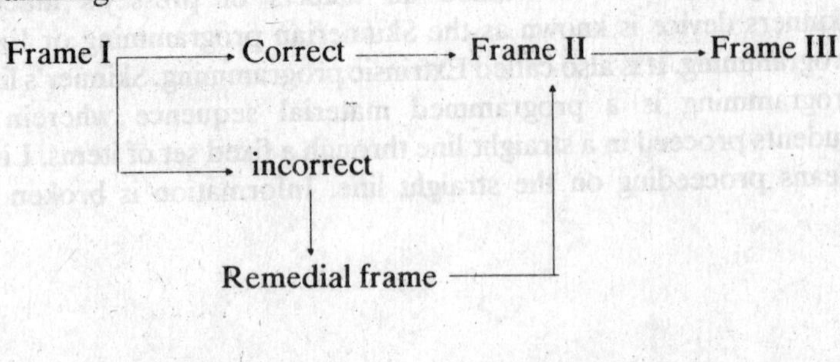

3. Brainer Programming

It is a hybrid of linear and branched programming. In this type the beginning of instruction is made with the branched programming and with every correct response, the learner has to go through a linear path of frames to get the right response.

4. Adjunct Programming

In this programming style the full lesson is taken as the learning step and it utilizes the students response made through multiple choice questions. It may use the printed material or normal lecture method for presenting the learning material. The material is repeated by the students till almost full correct response is given by the student on the multiple choice questions.

5. Mathetics

This style was developed by Gilbert. He laid more stress on learner's activity than presenting the learning material in linear frames. In this style units of learning in the form of exercises are presented to students. Further mathetics uses large learning steps and advocates the use of multimedia system as a vital support material for learning. Its highlight is that it caters for individual learning differences of students.

6.5 MERITS OF PROGRAMMED LEARNING

Following are the merits of programmed learning.

1. It helps the quality of life science teaching in our schools.
2. It helps the class teacher but is not a substitute for a teacher.
3. It makes use of a scheme of learning alongwith text books, the technique becomes very useful and the learning becomes quicker.

Text books, cards and other materials are used in this method but teaching machines have also been invented and they are being used with advantage.

6.6 TEACHING MACHINE

European countries are making use of teaching machines in programmed learning. Machines only need the answer. Students can feed the answer in the machine. These machines are different from other types of teaching aids.

Functions of a Teaching Machine

Following are the functions of a teaching machine:

1. The whole process is fool-proof.
2. The frames of programme are given individually.
3. It can act as a psychological reinforcement.
4. There are a predetermined and pre-planned programmes.
5. It is used for individual teaching.

Pressey's Teaching Machine

Pressey's teaching machine was the first of its kinds after the form of multiple choice items. Each question may have four options. Student has to choose one out of four options. The machine provides immediate feed back. Only when the student chooses correct answer, the machine will allow him to move to the next item. When he chooses wrong response he will have to repeat till he gets correct response. This machine has improved learning to a greater extent. Yet is was defective because the student had to choose from many options and the material was not arranged in sequential order.

6.7 MERITS AND DEMERITS OF PROGRAMMED TEACHING METHOD

Merits

1. It provides a chance to each child to experience and investigate.
2. A child learns according to his interest, ability and method of learning.
3. A good teacher gets recognition for hard work.
4. It places emphasis on novelty and innovation of the teacher.
5. Personality development takes place efficiently.
6. Individual needs of a student are best served under this method.

7. Child can proceed at his own speed.
8. Learning atmosphere, to motivation and encouragement are provided to the student in this method.

Demerits

1. It can be taken up only in a small class.
2. The provision for this method are difficult.
3. Suitable laboratories for this technique are not available.
4. Expert teachers for using this technique are not available.

Chapter 7

Life Science Laboratories

7.1 IMPORTANCE OF PRACTICAL WORK IN LIFE SCIENCES

No course in science can be considered as complete without including some practical work in it. The practical work is to be carried out by individual in a science laboratory. Most of the achievements of modern science are due to the application of the experimental method. At school stage practical work is even more important because of the fact that we 'learn by doing' scientific principles and applications are thus rendered more meaningful. It is a well known fact that an object handled impresses itself more firmly on the mind than an object merely seen from a distance or in an illustrations. Centuries of purely deductive work did not produce the some utilitarian results as a few decades of experimental work. Practical class room experiments help in broadening pupil's experience and develop initiative, resourcefulness and cooperation. Because of the reasons discussed above practical work forms a prominent feature in any science course.

7.2 PRACTICAL WORK IN BIOLOGY

Writing on the subject of practical work in biology Dorathy Dallas remarks, "Teachers need to look critically at proposed practical work – is it merely recipe – following without comprehension, the biological equivalent of sand and water play in the nursery school? or are the class really learning from it? A classic example of a waste of time and effort, with a high degree of anti-conservation is the work recommended in a section of the first edition of Nuffield-O-level biology which aims at helping pupils to see fertilization as it actually occurred".

Though such type of experience may provide joy to first year students but enough doubt exists about the capability of such a student to make use of a microscope in a proper way. However this project may ultimately help to make a 'film' of the events and such a 'film' may be more beneficial to use rather than the real thing.

Though many an experiments are included in 10 + 2 biology practicals about testing of 'food adulteration' yet only a few students ever perform these things in practical life.

Thus a word of caution about practicals is that beware of practicals 'to give them some thing to do' or 'to fill up the lesson'. There are teachers to whom practical work is a genuine extension of their own expertise and an excellent learning situation for their pupils. Others use it merely as a support for a ragging ego, while their pupils learn only bad habbits and poor science.

Self-discipline is essential in practical work. Teachers should plan the practical work in such a way as to create the least confusion. The next section is devoted to organisation of practical work.

7.3 ORGANISATION OF PRACTICAL WORK

Out of the various teaching methods discussed earlier the *Assignment method* is the only method that continues theory and practice in a harmonious manner and can be easily practiced in our schools. The *Heuristic method* is preeminently a *laboratory method*. However from this it should not be concluded that practical work in laboratory is impossible if the teacher makes use of any other teaching method. Thus irrespective of the method adopted by the teacher for teaching of science in the class, practical work in laboratory must be attempted. The following guide lines will help the science teacher to make his practical work effective.

Guide Lines for Teachers

For smooth working in the laboratory teacher should give due consideration to the following points.

(*i*) If teacher follows the demonstration method to teach theory, he should remember the most important principle that practical work should go hand in hand with the theoretical work. Thus if a class is doing theoretical work in physics it should also do practical work in physics during the practical periods.

(*ii*) An attempt be made to arrange the practical work in such a way that each student is able to do his practical individually. Thus for practical work individual working be preferred in comparison to working in groups.

(*iii*) In case of a large class, it is convenient to divide the class in a suitable number of smaller groups, for practical work. A practical group in no case should have more than 20 students. The limit on practical group is essential otherwise teacher will not be able to devote individual attention to the students.

(*iv*) To save time on delivering a lecture about do's and don'ts in laboratory, card system is used. This card which contains certain amount of guidance printed on it is given to each pupil. In some laboratories where card system exists each student is given a card containing instructions about the experiment that he has to perform. This card also contains the details of the apparatus required. Student can complete his practical work according to instructions given in the card.

(*v*) The apparatus provided should be good so that students get an accurate result particularly in those experiments in which the student is likely to compare the numerical value of his result with some standard. However, every science teacher should gaurd against 'Cooking' of results by his pupil. If this bad habit of cooking is not checked in the beginning it persists through out the students' career.

(*vi*) A true and faithful record of each and every experiment be kept by pupils. The record should be complete in all respects.

(*vii*) To check the habit of 'cooking' teacher should see that students enter all their observations directly in their practical notebook. The teacher should insist that the pupils do not go to the balance room without first entering the data in their note books.

(*viii*) Students should not be allowed to erase any figures. To change any wrong entry the same be crossed and correct figure entered only with the permission of the teacher.

(*ix*) Students should not be allowed to calculate results or write data on scrap papers.

(*x*) In practical notebook the right hand page be reserved for record while the left hand page be left for diagram and calculations. This practice be followed for Assignment method.

For any other method the laboratory work be done on left hand page of practical notebook and procedure etc. on right hand page of practical notebook.

(*xi*) Teacher should see that students complete their practical notebook in all respects and get it signed before they are allowed to leave the laboratory. Incomplete practical note books be kept in the laboratory and students be asked to complete it in their spare time.

(*xii*) Teacher should thoroughly check and critically examine the account written by students.

(*xiii*) Whenever a student is required to make use of a piece of apparatus for the first time it is the duty of the teacher to explain to his students the working of the apparatus. He should also explains reasons for necessary care and accuracy.

(*xiv*) Teacher should see that students find no difficulty to get apparatus and chemicals needed by them. In the absence of provision for laboratory assistants in our schools it is for the teacher that he arranges the apparatus in such a way that things frequently needed by students are easily accessible to them. Teacher should also emphasise proper and economical use of apparatus and chemicals.

(*xv*) While working with larger groups and with limited apparatus teacher can act as under:

(*a*) He may use assignment method.

(*b*) He may allow students to work in groups.

(*c*) He may devise alternate simple experiments and work with improvised apparatus.

(*d*) He may allow use of home made apparatus.

(*xvi*) Whenever the teacher is required to draw up suitable laboratory directions or instructions for practical work by pupils, be should keep the following points in mind:

(*a*) Beginner be given detailed directions.

(*b*) He should not tell the students what is actually going to happen.

(*c*) The main aim of the experiment should be made clear.

(*xvii*) During a practical class teacher should observe all children from his desk otherwise chances of accidents are there. Even when teacher has to move from his desk his power of control over the class should be such that students continue their work satisfactorily.

7.4 NEED FOR BIOLOGY LABORATORY

In the early stages of life when biology is simply 'nature study' biology should be taught outside the laboratory. However a separate biology laboratory becomes inevitable at the advanced level. In this stage field work has to be supplemented by laboratory work. Thus the effective and efficient teaching of life sciences require a good life science laboratory.

7.5 LIFE SCIENCE LABORATORIES AND THEIR KINDS

Of the various types of laboratories suggested by scientists and scholars the following are considerably important:

(*i*) Combined lecture room-cum-laboratory.

(*ii*) All purpose science room.

(*iii*) A biology laboratory for senior secondary schools.

Combined Lecture room-cum-Laboratory

Laboratory is a spacious room where in a group of students carry out their practicals. The work of designing and building a science room (laboratory and lecture room) is that of the architect but science master should collaborate with the architect in planning for what is best from the educational point of view. The plan of a combined lecture room and laboratory for use in schools upto matriculation standard, devised by Dr. R.H. Whitehouse, formerly principal of the Central Training College, Lahore, has been adopted as the official standard plan by Punjab Education Department. The plan is shown in Fig. 7.1.

CAPACITY : 40 STUDENTS FOR DEMONSTRATION, 20 FOR PRACTICAL WORK

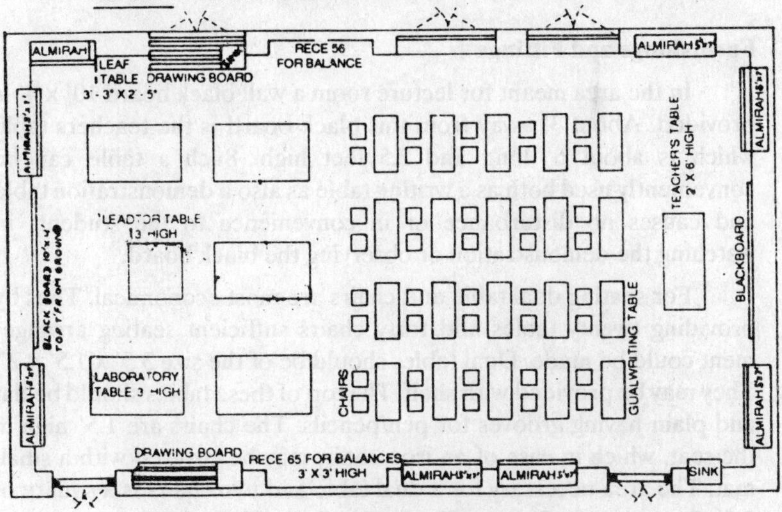

LABORATORY PLAN

Fig. 7.1. Laboratory Plan.

This plan combines laboratory and class room for science teaching. The suggested size of the room is 45′ x 25′ and it is meant for a class of 40 students which is sub-divided in two groups of 20 each for practical work.

The size of the room is most economical. Though the length of the room is 45′ but it should not be considered as disadvantageous because the teacher is expected to address a class of 40 students who will be occupying only about half the room.

For constructing such a room walls are to be of 1′ 6″ thick keeping Indian conditions in view, use of distemper be preferred to white wash for the walls. A perfectly smooth floor is preferable to one exhibiting any roughness. Such a floor is easier to clean of the two doors, one is used for lecture room and the other is reserved for laboratory part. To provide side lighting three large windows (6′ x 8′) are provided. One of these is provided near practical benches and two near seating accommodation. Doors as also windows should open outwards. The inner window sills may be used as shelves for carrying out experiments. To avoid flies wire gauze screens be provided to the windows. If necessary, in such a case, the windows be constructed with an upper and a lower half. The lower half is fixed so that the inner sills of windows could still be used as shelves.

Furnishings and Fittings

In the area meant for lecture room a wall black board 10′ × 4′ is provided. About 3′ away from this black board is the teachers table which is about 6′ long and 2.5 feet high. Such a table can be conveniently used both as a writing table as also a demonstration table and causes no disturbance or in convenience to the students in watching the demonstration or observing the black board.

For seating dual table and chairs are most economical. Thus by providing twenty tables and forty chairs sufficient seating arrangement could be made. Dual tables should be of the size 3.5′ × 1.5′ × 2′. They may be provided with shelf. The top of these tables should be flat and plain having grooves for pen/pencils. The chairs are 1.5′ high in the seat, which in case of an iron chair, may be covered with a small mat. The area necessary for a dual table and two chairs is a square of 3.5′. Passages of 1.5′ are sufficient for single file and 2.5′ to 3.5′ at the sides.

A sink is provided for use of the teacher. The size of the sink generally used is 18″ × 12″ × 6″.

The advantages of table and chair system are as under:

(*i*) They are quite economical.

(*ii*) They provide quite natural seats.

(*iii*) They allow enough space for easy passage of the students.

(*iv*) They can be easily moved while cleaning the room.

(*v*) They can be used for other purposes such as accommodating guests at various school functions.

Laboratory

In the laboratory part of the room are provided six laboratory tables which are made of wood and are perfectly plain. A black board is also provided on this side of the room. The laboratory tables are of the size 6′ × 3.5′ and are provided with a shelf on the working side just below the top. Four students can work on each table. The whole of each table except top should be stained dark. The top should be treated with wax ironed with a hot flat iron in order to fill the pores of the wood and to prevent the easy penetration of the liquids. The space between the tables and walls varies between 3′ and 4′ and passage-way at the end of the tables is 2′ wide. At school level the laboratory tables are not provided with any sink. Some of the reasons for not providing the sinks are as follows:

(*i*) *Economy:* A large economy is observed because much plumbing and a network of drains is avoided. Cost of sinks is also saved. For most of the experiments at school level a trough can serve the purpose.

(*ii*) *Usefulness:* The table is quite useful for both physics and chemistry. In absence of sinks more space is available for use as working space. Such a table can also be used for other purposes.

(*iii*) *Appearance and cleanliness:* The floor of the room is not broken for providing drains etc. It gives a better look.

(*iv*) *Tidiness:* The tables if provided with sink would make the room untidy because such tables invariably allow splashing of water which is likely to interfere with experiments and is likely to create problems.

As shown in the plan there are only three sinks, one for the teacher and two for the students. Of the two sinks for students one is placed in the window recess and the other in recess in the wall. Each of the sinks is provided with a drawing board having grooves arranged to drip over the sink. It is used for placing beakers, flasks, etc. for drying.

For placing balances, recess in walls may be used. They may be about a foot wide at a height of about 3′, 3′′. Such recess has the following advantages over wooden or stone shelf:

(*i*) It is very economical because only very small masonary is needed.

(*ii*) It is more substantial as compared to a bracket shelf.

(*iii*) It does not project into the room and so space economy can be made.

For providing ample accommodation for balances a length of 7′ to 7.5′ is sufficient.

In the plan provision has also been make for the storage of science apparatus, equipments etc. For this purpose there is a provision of eight almirahs (each with 7′ x 5′ dimensions). Each almirah is provided with shelves 1.5′ deep, of this 1′ is recessed in the wall and only 6″ projects out. These almirahs provided sufficient space for the storage of not only the apparatus, equipment etc. but can also serve the purpose of storage of science library.

Reagent shelves can be very conveniently placed on either side of the recesses for balances space can also be found, for placing notice boards for assignments of work, results of tests, etc., on the wall between the windows or just inside the doors.

Advantages

The combined lecture room-cum-laboratory discussed in previous pages has the following advantages:

(*i*) It is very economical.

(*ii*) It is compact and provides enough space for seating, working, storage etc.

(*iii*) It can be furnished easily and with meagre resources.

(*iv*) It provides enough and comfortable seating space for the students.

(*v*) In this room science atmosphere prevails.

(*vi*) It provides an opportunity for better control. For a better control following points be kept in view by a teacher.

(*a*) Every student has his assigned place which is indicated by his name written on a card placed in a brass card holder fixed on the leg of the table.

(*b*) The four boys working on any table be allotted number 1, 2, 3, 4 and number 1 of each table be asked to collect four sets of articles required for each table. Number 2 be asked to remove the dirty apparatus, after the period, to drain board and number 3 will remove clean apparatus. Number 4 will wipe down the table with a duster.

(*c*) Class monitors be named for cleaning dirty apparatus after school hours or during recess period.

(*d*) Students be made responsible for the correct alignment of their tables. For this black and white lines be pointed on the floor.

All Purpose Science Room

A special science room set aside for science facilities and materials is very desirable in an elementary school even where a self contained programme is conducted. This room can be specially planned in a new building, an unused class room, part of an art or shop room, or any other available space. This room can be used for special science projects, science equipment and supply storage, school green house, science fairs and exhibits. This room should contain the following if possible: running water, electrical outlets, working tables, a source of heat, work bench with assorted hand tools, several rolling carts for distribution of science materials and ample storage facilities.

This room will serve all aspects of general science work, both practical and theoretical but an effective teaching of special subjects may not be possible with this laboratory. The size of such a room convenient for 40 students is 45′ x 25′.

The elementary class room must serve the total elementary curriculum and so the plans be made in the regular class room for such science areas as *activity areas, storage areas, research and library areas, conference areas and display areas*.

Activity Areas

Most modern elementary class rooms contain much movable furniture. The centre of the room usually houses the movable desks or tables and chairs. The wall space areas provide opportunities for more stationary equipment and faculties. Science facilities be grouped as far as possible in one general area of the room. The needed equipment, supplies and other facilities should be readily and easily available for making, assembling, experimenting and demonstrating in science. This area should be well lighter, should contain running water if possible, electrical outlets and a source of heat. There should be an adequate space to work. When the room arrangement does not allow for work bench or table, it can be done on desks. The desk tops should be protected by laying sheets of card board, masonite or other suitable material.

Temporary work areas can be improvised by putting boards or plywood across two wooden boxes or saw horses. Schools can purchase standard work benches in any size to fit the age and size of the children who will use them.

Work Area Storage

By simply enclosing the bottom of a working bench, considerable storage area is made for construction supplies and hand tools. An attempt can be made to solve the storage problem by providing portable laboratory table or work bench that can be moved from room to room. Any table around school preferably 6′ × 6′ can be mounted on wheels. The lower level of the table can be used for the storage of supplies and equipment. Such tables are extremely useful because they can be moved out the way when space is needed

Same bench made more useful by boxing in the ends and back and adding a shelf or two inside.

Fig. 7.2.

Having one of these for each two rooms is extremely useful since they can be moved out of the way when the space is required. The custodian in the school could probably make a portable table within a couple of hours. The cost of converting such a table would be very little since the basic table would be available in the school. Occasionally parents can be asked to help with such projects.

Making Storage Cabinets

Storage space for a science programme can be improvised by using orange crates or other partitioned wooden boxes. Besides being either free or extremely inexpensive, the crates are easy to use as is shown. These boxes can be arranged side by side in a row along the wall in the science area. Casters could be attached to the bottom of the crates so that they could be moved around the room or from room to room. A piece of plywood attached to the back and extending over the top of the crate can supply display space. The possibilities for a variety of uses for these crates is limited only the ingenuity of the children and teachers.

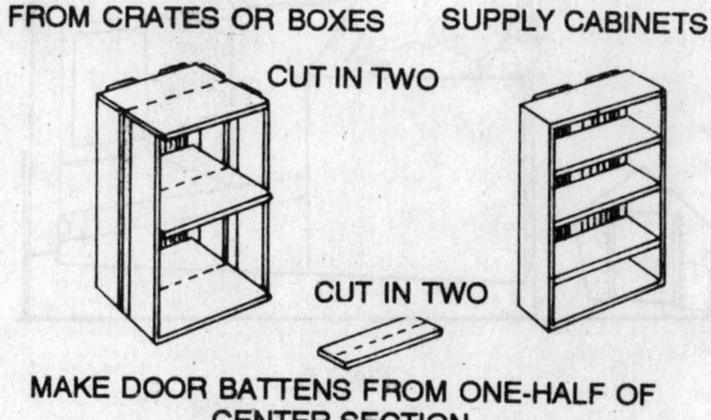

Fig. 7.3

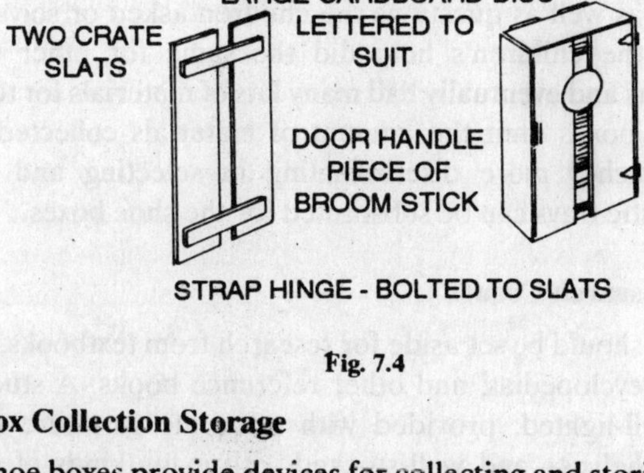

Fig. 7.4

Shoe Box Collection Storage

Shoe boxes provide devices for collecting and storing the readily available science maticular science area. For example, let us assume

Fig. 7.5

that the fifth class has just completed a science study of children collected bits of wire, bells, and light sockets; they made switches and telegraph sets. The teacher decided to put the collected magnetism and electricity materials in a shoe box with directions on how to make and use them as well as questions the children asked or solved. The teacher with the children's help did the same for other science curricular areas and eventually had many kits of materials for teaching science. Shoe boxes limit the amount of materials collected which makes the teacher more discriminating in selecting and storing materials. Plastic trays can be substituted for the shoe boxes.

Classroom Research Corner

An area should be set aside for research from textbooks, charts, pamphlets, encyclopedias, and other reference books. A study area should be well-lighted, provided with adequate furniture—tables, chairs, book-shelves—and well-stocked with many kinds of supplementary science materials. Efforts should be made to include as wide a range as possible of reading levels and interests and areas of science. It should be a place where children can go for finding answers to some of their scientific questions. Encouragement should be provided by the teacher for stimulating the use of this area. The teacher can also point out to children that scientists, especially in large laboratories, also require great amounts of reading from these materials. Directions for use of the area should be worked out co-operately between the teacher and the students. Stress should be made on the use of many references and not upon just one source of information. The children can be encouraged to bring in science reading materials to add to the ever-growing science research corner.

Conference Area

There is very often need for the teacher and children to hold small conferences or carry on group planning in the science programme. An area can be set aside for this a purpose. Generally a table and six chairs is satisfactory if it is placed away from distracting influences. Occasionally the classroom research area can be as the conference area. Occasionally it merely means moving six chairs to the back of the room. However it is done, the conference area should allow small groups to confer and plan quietly without being disturbed or disturbing others.

Display Area

Bulletin boards and displays are essential tools for teaching science. They can arouse curiosity, stimulate interests, and raise questions. By doing so, these devices involve children in planning and developing the content and activities of the particular science study. Bulletin boards and display boards also provide all children with materials that may not be available in sufficient quantity. It can easily be seen that classrooms presenting science bulletin boards and display board places value and emphasis on science. This in itself is stimulating for children.

Construction of science display board and bulletin boards is the same as for any curricular area. By planning for such display board in advance, children and teachers can collect pictures, charts, models, and other materials long before they are required. Children, after working with the teacher, can assume much of the responsibility for the planning, collecting, and arranging of such display articles and bulletin boards.

List of common articles and apparatus is given below:

1. Microscope
2. Toothpicks
3. Tweezers
4. Optical lens
5. Euglena
6. Microscope slides
7. Test tube rack
8. Jar
9. Cover glass
10. Dropper
11. Iodine stain
12. Methylene blue
13. Rosin
14. Kosher salt
15. Brown sugar
16. Pond water culture
17. Paramecium caudatum
18. Soda straw balance
19. Amoeba proteus
20. Calcium chloride
21. Sugar
22. Calcium chloride
23. Straws
24. Empty bottle
25. Molasses
26. Vinegar
27. Coffee tin lid
28. Hotplate
29. Yeast
30. Measuring cup
31. Meas. spoons

32. Vegetables
33. Spoon
34. Knife
35. Weeds
36. Test tubes
37. Bottle brush

7.6 LABORATORY PLANNING FOR SENIOR SECONDARY SCHOOLS

In a senior secondary school the arrangements are made to provide education in physics, chemistry and biology as elective subjects in addition to teaching of general science. In senior secondary school a provision has to be made for four laboratories, one each for physics, chemistry, biology and general science. The laboratories in senior secondary schools are almost the same as in colleges. Each laboratory is provided with a preparation-cum-store room attached to it. The size of the laboratory will depend on the number of students likely to work in it at a time. About 30 sq. ft. space be provided for each student. The structural details are generally provided by the architects but the following points be kept in mind.

Planning

It would be better if science teacher is consulted and for this there should be frequent conferences between the science teacher and the architect. Various points be thoroughly discussed. Some of the points of consideration are as under:

(*i*) Laboratories and class rooms should not be mixed on the same corridor.

(*ii*) Laboratories be situated, as far as possible, away from crafts room, music room, play fields, main gate etc.

(*iii*) The consideration be given to proximity of stores, preparation room, balance room, green houses etc.

Following points be given due consideration while planning individual laboratories

(*i*) Each student is easily accessible to the teacher.

(*ii*) There is minimum of movement.

(*iii*) Each student has a cupboard, bottles, heating point and a sink near him.

(*iv*) Teacher can easily watch each student.

(*v*) Black board is visible to each student.

(*vi*) Each student can easily see the demonstration.

(*vii*) There is enough space (4.5′) between two laboratory tables.

(*viii*) Master switches be provided to control electricity, gas, water etc. in each laboratory.

Lighting

Proper lighting arrangements be made for laboratory tables and class rooms. Special attention be given to the lighting of demonstration table and black board. It would be preferred if a provision could be made for electrical lights over tables through pulleys so that their height may be varied from 2 to 8 ft. Two way switches be provided for controlling the main lighting from doors and preparation rooms. Dark blinds or curtain must be provided for each laboratory.

Ventilation

It possible each laboratory should be surrounded by a 6′ verandah on all sides to keep away the direct heat of the sun. Ventilators be provided as usual. In case of chemistry laboratory ceiling should be high and exhaust fans must be provided

For laboratory ventilation full height windows are desirable. To avoid direct draughts even when the windows are open windows should be designed as under.

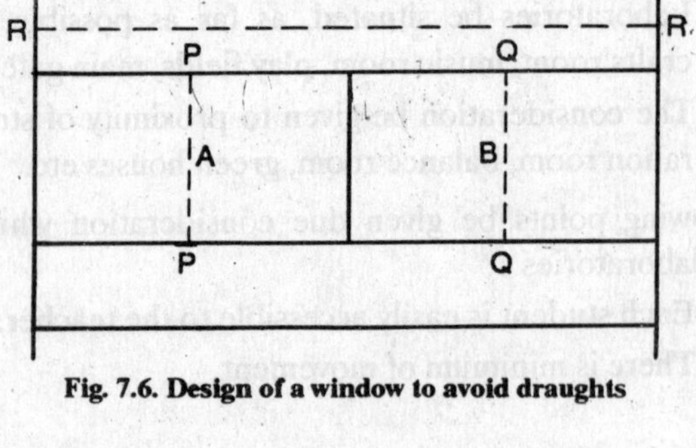

Fig. 7.6. Design of a window to avoid draughts

Windows A and B are side hung or pivoted along the axis PP and QQ. Window C is pivoted along RR. If this plan is used them windows can open in different ways depending on the wind direction. In dark room the ventilation can be provided by deflecting incoming and outgoing air by opaque partition. A no door arrangement as shown on next page may be made.

Water Supply

Provision of water supply must be made in every laboratory. Water supply is most essential item and for this purpose proper arrangement of water taps and sinks is a must in every laboratory. In case of non-availability of adequate water supply from municipal/local sources alternate arrangements have to be made. For making alternate arrangements suggestion given below be considered.

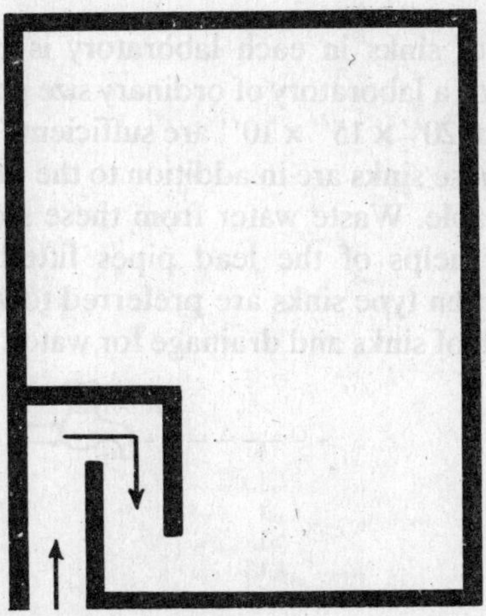

Fig. 7.7. A 'no-door' Dark Room

A water storage tank having a capacity of 1000 to 5000 litres be constructed with concrete and cement or a readymade tank of synthetic material be purchased and such a tank be then placed at the roof of the room. Water be then lifted using electric pump for filling this tank. The water supply is then provided from this storage tank to the laboratories. A tentative scheme for storage and supply of water is shown in Fig. 7.8.

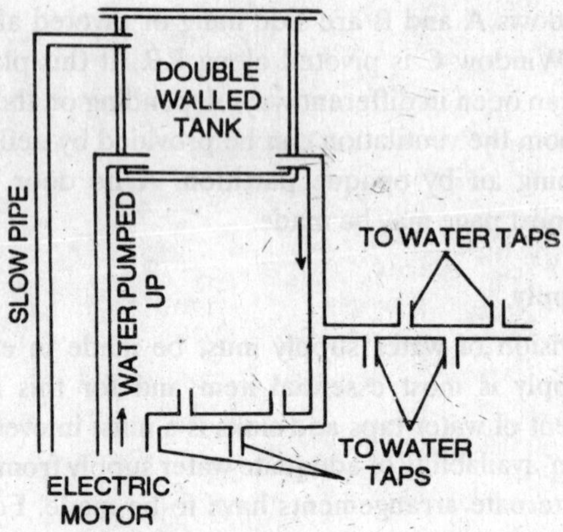

Fig. 7.8

Sinks

Provision of sinks in each laboratory is one of the essential requirements. For a laboratory of ordinary size generally four sinks of 15″ x 12″ x 8″ or 20″ x 15″ x 10″ are sufficient. These sinks be fitted on side walls. These sinks are in addition to the one provided with the demonstration table. Waste water from these sinks is carried to the drains with the helps of the lead pipes fitted with the sinks. In laboratories kitchen type sinks are preferred to wash basin type. Fig. 7.9 gives a sketch of sinks and drainage for water.

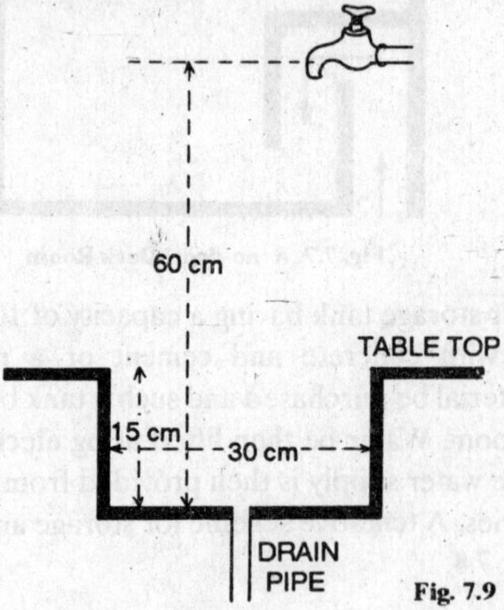

Fig. 7.9

Waste Disposal

In laboratories two types of wastes (*i.e.* liquid and solid) are often encountered. Arrangements have to be made for disposal of these wastes. For disposal of liquid wastes use of lead pipes or earthen ware pipes is considered most suitable. However care be taken to avoid the flow of solids like pieces of filter paper, cork, broken glass pieces etc. through these pipes, otherwise these pipes get chocked. For disposal of such solid wastes metal boxes or wooden boxes be provided. Such boxes be placed in the corners of the laboratory and students be asked to put all solid wastes in these boxes. Such waste boxes can even be placed under the sinks as shown in Fig. 7.10.

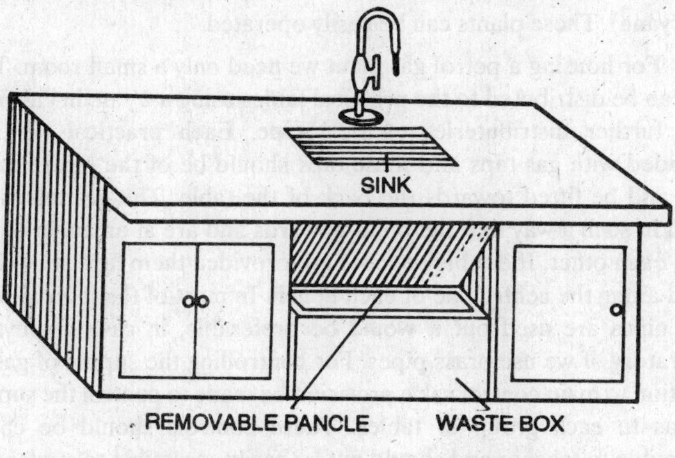

Fig. 7.10. A space saving position of a disposal box

Pipe Lines

Installation of water pipes and gas pipes is another important aspect for furnishing a science laboratory. While installing pipes some of the points that be given due consideration are given below:

(*i*) Not more than 4 or 5 half inches pipes be led from any 1″ pipe for purpose of supply of water or drainage of water.

(*ii*) In case of physics laboratory all efforts be made to avoid iron pipes.

(*iii*) Pipes should never be placed on the laboratory tables.

(*iv*) It is convenient if the pipe fittings are not underground.

Gas Supply

For adequate supply of fuel gas to the laboratory generally any one of the following arrangements is made.

(*i*) Kerosene oil gas plant is installed.

(*ii*) Coal gas plant is installed.

(*iii*) Petrol gas plant is installed.

(*iv*) Gobar gas plant is installed.

The petrol gas plant is preferred as such a plant is economical and such plants are available in various capacities. A moderate capacity plant can feed 10–20 gas taps. Petrol gas plants are readily available and such plants are also manufactured at Ambala (Haryana). These plants can be easily operated.

For housing a petrol gas plant we need only a small room. The gas can be distributed to the practical tables using a 2″ main gas pipe with further distributeries of 1/2″ pipe. Each practical table is provided with gas taps and these taps should be of the rigid nozzle type and be fitted towards the back of the table. The gas tables be fitted in such a way that the point upwards and are at an angle of 45° from each other. If double benches are provided them taps should be fitted along the centre line of each bench. In most of the laboratories iron pipes are used but it would be preferable, in case of physics laboratory, if we use brass pipes. For controlling the supply of gas in addition to main control valve provision be made to control the supply of gas to each group of tables. These controls should be easily accessible to teacher and should not be easily accessible to students.

Laboratory Tables

The provision of laboratory tables as a must for each laboratory. The taps of laboratory tables be preferably made of teak wood. However other hard wood such as sheesham or deodar can also be used for making tops of laboratory tables. These tops are generally 1″ thick. Other parts of the table *i.e.* legs, drawers etc. may be made of any other type of locally available wood. Plywood or hardboard can also be used for drawers. In physics laboratory tables without drawers are preferred but in chemistry laboratory such drawers are provided with the laboratory tables.

In addition to these provision for boards be made in the laboratories. For this either wall black boards be provided or movable wooden black boards with stands can be used.

The organisation of laboratories in secondary schools was also discussed at a seminar (All India) on the teaching of science in secondary schools. This seminar was held at Tara Devi (Simla) and it made some recommendations. Its recommendations under various heads are given below.

Lay out

(*a*) Provision be made for one general science laboratory and one laboratory for each of the three elective subjects *i.e.* physics, chemistry and biology, in every higher secondary school.

(*b*) A floor space of 30 sq. ft. per student be provided in each laboratory.

(*c*) Adjacent store room be provided with each laboratory.

(*d*) A part of store room may be earmarked for use as a preparation room.

(*e*) In science wing, some suitable place for work benches with tools, be provided.

(*f*) A minimum of two class rooms provided with galleried seats be provided in each school.

Equipment

The list of equipment for each laboratory as recommended at the Tara Devi (Simla) seminar is given below:

Science Room

Science room should be provided with

(*i*) Galleried seats

(*ii*) One demonstration table (8′ x 4′) having cupboards, gas and water fittings.

(*iii*) A black board or wall board.

(*iv*) Black curtains for covering doors, windows and ventilators.

General Science Laboratory

It must have the following equipment:

(*i*) Working tables (ordinary) with drawers.

(*ii*) Demonstration table (8′ x 4′) provided with gas and water points.

(*iii*) A minimum of two sinks be provided in the corners of the laboratory.

(*iv*) A wall board or black board.

(*v*) Stools (in two sizes).

(*vi*) Almirahs (wooden or steel).

Biology Laboratory

Biology laboratory should be equipped with the following:

(*i*) Tables (6′ x 2′ x 2.5′) with water fittings and drawers.

(*ii*) Two sinks at the corners of the laboratory

(*iii*) Almirahs

(*iv*) Stools (in two sizes)

(*v*) Wall board or black board

(*vi*) Small table racks.

(*vii*) Wall shelves.

(*viii*) A froggery, where necessary

Special attention be paid to lighting arrangement in biology laboratory. It should have glass panes on the northern side and pendant lights over the tables.

General

Store rooms attached with the laboratories should be well equipped with almirahs, racks, sink etc. For storage of inflammable and poisonous substances separate shelter be provided.

In schools having larger number of students a provision be made for separate workshop which should have work benches and tool cabinet. However in smaller schools a few work benches may be placed in science wing.

Provision of a first aid and fire extinguishing apparatus be made near each laboratory. Arrangements for water supply and gas supply to each laboratory must also be made.

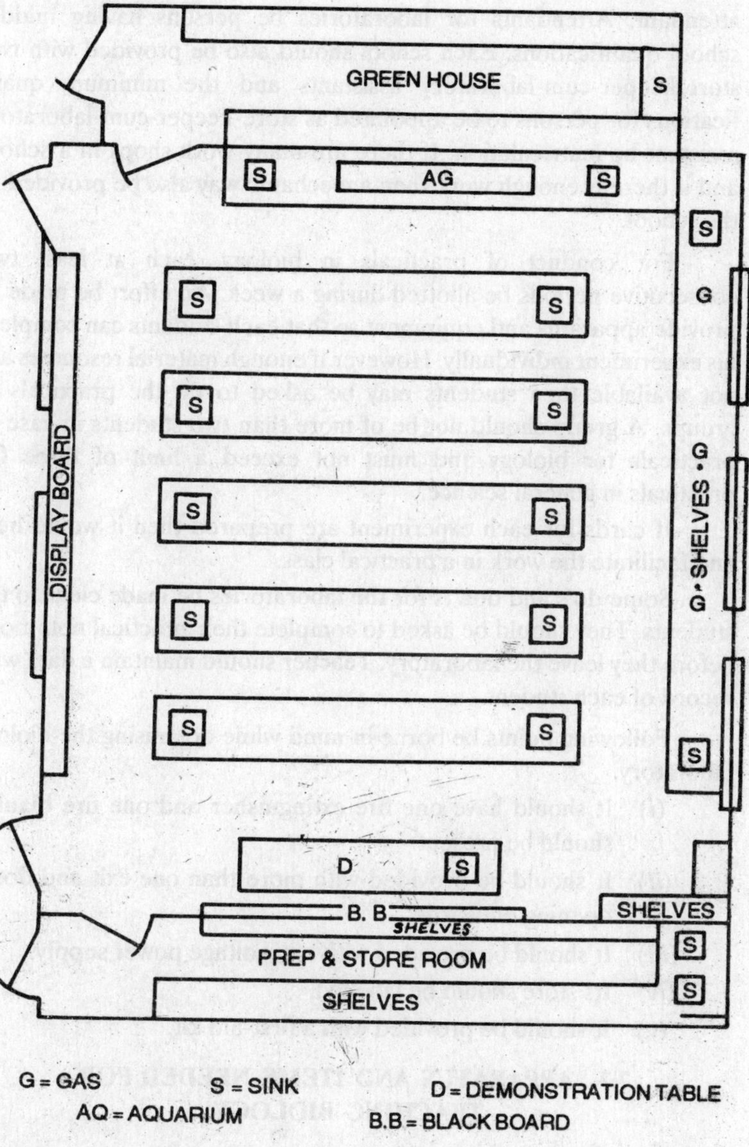

Fig. 7.11. A Biology Laboratory

Administration

Each laboratory be under the supervision of a laboratory attendant. Attendants for laboratories be persons having middle school qualifications. Each school should also be provided with two store-keeper-cum-laboratory assistants and the minimum qualifications for persons to be appointed as store-keeper-cum-laboratory assistant be matriculation. If there are many work shops in a school and if there is enough work then a mechanic way also be provided to the school.

For conduct of practicals in biology, each at least two consecutive periods be allotted during a week. An effort be made to provide apparatus and equipment so that each students can complete his experiment individually. However if enough material resources are not available then students may be asked to do the practicals in groups. A group should not be of more than two students in case of practicals for biology and must not exceed a limit of three for practicals in general science.

If cards for each experiment are prepared then it would help and facilitate the work in a practical class.

Some do's and don'ts for the laboratories be made clear to the students. They should be asked to complete their practical note-book before they leave the laboratory. Teacher should maintain a date wise record of each student.

Following points be borne in mind while organising the biology laboratory.

(*i*) It should have one fire extinguisher and one fire blanket should be present.

(*ii*) It should be provided with more than one exit and doors opening outwards.

(*iii*) It should be provided with low-voltage power supply.

(*iv*) Its store should be labelled.

(*v*) It should be provided with a first-aid kit.

7.7 APPARATUS AND ITEMS NEEDED FOR TEACHING BIOLOGY

The most important apparatus and items required for the teaching of biology are:

(*i*) Refrigerator.

(*ii*) Centrifuge.

(*iii*) Thermostatically controlled oven.

(*iv*) Thermostatically controlled water baths.

(*v*) Electric blender.

(*vi*) Pressure cooker or Autoclave.

(*vii*) Deioniser.

(*viii*) Standard reagents like Acetocarmine, Alcohol, Agar, Barium sulphate, Bicarbonate etc.

7.8 LABORATORY DISCIPLINE

The life science teacher faces more problem in the laboratory than in the class room. It is so because pupils doing the same work wish to talk and discuss with others. Modest talking is inevitable in laboratory. Yet talking and walking about in the laboratory may result in indiscipline causing serious dangers. Hence, the life science teacher has to follow certain rules in the laboratory.

Rules for Teacher

(*i*) The teacher should not be late unduly.

(*ii*) Students should enter and go to their seats silently when permitted by the teacher.

(*iii*) Teacher should wait for silence before beginning his lesson.

(*iv*) The teacher should address the whole class while delivering his lesson.

(*v*) There should be absolute silence while the teacher talks.

(*vi*) The teacher should vary his pitch and loudness to add interest to his talk.

(*vii*) Teacher should keep the class busy.

(*viii*) Variety of teaching methods be used.

(*ix*) The teacher should remove the possible causes of trouble.

(*x*) The teacher should not try to produce rigid discipline.

Rules for Students

(*i*) They should not take out any thing from the laboratory without the permission of the teacher.

(*ii*) Apparatus and materials should be used for specific purposes.

(*iii*) Any mistake should be immediately reported to the teacher.

(*iv*) Apparatus must be kept clean and tidy in their original position after the experiment is over.

(*v*) Materials must be used economically.

(*vi*) Teacher's help or advice must be sought in case of doubts.

7.9 COMMON ACCIDENTS AND THEIR REMEDIES

Burns

Burns by Dry Heat (*i.e.* by flame, hot objects etc.). For slight burns apply *Burnol* and *Sarson oil.*

In case of blisters caused by burns apply *Burnol* at once and rush to dispensary.

Caution. *Heat burns should never be washed.*

Acid Burns

Wash with water and then with a saturated solution of sodium bicarbonate and finally with water. Even after this if burning persists, wipe the skin dry with cotton wool and apply *Sarson oil* and *Burnol.*

Caution. In case of conc. sulphuric acid, wipe it from the skin before giving the above treatment.

Alkali Burns

Wash with water and then with 1% acetic acid and finally with water. Dry the skin and apply *Burnol.*

Cuts

In case of a minor cut allow it to bleed for a few seconds and remove the glass piece if any. Apply a little methylated spirit or *Dettol* on the skin and cover with a piece of leucoplast.

For serious cuts call the Doctor at once. In the mean while try to stop bleeding by applying pressure above the cut. The pressure should not be continued for more than five minutes.

Note. Minor bleeding can be stopped easily by applying concentrated ferric chloride solution or alum.

Eye Accidents

Acid in Eye. At once wash the eye with water a number of times. Then wash it with 1% sodium carbonate solution by means of an eye-glass.

Alkali in Eye. At once wash with water and then with 1% boric acid solution by means of an eye-glass.

Foreign Particles in Eye. Do not rub the eye. Wash it by sprinkling water into the eye. Open the eye and remove the particle by means of a clean handkerchief or cotton wool. Again wash freely with water.

Poisons

If a solid or liquid goes to the mouth, but is not *swallowed*, spit it at once and repeatedly rinse with water. If the mouth is scalded, apply olive oil or *ghee*.

Acids. Dilute by drinking much water or preferably milk of magnesia.

Caustic Alkalies. Dilute by drinking water and then drink a glass of lemon or orange juice.

Arsenic of Mercury Compounds. Immediately give an emetic *e.g.* One table spoon full of salt or zinc sulphate is a tumbler of warm water.

Inhalation of Gases

Pungent gases like chlorine, sulphur dioxide, bromine vapours etc. When inhaled in large quantities often choke the throat and cause suffocation. In such a case remove the victim to the open air and loosen the clothing at the neck. The patient should inhale dilute vapours of ammonia or gargle with sodium bicarbonate solution.

Fire

Burning clothing. It clothes have caught fire then lay the victim on the floor and wrap a fire-proof blanket tightly around him. The fire in the burning clothes will thus be extinguished. *Never throw water on the person* as it will cause serious boils on his body.

Burning Reagents. In case of fire on the working table at once turn out the gas taps and remove all things which are likely to ignite. Following methods be used to extinguish the fire.

(*i*) If any liquid in a beaker or flask has caught fire, cover the mouth of the vessel with a clean clamp cloth or duster.

(*ii*) Most of the fire on the working table can be extinguished by throwing sand on them.

(*iii*) If any wooden structure has caught fire it is put up by throwing water on it.

(*iv*) *Never throw water on burning oil or spirit*. Since it will only spread the fire. Throwing of a mixture of sand and sodium bicarbonate on the fire is most effective.

7.10 FIRST AID BOX

A first aid box should be provided in every laboratory. It should contain the following materials.

Bandages (3-4 rolls of different sizes), gauze, lint, cotton wool, leucoplast.

A pair of forceps, a pair of scissors, safety pins.

Glass dropper, two eye-glasses.

Vaseline, boric acid powder, sodium bicarbonate powder, a tube of Burnol.

Sarson oil, olive oil, glycerine

Picric acid solution, Tannic acid solution 1% acetic acid, 1% boric acid, 1% sodium bicarbonate, saturated solution of sodium carbonate.

Methylated spirit, rectified spirit, Dettol.

7.11 SAFETY IN BIOLOGY LABORATORY

In addition to the usual hazards that the students face in teaching of physical sciences, biologists must be aware of some others such as potential danger from animals and microbiological hazards, problems of ethics of using animals and problems of ethics of using animals and problems of hysteria about dissection. Some times there may be parental disapproval of sex education.

In addition to various laboratory etiquetes that a teacher attempt to inculcate in his students, he should also pay due attention to the safety considerations in biology laboratory. However the laboratory discipline should not put too much reliance on teacher's presence in laboratory rather should grow during secondary education through conscious organisation of experience.

Chapter 8

Life Science Teacher

8.1 INTRODUCTION

The success of failure of a science course rests mainly with the teacher. He may be provided with all the possible facilities in terms of laboratory, apparatus and equipment, given an ideal syllabus and a sufficient time for teaching of science but unless he is enthusiastic about his work, knows the subject and really knows how to teach science, he is not likely to achieve success. On the other hand a keen and well informed teacher who loves his subject and believes in its value will succeed inspite of difficulties and handicaps.

In this regard the Kothari Commission report (1966) says, "*of all the different factors which influence the quality of education and its contribution to national development, the quality, competence and character of teachers are undoubtedly the most significant*".

Dr. S. Radha Krishan emphasises the role of teacher in the following words, "*The teachers place in society is of vital importance. He acts as the pivot for transmission of intellectual traditions and technical skill from generation to generation, and helps to keep the lamp of civilisation burning. He not only guides the individual, but also, so to say, the destiny of nation. Teachers have therefore to realise their special responsibility to the society. On the other hand it is incumbent on the society to pay due regard to the teaching profession and to ensure that the teacher is kept above want and given the status which will command respect from his student.*

8.2 QUALIFICATION OF LIFE SCIENCE TEACHER

A science teacher is expected to possess certain academic qualification as also certain professional qualifications.

As regards the academic qualifications it is usually a pass in matriculation/senior secondary examination for becoming a science teacher in a primary school. A pass in B.Sc. examination for being a science teacher in a middle or high school and a pass in M.Sc. examination in the respective subject for becoming a teacher to teach an elective science subject in a senior secondary school (grade 11 and 12).

In addition to the minimum academic qualifications any one who wish to be appointed a teacher in science has to undergo a teachers training course. For this purpose a person for appointment as a teacher in a primary school has to undergo 1 or 2 years Junior Basic Training (J.B.T) course and for appointment in high and higher secondary school the graduate or post-graduate teacher has to under a B.T. or B.Ed. course. This professional training is all the more important these days when new techniques of teaching, evaluation etc. are being introduced. Trained science teachers also require the stimulus of a refresher course to keep himself informed about the latest methods of teaching and to refresh his knowledge of science. Such a refresher course also provides him with an opportunity to see some of the latest books and apparatus concerning science teaching and to obtain instructions in arts and scientific hobbies. During such refresher course he also gets practical training in the organisation of science clubs, science fairs etc. For keeping himself in touch with latest in science the science teacher may visit some nearby schools where science is taught by new methods. He can also take up the membership of a good library or good science association. He can think of other such institutions and industrial houses nearby from where he can get the latest knowledge of science. All this is quite essential because a good teacher must always keep himself informed of the latest developments in the field. This aspect of a teacher has been brought out in the following words by Dr. Rabinder Nath Tagore, "*A teacher can never truly teach unless he is still learning himself. A lamp can not light another lamp unless it continues to burn its own flame*".

8.3 QUALITIES OF A LIFE-SCIENCE TEACHER

The secondary education commission in its report emphasises the fact that quality of education would depend upon the quality of teacher. It has been pointed out, "of all the different factors which influence the quality of education and its contribution to national development, the quality, competence and character of teachers are undoubtedly the most significant". Nothing is more important than securing a sufficient supply of high quality recruits to the teaching profession, providing them with the best possible professional preparation and creating satisfactory conditions of work in which they can be fully effective.

The foremost basic qualities of a life science teacher are as under:

(*i*) Basic academic qualification.
(*ii*) Trained in modern methods and techniques of teaching.
(*iii*) Master over child psychology.

For a teacher having the expertise in the following, the teaching becomes a play thing.

(*i*) Planning of lessons and methods of teaching.
(*ii*) Organisation and maintenance of laboratories.
(*iii*) Technique to run a science museum.
(*iv*) Preparation of instructional material for pupil.
(*v*) Organisation of instructional material.
(*vi*) Knowledge of child psychology.
(*vii*) Acquaintance with learning process.

Following points will be quite helpful for a life science teacher to improve his performance.

1. He should have complete mastery of the subject.
2. He should plan his lessons scientifically
3. He should try to use inductive method in teaching.
4. He should encourage more practical work.
5. He should teach the latest in the field.
6. He should freely use guides, handbooks, manuals and other aids.

8.4 PROFESSIONAL GROWTH OF A LIFE SCIENCE TEACHER

It has been rightly said, by Tagore "A teacher can never teach unless he is still learning himself. A lamp can never light another lamp unless it continues to burn its own flame".

Tagore further says, "The teacher who has come to the end of his subject, who has no living traffic with his knowledge but merely repeats his lessons to his students, can only load their mind, he cannot quicken them. The greater parts of our learning in schools has been a waste because, for most of our teachers, their subjects are like dead specimens of once living things".

Another philospher writes about life science teacher, "The life science teacher should not devote all his time in theoretical teaching. He should make the teaching a lively thing. He should devote much time in those activities in which the students participate with keen interest".

Steps for Professional Growth

Following are some of the important steps that have been taken for the professional growth of a life science teacher.

1. Unitary institutes.
2. Sequential institutes.
3. Special institutes.
4. Project technology institutes.

All these different types of summer institutes are run in India for offering in service training. The basic aim of these institutes is to keep life science teacher abrest of changing subject.

However the results of summer institutes and in service training programmes in India have become discouraging. The reasons for it are:

(*i*) Lack of coordination between the summer institutes and other programmes.

(*ii*) The lukewarm attitude of the state education departments towards organising summer institutes.

(*iii*) Rigid course content based on the external examination system.

(*iv*) Lack of incentive for the participants of in service training programmes.

Steps to make In-service Training Effective

In service training could become effective by observing the following:

(*i*) Activities of summer institutes and in-service programmes should be closely relevant and related to class room work.
(*ii*) Proper organisation of follow-up programmes.
(*iii*) Teachers undergoing intensive training should be duly recognised.
(*iv*) State Education Department should be fully involved in the organisation of summer institutes and in-service training programmes.
(*v*) Source-books and science-books be prepared in regional languages.
(*vi*) Strengthening the All India Science Teacher's Association and subscribing for journals on science teaching.

8.5 TIME ALLOTTED FOR SCIENCE TEACHING

We have already discussed it and given the allotment of time for science teaching in various countries. It can be conveniently assumed that about 100 hours are available in a year for teaching of science at elementary stage in India. This time should preferably be divided as under.

(*i*)	Excursions, visits etc.	20 hours
(*ii*)	Projects and allied activities	50 hours
(*iii*)	Class room teaching	30 hours.

Generally two lessons of about half an hour per week should be sufficient at the primary stage.

At the middle stage three periods of 40-45 minutes per week should suffice. One of the three periods in a week be given to practicals and the remaining two to teaching.

At the high school stage an allotment of a minimum of three hours per week be made for teaching of science. Generally six periods of 40-45 minutes per week are allotted which includes laboratory work also. It would be more sound if an allotment of four periods for practical and two periods for theory is made. The four periods of practical work may be turned into two double periods of an hour and a half each.

If possible a free period be allowed to science teacher before his class so that he can prepare the experiment and the practical periods be so adjusted that they are just before the recess or in the last periods. Such an arrangement is useful because the teacher can allow some more time to the students to finish their practicals.

If instead of having two double periods for practical work, we have one double period and two single periods for this work and two single periods for class room work, the science teachers time table will be some thing like the one given below.

Days	*1st period*	*2nd period*	*6th period*	*8th period*	*9th period*
Mon.	Preparation	Demonst. X			Demnost. IX
Tue.	Preparation	Demonst. IX		Preparation	Demnost. X
Wed.	Preparation	Demonst. X			
Thurs.	Preparation		Demonst. X		
Fri.				Practical IX	Practical IX
Sat.	Preparation	Demonst. IX		Practical X	Practical X

This is for a school having nine periods and providing a recess period after the 6th period.

8.6 SCIENCE TEACHER'S DIARY

Just like other teachers the science teacher should also keep a diary. In this diary the record of syllabus drawn up by science teacher be maintained. It should clearly indicate the particulars of quarterly and weekly distribution of work. A copy of the time-table be also kept in diary. The time table should clearly show the distribution of available time for (*i*) class room and laboratory work (*ii*) projects and other allied activities and (*iii*) out door activities (excursions, visits etc.).

A record of daily work be entered in the diary regularly and it should be dated. In keeping this daily record teacher should clearly mention the details of lecture-cum-demonstration work, individual experimental work, slides etc. to the shown and any such other details. He should also enter in his diary (*i*) those parts of the proposed work that have been accomplished (*ii*) those parts of the proposed work that could not be accomplished and (*iii*) any other extra work that has been attempted.

The diary should also show the details of written work, questions set. Entries of any comments on assignments and practical work must also find a place in teacher's diary.

If possible teacher should also mention the mistakes that were committed by a majority of students. Such an entry will be helpful to the teacher and he can explain these mistakes to the class.

The results of class tests and house examinations must also be recorded in teacher's diary. Science teacher can also keep a record of apparatus or chemicals to be ordered for his reference in his diary. Such a record will be quite useful for him when he is placing the orders at the beginning of the year.

8.7 STUDENT'S NOTE BOOKS

It is expected of each student to have three note books. One of these should be a practical note book, the remaining two are to be ordinary note books. One of these be used for taking notes and copying black board summaries and the other for assignments. It would be much convenient if all the students have same type of note books and the two note books to be used for taking notes and for assignment purposes are of different colours. Teacher should emphasise that all note books must be kept clean and maintained properly. It would be useful if right hand page is used for writing and left hand page is left blank for corrections, diagrams and calculations. This blank page can also be used for further notes from text books, library books, etc.

Record of individual practical work should be kept in the practical note book. The observation should always be directly recorded in fair practical note books.

For practical class some teachers use printed note books but such note books be avoided in high classes.

Note Taking

It is not possible even for a brilliant boy to take full notes of a lecture-cum-demonstration lesson during the class period. In class room the teacher say a good deal more than what a student can note down. Students fails to discriminate between essentials and non-essentials and it is only with a lot of practice and guidance of teacher that be learns to note down the important points of a lesson. The best way for taking down notes for the beginners is to copy the teacher's notes from the black board and then develop them at home. A record of the notes can be kept in any of the following two ways:

(*i*) The rough notes are taken down in the class and these are then noted down in a fair note book at home.

(*ii*) The notes are taken in a fair note book directly.

Both the above methods have some advantages. In the first method student will be able to write in fair note book neatly and would be able to draw neat and labelled diagrams. In second method the student acquires the habit of careful work and it also saves time.

Home Work

In science home work consists of preparatory part of assignment set, or of learning the work covered in a demonstration lesson or to write answers to one or two questions on the topic of demonstration. Occasionally keeping in view the availability of time teacher may ask his students to read from some popular science books, magazines etc. and even ask them to write some thing on them. A science student is also expected to keep a record, of individual experimental work done by him, in his practical note book.

Home work must be corrected and corrected properly by science teacher. The correcting and marking of note books take a lot of teachers free time but it is useless to assign work to students if the teacher does not find time to correct and mark their work. All efforts be made to reduce this work to a minimum. For this teacher may use some selected code of symbols to make corrections and ask the students to make corrections themselves.

While making correction all efforts be made by science teacher to point out mistakes in style and language. He should encourage the students to use a simple and straight forward language.

8.8 CO-OPERATION OF PUPILS OUT OF SCHOOL HOURS

Science teacher is required to take help of students during and even after school hours. During school hours be expects the help from students during a demonstrations-cum-lecture lesson. He seeks the help of students and asks them to read temperatures, light spirit lamps, hold a test tube etc.

Teacher can also take help from some sincere, brilliant and willing students who are keenly interested in science by assigning them work outside school hours. Such students may be asked to contribute to science museum, make some scientific models, charts etc. They can also be asked to clean science apparatus and arrangement of this apparatus in a proper way. Their help can also be sought to keep laboratory clean and tidy. Allotment of such work to students provides an excellent chance to a science teacher to channelise the energies of some naughty students. It also provides an opportunity to the teacher to assess the qualities of leadership and sense of responsibility in his students.

8.9 INSPECTION OF A SCIENCE DEPARTMENT

A regular inspection of science department is essential for its efficient running. A thorough inspection should be carried out at least once a year. The inspection be carried out by a team which must include at least one expert in science. While carrying out the inspection the inspection team should pay special attention to the following points.

(*i*) *Teacher.* The inspection team should see that the science teacher possesses the required academic and professional qualifications. The team should also pay attention to his teaching method. The individuality of teacher's method should be respected and the team if it so feels may suggest an alternative method but it should not be insisted upon. The inspection team should see that the science teacher practices proper correlation and coordination of science with other science subjects and also with other school subjects and environment.

(*ii*) *Scheme of Work.* Inspection team should see that the teacher prepares a quarterly and weekly scheme and such a scheme as shown in his diary is followed by him.

(*iii*) *Teacher's Diary.* The inspection team should see if the science teacher is maintaining his diary properly. Whether or not is he keeping a daily record of work done both in theory and practical, home work assigned etc. Has he noted down his time-table in diary? Is he having a good time-table? Is he having enough time for practicals? Is he teaching some other subjects? etc.

(*iv*) *Text Books and Library Books.* Are the students using approved and standard text books? What type of books are available in library? Are the students using library books?

(*v*) *Laboratory and Equipment.* The inspection team should see that adequate space and apparatus etc. are available in school. In the laboratory there is a provision for the proper storage of the apparatus, equipment, chemicals etc. Inspection team must make a report about the upkeep and tidyness of the laboratory. While making remarks about laboratory the following points be clearly mentioned.

(*a*) Were the pictures, charts, models etc. properly displayed in the laboratory?

(*b*) Did the arrangement exist in the laboratory for supply of water, disposal of waste water, first-aid box etc.?

(*vi*) *Stock Registers.* Maintainance of stock registers is one of the duties of science master and inspection team is expected to see that various stock registers are being maintained properly, accurately and regularly. It would not be improper if the inspection team carries out the physical verification of some items and find out for themselves if the actual stock agrees with the balance shown in the stock register. The checking of stock register includes the checking of requirements register and the preparation of indents etc.

(*vii*) *Class work and Home work of Students.* It can easily be seen from the note-books maintained by the students. The inspection team should satisfy itself that the amount of written work done by the students is sufficient. Practical note books and assignments have been checked properly and regularly by the teacher and the mistakes have been pointed out to the students.

(*viii*) *Science Library and Science Museum.* The importance of science library and science museum for teaching of science is given elsewhere in the book. The inspection team write carrying out the inspection of science department in a school should find if a science library and science museum of some good standard exist in the school? Is the school library being used properly by the students? Are there arrangements for regular issue and return of books from science library? What method is used by science teacher to satisfy himself that his students regularly devote some time to the study of library books?

(*ix*) *Extra-curricular Activities*. The existence of a science club is a school provides an opportunity for carrying out extra-curricular activities. Inspection team should report, whether a science club exist? What are the activities of science club? How many tours excursions etc. have been arranged? How many of such excursions, tours were arranged to visit places of scientific interest? Has the school arranged any science fair during the year? How many films/slides shows were arranged during the year? What steps were taken to encourage students to prepare home-made apparatus? Have the students contributed any good charts/models during the year? Have any debate/declamation/paper reading contest/quiz contest etc. arranged?

The inspection team should also ask for the record of all such activities carried out by the school during the year.

In addition to carrying out the inspection the inspection team is expected to give some constructive suggestions to the science master for all the activities for making improvements in science teaching in schools. Such suggestions should not be forced on science teacher and only those of these suggestions be implemented by the science teacher which are likely to bring about a qualitative, change in science teaching.

Chapter 9

Co-curricular Activities in Life Sciences

9.1 INTRODUCTION

For supplementing the teaching of life science in class room and to widen the knowledge of his students a good science teacher can involve his students in a number of co-curricular activities such as the *science club, scientific hobbies, visits of places of scientific interest, broad-cast talks, gramophone lectures* etc. Though there is no limit to such extracurricular activities and teacher is free to undertake one or more such activities in his school for the benefit of his students.

Some of these activities, their organisational and other aspects, are taken up in the next few pages.

9.2 SCIENCE CLUB

To channelise the energies of students and to make proper use of talent of the students science clubs may be organised in schools. Such a club then forms the backbone of the co-curricular activities in the school. Such clubs, if properly organised, will be of great help to create interest in teaching of science and so now the importance and educational value of such clubs is duly recognised. Such clubs provide better chances to acquaint the students with various facts and principles of science. Students can take up any project or a scientific hobby of his choice while participating in a science club activity. Such a participation of a student in science club activities helps to link his theoretical knowledge to the outside world and he gets more opportunities for self-expression and creativity. Participation in various activities of science club also helps to develop manual skills of the student and he gets interested in learning of science.

The importance of science clubs in schools in words of Dr. W. Davis is, "*If the future belongs to youth and to science, then there is a vastly more important place for science clubs, in the scheme of things*".

Mckown has opined as follows while stating the advantages of science clubs over usual class room teaching.

"The club offers the pupil an opportunity for specialisation which he does not have in the class room. In the class room his work is formal; in the club it is informal; in the class room he is told what to do, in the club he chooses; in the class room his method of dealing with a topic is clearly outlined by teacher imposed restrictions, in the club programme the method is of his own desiring; in the class he tries to please the teacher, in the club he works for his own and his club's interest and for the joy of doing his works; in the class room he confirms to a system, in the club he suits his own convenience".

From the views expressed above we can clearly see that there is complete freedom for the students to pursue his interests in a science club and he can choose his own project and also his own method to pursue the project so chosen. This atmosphere that prevails in a science club is totally different from the one that prevails in a class room. The club represent freedom and expression where as the class room represents conformity and repression.

Science class are very popular in Russia and America. They are also encouraged in India. Government also provides financial help for organisation of science clubs. NCERT provides non-recurring grants to the schools which have science clubs.

Science clubs can play an important role in educational process.

Objectives of Science Club

These can be summarised as under:

1. To maintain neat and healthy living conditions.
2. To make students in particular and public in general, science oriented.
3. To help exploration and creative spirit.
4. To use science in life-situations.
5. To create interest for new advances in science.

6. To inculcate scientific attitudes and teach scientific method.
7. To provide encouragement to work by hand.
8. To develop in students the keen observation power.
9. To grow cooperation initiative and enterprises.
10. To exchange views and information mutually.
11. To encourage a healthy competition among pupils.

Types of Science Clubs

Broadly speaking science clubs can be classified as

(i) The Specialised Interest Science Clubs

In this catagory the clubs take up such projects which deal with some specialised subject. Such clubs are Radio club, Photographic club, Nature study club, Aviation club, Astronomical club, etc.

(ii) General Science Club

These clubs take up any type of science activity and such clubs are generally known as chemical society, zoological society, botany club, physics association etc.

Though both types of clubs have their advantages but experience has shown that specialised clubs are only short lived and so a science teacher should prefer general science club. He can undertake some specialised activity as a part of programme of such a general science club for a short duration of time.

Aims of Science Club

The major aims of science club can be summarised as under:

(*i*) To make proper use of leisure time.

(*ii*) To develop individual and group initiative.

(*iii*) To create students' interest in his everyday experiences and his environment.

(*iv*) To develop scientific attitude among students and to inculcate a training in scientific methods and to broaden his scientific outlook.

(*v*) Provide the student with opportunity to develop his explorative, creative, and inventive faculties.

(*vi*) To develop a habit of cooperation in the students.

(*vii*) To encourage students participation in teaching-learning process.

(*viii*) To provide encouragement to club members for undertaking some difficult, complicated and even risky experiments which are not permitted to be undertaken in regular class.

(*ix*) To allow opportunities to young students to learn practical applications of science.

(*x*) To identify and nurture the would be scientists of the country.

(*xi*) To familiarise the students with recent advances in science.

(*xii*) To provide students vocational and educational guidance.

(*xiii*) To exchange information with other science clubs.

Organisation of a Science Club

A science club, if properly organised, will be a great help in enlivening the teaching of science. Such a club should be run by the students under the guidance and supervision of the teacher. For proper running of a club the most important thing is the preparation of a draft constitution of the club. This draft be prepared by the science teacher in consultation with the head of the institution. This draft constitution should provide all important details about the name of the club, aims and objectives of the club, details regarding membership and the fees etc. to be paid by members, purposes for which the expenditure can be incurred and the person competent to approve such an expenditure. Various offices available to members and the procedure for filling up such offices. Any other relevant details.

For efficient and successful working of science clubs an expert body has suggested the organisation as under:

(*i*) Such a club should have the head of institution as its pattern.

(*ii*) One of the senior science teachers be asked to be the sponsor of the club.

(*iii*) Membership of the club be open to all the science students of the school.

(*iv*) Associate-membership may be allowed to some other students interested in science.

(*v*) The club may have an elected executive committee. The members of executive should include the following and should be elected or nominated from amongst the students.

(*a*) Chairman

(*b*) Secretary

(*c*) Asstt. Secretary.

(*d*) Treasurer

(*e*) One or two class representatives from each class.

The executive committee may also include a librarian, a store keeper and a publicity officer.

(*vi*) Only a nominal membership fee be charged from the members.

(*vii*) The club members be asked to tap other resources and carry out the club activities in their own locality.

Assignment of Duties to Office Bearer of a Science Club

For a cohesive and efficient functioning of a club, there must be a clear demarcation of duties to be assigned to its office bearers. Following suggestions have been made in this regard.

Patron. He is expected to take a keen interest in all the activities of the club and to extend all the possible facilities to the club.

Sponsor. He is the main force to start the club and he has to take initiative to start such a club and made it a hub of activities. His role should be that of an advisor, guide and supervisor and he should refrain from becoming a dictator. He should always be alert to avoid any mishap. He should keep a strict watch on the activities of the club members.

Chairman. He being the elected representative of the student should be asked to preside over all the formal functions organised by the club. He has also the convene and preside over the meetings of the executive committee of the club.

Secretary. He is also an elected member and is to look after and maintain a proper record of various activities of the club. He should call a meeting of the executive committee in consultation with the chairman and in accordance with the constitution of the club. He should keep a true record of the meetings of the executive committee. He is also responsible to carry out all correspondence on behalf of the club and to extend invitations to speakers and guests for various functions of the club.

Asstt. Secretary. His main role is to assist the secretary in performance of his duties. In the absence of secretary he has to carry out all the functions of the secretary.

Treasurer. He is the person who is responsible for collection of subscriptions/membership fee for the club. He has also to maintain a proper account of receipts and expenditure of the club. He must present his accounts to the executive for audit and scrutiny at least once a year.

Members of Executive Committee. A member of executive committee is expected to extend his active cooperation and participate actively in formation of club's policy and programme. He should use his contacts and influence to make the programmes of the club a success.

Suggested Activities for a Science Club

(*i*) Interesting experiments may be undertaken in the club to enable students to develop skills and abilities for research work.

(*ii*) Club members may be asked to make collections of specimen, prepare charts and models etc.

(*iii*) Club can arrange excursions to places of scientific interest.

(*iv*) Science clubs may be asked to arrange science fairs and science exhibitions.

(*v*) Under the ages of the club some quiz contest, paper reading contest, essay competition and some such other competitions can be arranged.

(*vi*) Science clubs must celebrate science days. On such occassions they should put up tabuleaux and plays.

(*vii*) Some eminent scholars be invited to deliver extention lectures.

(*viii*) Science clubs can render school service in health and sanitation.

(*ix*) Members of the club can also render community service in realm of public health.

(*x*) If possible a science club should take initiative to organise a camp in which participants be educated to actively participate in national programme of health and family planning. They may be asked to inculcate sound health habits.

(*xi*) The club can take up the production of some common things like ink, soap, phenyl, shaving cream, boot polish, nail polish etc.

Science Club and Classroom Teaching

The activities of science club are a supplement to classroom teaching. Such clubs play an important role in making science education more meaningful and effective. Various charts, models, improvised apparatus prepared by members of the club can be used as important teaching aids for teaching of science in the classroom. References could be made to various science projects undertaken by the club members and the club members may be asked to explain their projects in the class. The explanation of a project by a student in a class may then be put to open discussion in the class which would make other students more interested in learning science.

To make best use of the trips and excursions arranged by the science club, the students be given a questionnaire so that students may be more attentive to provide their answers. Answers given by the students may then be discussed in the classroom and teacher can coordinate all the facts observed by the students into a complete lesson.

Some method can be used to correlate and coordinate various club activities with classroom teaching.

There is no doubt about the fact that if the club activities are organised properly they will never interfere with classroom teaching. Various activities of the club are expected to develop the skill of the student, his power of reasoning, understanding, his power to distinguish between relevant and irrelevant etc.

Evaluation of a Science Club

To find out the extent to which a club has succeeded in achieving its stated objectives it is necessary to carry out regular periodical evaluation of the activities of the club. Such an evaluation may be external or internal or it may be a mixture of both. For internal evaluation the views of patron, sponsor about the activities of the club may be obtained. They should express their views along with their suggestions for improvement in the working of the club. For external evaluation the sponsor of some other near by science club be asked to visit the club activities and express his opinion. He may also be asked to give suggestions for improvement. An effort be then made to further improve the working of the club in the light of suggestions given for improvement.

9.3 SCIENTIFIC HOBBIES

Scientific hobbies can also be undertaken as a part of activities of science club. Now that more and more attempts are being made to give a technical bias to our education and hobbies with a scientific basis are becoming more and more popular, the science master can make a valuable contribution by encouraging a number of hobbies that bear directly on education in science, students will be found only too enthusiastic and even willing to spend money in addition to their time to pursue such hobbies if the science teacher is keen and knows the particular hobbies he is going to start. In the beginning an attempt be made with one or two simple and less expensive hobbies. There is a large number of such hobbies having a scientific basis *e.g.* ink making, soap making, making hair oils and face creams, phenyl making, preparation of James and Jellys, achars and chutneys etc. The list can be enlarged to include gardening, making of charts and models, rendering first aid etc.

Uses of Hobbies Class

A hobbies class provides the student the best way of utilizing his leisure time and as such a hobbies class fulfills one of the chief aims of education *i.e. to train the child to use his leisure time properly*. The students get a good opportunity to keep himself busy in a constructive way by attending such hobby classes. It helps the students to keep himself away from adolescent disturbances that helps him to adjust in later years of life. Hobbies class also provide the student a knowledge of technical side of science and also helps in correlating the teaching of science with the everyday life and environment of the student.

Following hobbies can be undertaken under the aspices of science club:

1. Debates and seminars.
2. Museum and exhibitions.
3. Reading reference books.
4. Preserving specimen.
5. Collection of specimen.
6. Vivarium.
7. Aquarium.
8. Bee-keeping.
9. Poultry farming.
10. Animal keeping.
11. Farming.
12. Gardening.
13. Drawing charts etc.

Suggestions

Teachers should encourage the students to take one or more hobbies and should give proper guidance. Hobbies selected should not be time consuming and students be able to pursue them in their leisure time. The hobby should merely be a side affair.

9.4 SCIENCE FAIRS AND EXHIBITIONS IN SCHOOLS

We find that functions such as prize distribution, parents day, sports day etc. form a regular feature of most schools. Just like these functions an effort should be made to hold an annual science fair or exhibition may be along with any of these days. A science fair provides an excellent opportunity for display and dissemination of various activities that are being carried over by the science club. A science fair can also serve the purpose of acquainting the parents in particular and people of locality in general with the diverse nature of scientific work that is undertaken in the school. The organisation of a science fair or a science exhibition can easily be entrusted to the school science club. In recent years various government agencies encourage the organisation of science fairs and science exhibitions. The encouragement is provided in the form of financial and other help. Such fairs are encouraged by NCERT and SCERT of various states.

NCERT (National Council of Educational Research and Training) has outlined the following objectives for organising science fairs.

(*i*) To give impetus and provide encouragement to students to try out their ideas and to apply their knowledge of science into some creative channel.

(*ii*) To provide opportunities to students to see for themselves some achievements of their colleagues and in this way stimulate them to plan their occur projects.

(*iii*) To make science activities more popular amongst the students thereby hoping to improve standards of performance.

(*iv*) To encourage bright and enthusiastic students having special science talent.

(*v*) To identify talented students in science and nature the future scientists.

(*vi*) To provide an opportunity to the people of area to come in contact with school and to meet the teachers and students.

(*vii*) To provide a competitive forum to various science clubs in the area.

Organisation of a Science Fair

When ever a science teacher plans to organise a science fair he should inform his students about it well in advance. Then he should start to find a good and suitable location in the school where such fair can be organised. Having located a suitable place he should start planning or arrangements of exhibits.

Planning. It is essential that planning be thoroughly done. During planning the limits of the fair, the procedure, and other factors should be discussed and decided upon. During planning the following aspects should be considered.

(*i*) Objectives and aims of the fair.

(*ii*) Scope of the fair-whether to limit to school or open to other schools.

(*iii*) Type of programmes etc.

(*iv*) Procedure.

(*v*) Financing.

(*vi*) Place, time and duration.

(*vii*) Other factors and facilities.

Distribution of Work. After planning, the work should be assigned to different individuals or groups. A number of committies may be formed which look after different programmes and sections of the fair. There may be advisory, executive, recording, reception, general management sectional seating, publicity committees and sub-committees. All these committees are guided and directed by the teacher-in-charge in consultation with the students. While distributing the work the interests and the talents of the students should be kept in view.

He should then train some selected students to act as students guide. Science teacher should see that there students volunteers can guide the visitors and can explain to them various scientific principles involved in any exhibit.

Exhibits. There could be a variety of exhibits in a science fair. For exhibiting in a science fair the science master can select a few interesting experiments, charts, working models of useful appliances specimen collected by students during excursions, applications of scientific principles to daily life, scientific toys etc. For sake of convenience exhibits can be classified as under:

(*i*) Experiments

(*ii*) Models

(*iii*) Specimens

(*iv*) Collections

(*v*) Improvised apparatus

(*vi*) Charts and diagrams

(*vii*) Investigatory projects

Evaluation. To encourage the participants some prizes in the form of general science books or merit certificates may be instituted and awarded to pupils whose exhibits have been adjudged best by a panel of judges. For purpose of award of prizes various exhibits at a science fair be classified in various catagories and prizes be awarded separately for some good entries in each class. While judging an exhibit some criteria on the following lines may be used by the judges. Various aspects be given the following weightage.

1.	Scientific approach	30%
2.	Originality	20%
3.	Technical skill	20%
4.	Thoroughness	10%
5.	Dramatic value	10%
6.	Personal Interview	10%

Uses of Science Fairs

"The science fairs have social, intellectual, psychological and educational values. The students take part in group projects and activities and learn many things which cannot be learnt through class-room teaching. They develop not only intellectually but also socially, psychologically and educationally. The instincts of construction, acquisition, curiosity etc. also get satisfaction. Their talents are recognised and stimulated. They develop a keen taste and interest for scientific investigations and in solving scientific problems. Science fairs also provide an opportunity for discovering and encouraging science talent.

Chapter 10

Teaching Aids

10.1 INTRODUCTION

For teaching effectively and for realising the stipulated objectives of life science teaching, the life science teacher wants an effective communication with his students in quite interesting and useful way. For such a communication the teacher some times resorts to some aids which are referred to as *teaching aids*. Such aids are used to supplement the process of teaching. Most of the teaching aids are sensory and their function is to make teaching concrete, effective and interesting.

The most important teaching aids used in teaching of biology are:

(*i*) Aquarium
(*ii*) Terrarium
(*iii*) Green House
(*iv*) Nature-Study Garden
(*v*) Museum
(*vi*) Biology Text Books etc.

10.2 IMPORTANCE AND NEED OF TEACHING AIDS

(*i*) These aids help the teacher in getting the attention of his students.

(*ii*) These aids help in creating the interest of the student in the topic and activate the mental process of the students.

(*iii*) The student gets an opportunity to get a first hand experience by visualising some concrete things, living specimens and actual demonstrations etc.

(*iv*) Use of teaching aids help to have a clear conception of ideas, information, facts and principles.

(*v*) It helps the students in understanding some complicated and difficult concepts.

(*vi*) They provide an opportunity for a change in the monotonous atmosphere that generally prevails in a class room.

(*vii*) They provide an opportunity for a better support between the teacher and his pupil.

(*viii*) They help the students to develop a scientific attitude.

(*ix*) They provide a training in scientific method.

(*x*) They can be used in bigger classes.

(*xi*) Use of such aids is based on the principles of psychology.

10.3 PRINCIPLES FOR USE OF TEACHING AIDS

Teaching aids should be used properly to make teaching more effective. Teaching can because more effective if such aids are used widely but the use of such aids cannot provide a guarantee of good teaching. Following points are important for a proper use of teaching aids.

(*i*) Teaching aids should be woven with class room teaching and these aids should be used only to supplement the oral and written work being done in the class.

(*ii*) While making use of any teaching aid an effort be made that the teaching aids being used in any class are in confirmity with the intellectual level of the students and is in accordance with the previous experience of the students.

(*iii*) Only such aids the preferred which provide a stimulus to the students for greater thinking and activity.

(*iv*) If possible actual specimens be preferred to a photograph or a slide of a specimen.

(*v*) The teaching aid used should be exact, accurate and real as far as practicable.

(*vi*) The Teacher should use a teaching aid only when he is quite sure about handling a specific teaching aid. For handling some aids (*e.g.* operating a projector etc.) training is provided by various authorities. For this purpose more information can be obtained from local SCERT or directly from NCERT, New Delhi.

(*vii*) Teaching aids used be such as are closely related to pupils experiences.

(*viii*) The teacher should use a teaching aid only after a proper planning so that the aid is used exactly at the point; in the process of teaching, where it best fits in the process of teaching.

(*ix*) Teacher should see that a follow up programme follows the lesson wherein a teaching aid has been used.

(*x*) Teacher should carry out occasional evaluation about the use, function and effect of a teaching aid on the learning process.

10.4 TYPES OF TEACHING AIDS

For convenience of discussion the teaching aids may be grouped as under:

General Classification of Teaching Aids

The general classification of audio-visual aids are as under:

(*i*) The Black board and bulletin boards.

(*ii*) *Charts*. Table, stream and tree and organisation of flow.

(*iii*) *Dramatics*. Pantomime, pagent, puppet show, shadow play.

(*iv*) *Flat Pictures*. Photographs, prints and post cards.

(*v*) *Graphs*. Pictorial statistics, bar, diagram.

(*vi*) *Maps*. Flat, relief, projection, electric, globe etc.

(*vii*) *Models*. Objects and specimen.

(*viii*) *Motion pictures*. Silent and sound.

(*ix*) Phonographs, records and transcriptions.

(*x*) Poster, Cartoons, Clippings.

(*xi*) Radio, dictaphone and loud speaker.

(*xii*) Stereoscope.

(*xiii*) *Pictures*. Still and projected.

(*xiv*) Trips, journey, tours and visits.

Specific Classification

A report has given following four types of audio-visual aids for teaching.

(*i*) *Audio aids*. Examples of this type of teaching aids are radio, tape recorder etc. This type of aids help the learner in acquiring knowledge through his auditory senses.

(*ii*) *Visual aids*. Examples of this type of teaching aids are charts, pictures, models, epidiascope, micro-projector, film-strips etc. This type of aids are help the learner in acquiring knowledge through his visual senses.

(*iii*) *Audio-visual aids.* In this type are included those teaching aids which involve the use of two of our senses *i.e.* hearing and seeing (or auditory and visual senses) for gaining the desired learning experiences. For example T.V., motion picture, video film, living objects etc.

(*iv*) *Activity aids*. This refers to those teaching aids in which students learn by engaging themselves in some useful activity. This type of aids help the learner in acquiring knowledge through sight and sound as well as through doing. For example science excursion and visits, science exhibition and fairs, Science Museum, Nature study garden, Botanical garden, Zoological place, Aquarium, Vivarium, Terrarium, Experimentation in the laboratory and work shop.

Some of these aids are discussed in the following pages.

I. Visual Aids

Under this head we will take of following types of teaching aids.

(*a*) Display Boards such as Chalk boards or Black boards, Flannel boards, Bulletin boards, Magnetic board etc.

(*b*) Charts, pictures and models.

Visual aids are those which can be appreciated and understood by seeing them only.

(*a*) **Display Boards**

It is any flat surface that can be used to white information to be communicated. At present for this purpose the use is made of *black board* or *chalk board, bulletin board, flannel board, magnetic board* etc.

Though material for display on such a board can be collected from any source even from a text book but for being effective the material should be displayed in such a way that it is eye catching, colourful and purposeful.

Black Board or Chalk Board

It is one of the most common visual aids in use. It is a slightly abrasive writing surface made of wood, ply, hard board, cement, ground glass, asbestos, state, plastic etc. with black, green or bluish green paint on it. Details of various types of chalk boards and their arrangement for a science room or science laboratory have been given in the lessons dealing with these topics. A chalk board is generally installed facing the class which is either built into the wall or fixed and framed on the wall and provided with a ledge to keep the chalk sticks and duster. Portable chalk boards are also available these days. Such chalk boards can be placed on a stand with adjustable height. Generally white chalk sticks are used for writing on the black board or chalk board but some times coloured chalk sticks are also used. The coloured chalk sticks are used for better illustration.

Characteristics of a Good Chalk Board. Some of the characteristics of a good chalk board are as follows:

(*i*) Its surface should be rough enough so that it is capable of holding the writing on the board.

(*ii*) Its surface should be dull so that it can eliminate glare.

(*iii*) Its surface should be such that the writing on the board can be easily removed by making use of a cloth or a foam duster.

(*iv*) Its height should be so adjusted that it is within the easy reach of the teacher and is easily visible to the students.

Effective Use of Chalk Board. We find that chalk board is the most common teaching aid used by the teacher for writing important points, drawing illustrations, solving problems etc. The science teacher should keep the following points in mind to use the chalk board effectively.

(*i*) Write in a clear and legible handwriting the important points on the chalk board but avoid over crowding of information on the chalk board.

(*ii*) The size of the words written on black board should be such that they can be seen even by the back-benchers. The letters should not be less than one inch in height. The recommended height of letters on a chalk board in between 6 cm to 8 cm. For this the teacher should frequently inspect his own chalk board writing from the view point of the back-bench on a corner seat.

(*iii*) There should be proper arrangement of light in the class room so that the chalk board remains glare free.

(*iv*) To emphasise some points or parts of a sketch or a diagram coloured chalks be used.

(*v*) Rub off the information already discussed in the class and noted down by the students.

(*vi*) Draw a difficult illustration before hand to save the class time.

(*vii*) Stand on one side of the chalk board while explaining some points to the students.

(*viii*) Make use of a pointer for drawing attention to the written material on the chalk board.

(*ix*) Students may be allowed to express their ideas on chalk board, or to make alterations or corrections. Some times teacher may intentionally draw some incorrect diagram and ask the students to make necessary correction, alteration etc.

(*x*) For maintenance of proper discipline in the class the teacher should always keep an eye on his class while writing on the black board.

(*xi*) For proper writing on chalk board the chalk stick be broken into two pieces and the broken end of the piece be used to start writing.

(*xii*) While writing on a chalk board keep your fingers and wrist stiff and move your arm freely.

Advantages of Chalk board. Some of the advantages of chalk board over other visual aids are as follows:

(*i*) It is a very convenient teaching aid for group teaching.

(*ii*) It is quite economical and can be used again and again.

(*iii*) Its use is accompanied by the appropriate actions on the part of the teacher. The illustrations drawn on the black board captures students attention.

(*iv*) It is one of the most valuable supplementary teaching aid.

(*v*) It can be used as a good visual aid for drill and revision.

(*vi*) These boards can be used for drawing enlarged illustrations from the text books.

(*vii*) It is a convenient aid for giving lesson notes to the students.

Limitations of the Chalk board. Some of the important limitations of a chalk board are as under:

(*i*) The use of chalk board makes students very much dependent on the teacher.

(*ii*) It makes the lesson teacher paced.

(*iii*) It makes the lesson dull and of routine nature.

(*iv*) It gives no attention to the individual needs of the students.

(*v*) Due to constant use chalk boards become smooth and start glaring.

(*vi*) While using chalk-sticks to write on chalk board the teacher spreads a lot of chalk powder which is inhaled by teacher and students and it may affect their health.

Bulletin Boards

It is a display board on which learning material on some scientific topic is displayed. It is generally of the size of a black board but some times even bigger depending on the wall space available. It is generally in the form of a framed soft board or straw-board or cork board or rubber sheets. Such bulletin boards can be specified for individual branches of science or even for some specified science topics *e.g.* science puzzles, science news, science cartoons etc. such a board can also be used for displaying the best work of students. However for a all purpose bulletin board the following type of display material in recommended:

(*i*) Interesting science news.

(*ii*) Book Jackets of recently published science books.

(*iii*) Brochures.

(*iv*) Cartoons.

(*v*) Poems.

(*vi*) Sketches.

(*vii*) Pictures.

(*viii*) Photographs.

(*ix*) Thoughts.

(*x*) Announcements etc.

An effort be made to change the material on bulletin board as frequently as in practicable. Whenever the teacher starts a new topic he may ask the students to display the concerned material on the bulletin board and the teacher should specifically mention to the students the display material on the bulletin board while teaching a topic to the class. Students be asked to take the charge of bulletin board by rotation.

How to use A Bulletin Board. To make use of bulletin board as a useful teaching aid the bulletin board be used for creating interest amongst students an specific topics. For effective use of bulletin board as a teaching aid following points be kept in mind:

(*i*) Effort be made jointly by the teacher and the students to procure material from various sources on a given subject or topic.

(*ii*) Before displaying the material on the board sort out the material relevant to a specific subject or topic.

(*iii*) Make best use of your aesthetic sense to display the material on the bulletin board.

(*iv*) Do fix a title for the specific subject/topic of display material on the top centre of the bulletin board.

(*v*) It is desirable if a brief description about the specific subject or topic is fixed below the title.

(*vi*) The height of bulletin board from ground level be about 1 m.

(*vii*) The bulletin board be fixed in an area where enough lighting can be provided.

(*viii*) The material displayed should be large enough and should be provided with suitable headings.

(*ix*) Over crowding of material on bulletin board be avoided.

Advantages of Bulletin Boards. Some of the advantages of bulletin board as a teaching aid are as follows:

(*i*) It is a good supplement to class room teaching.

(*ii*) It helps in arousing the interest of students in a specific subject/topic.

(*iii*) It can be effectively used as a follow up of chalk ɔoard.

(*iv*) Such boards add colour and liveliness and thus also have decorative value in addition to their educational value.

(*v*) Such boards can be conveniently used for introducing a topic and for its review as well.

Limitations of Bulletin Board. Some limitations in the use of bulletin boards as teaching aids are as follows:

(*i*) They cannot be used for all inclusive teaching.

(*ii*) They can be used only as supplementary aids to some other teaching aid.

(*iii*) At times it becomes very difficult to make proper selection of the display material for certain topic.

Flannel Board

It is also some times referred to as *flannel graph* or *felt board*. It is made of wood, card board or straw board covered with coloured flannel or woolen cloth. It is one of the latest devices effectively used for science teaching. Display materials like cut-outs, pictures, drawings and light objects backed with rough surfaces like sand paper strips, flannel strips etc. will stick to flannel board temporarily.

For display purposes a flannel board of 1.5 x 1.5 m is generally used. It can be fixed next to the black board or can be placed on a stand about one metre above the ground.

How to use a Flannel Board. Following points be kept in mind for effective use of flannel board as a teaching aid:

(*i*) The teacher should collect a large number of pictures or wall cut diagrams etc. and back them with sand paper pieces. He may then make use of these by displaying these on the board one by one, after proper selection.

(*ii*) Display the material on the flannel board in a sequence to develop the lesson.

(*iii*) Make proper use of flannel board for creating proper scenes and designs relevant to the lesson.

(*iv*) Change the display material on the board as frequently as required.

(*v*) Flannel board can be used quite effectively for showing relationship between different parts or steps of a process.

Advantages of Flannel Board. Some of the advantages of using flannel board as a teaching aid are as follows:

(*i*) It is quite economical and easy to handle and operate.

(*ii*) The pictures or cuttings can be easily fixed and removed when required, without spoiling the material. Thus same material can be used for display many a times.

(*iii*) Any display material on the board holds the interest of students and arrests their attention.

(*iv*) Such boards enable a teacher to talk along with changing illustrations to develop a lesson.

Magnetic Chalk Board

It is a framed iron sheet having porcelain coating in black or green colour. Such a board can be used either to write with chalk sticks, glass marking pencils and crayons or to display pictures, cut-outs and light objects with disc magnets or magnetic holders.

Thus such a board functions both as a chalk board and as a flannel board. We can display visual learning material on such a board while writing key points on it. Such a board provides the flexibility of movement of visual material. It is possible to display even a three dimensional object on such a board using magnetic holders.

Since the magnetic chalk board functions both as a chalk board and as a flannel board so various points discussed for the effective use of these boards be kept in mind while using magnetic chalk board as an effective teaching aid.

Advantages of Magnetic Chalk Board. Some of the advantages of magnetic chalk board are as follows:

(*i*) It is a versatile teaching aid that combines the advantages of both a chalk board and a flannel board.

(*ii*) It is possible to move visual material by sliding it along the surface of the board such a movement is not possible on a flannel board.

(*iii*) It is very light and can be easily taken from one place to another.

(*iv*) Such a board can be easily got prepared in the school from an iron sheet and painting with some good paint.

(*b*) Charts, Pictures and Models

Charts, pictures and models also are an important teaching aids.

Charts. Sometimes charts are needed by the teacher to supplement his actual teaching. There are certain charts where in the interior of some thing is depicted *e.g.* various systems of human body, internal combustion engine, motor car etc.

Following points be kept in view while using charts as teaching aids:

(*i*) An effort be made to use charts prepared by students under the guidance of the teacher, however some charts may be purchased.

(*ii*) Only such charts be purchased which have bold lines and in which such colours are used as could be seen and distinguished even by the back-benchers.

(*iii*) Charts should give only the essential details.

(*iv*) Charts should be properly and clearly labelled in block letters.

Sources for Procurement of Charts

(*i*) Charts can be prepared by students and teacher.

(*ii*) Charts can be purchased.

(*iii*) Charts can be procured on a very nominal cost from the following sources:

(*a*) Ministry of Education, Government of India, Delhi.

(*b*) NCERT, New Delhi.

(*c*) Director, Extension Service of College of Education in the State.

(*d*) SCERT of the state.

(*e*) District Public Relation Officer.

Advantages of Charts

(*i*) They can be made quickly.

(*ii*) They have a better appeal.

(*iii*) Only bare essentials can be shown in the chart and unnecessary details can be avoided.

(*iv*) Charts are available from various sources.

Pictures. Pictures of gas-works, steamships, and locomotives and portraits of great men of science – physicists, chemists, biologists and astronomers – will be of great help in teaching of science provided a reference in made to them. Portraits of great scientists if displayed in science room give it the proper scientific atmosphere. These pictures, portraits etc. can be used as teaching aids and they are quite useful in a demonstration lesson. Everything a child learns can be presented graphically with the aid of pictures and brightly coloured diagrams which will excite his interest.

Following points be given due consideration while using pictures as teaching aids:

(*i*) Pictures should be bold, direct and sufficiently large.

(*ii*) Pictures should not be over loaded with information rather they should stick to the maxim, '*one picture, one idea*.'

Models. In teaching of science models are very frequently used. Various costly models are available and some of these may be available and in school laboratory. However the cost of such models should not be any hindrance to the use of models as teaching aid because a science teacher can prepare almost all types of models by making use of ingenuity. It is also possible to take some very costly models on loan or such models can even be hired. Models are very helpful in making the subject clear to the students and they also give the student an idc of the actual shape/size etc. of the article under discussion.

In using charts, pictures and models as teaching aids the teacher should be careful to plan their proper display. These should be displayed in such a way and at such a height that each student can have a detailed view of it.

Following is the list of some firms from whom scientific charts and models can be procured:

1. M/s Scientific Instruments Stores, J-355, New Rajinder Nagar, New Delhi.
2. M/s Educational Aids and Charts, 20, I Block, Kumara Park, West Extension, Bangalore-20.
3. M/s Variety Teaching Aids, Bagalkot, Distt. Bijapur.
4. M/s Educational Emporium, 15-A, Chittranjan Avenue, Calcutta-7.
5. M/s Oxford University Press, Appollo Bunder, Bombay.
6. M/s School Aids Manufacturing Co., 12-Gun Boat Street, Fort, Bombay-1.
7. The Director, Survey of India, Hathi Barkala Road, Dehradun (UP).
8. M/s Hobby Centre, Mount Road, Madras-2.

II. Aural Aids

In this type the following aids are considered:

(*i*) Broadcast talks,

(*ii*) Gramophone lectures, and

(*iii*) Tape recordings.

Broadcast Talks

All India Radio has in its regular feature some programmes meant for school children. In such a programme gene- rally talks on educational matters or on scientific topics are broad- casted. Such a talk in quite useful for students as also for science teacher. The topic, date and time of broadcast of such talks are given in advance by All India Radio. A school can take benefit of such talks only if it possesses a good radio set and a period is provided in the school time-table for listening such talks. Such an arrangement can be worked out by the school authorities and then teacher can refer to such talks while teaching his class. It is also possible to synchronise the broad cast talk on some topic with the actual teaching of that topic in a class.

Some handicaps of such broadcast task are listed here.

(*i*) Sometimes when the receiving set is not working satisfactorily there prevails a sense of strain in the class room.

(*ii*) Some students are poor listeners and may not be benefited by such talks although they benefit by normal teaching through questions, demonstrations and reading.

For the maximum utility of such talks following points be kept in view:

(*i*) The students with bad hearing be seated on front seats.

(*ii*) To keep students interest alive in such talks teacher should tell his students in advance a few questions which they have to answer after the talk.

(*iii*) Only short duration talks be arranged.

Such talks cannot be a substitute to the actual teaching and such a talk is only to help in teaching.

Gramophone Lectures and Tape Recordings

Another teaching aid available to a science teacher is records of short talks an interest- ing scientific topics by eminent scientists, doctors etc. Magnetic tapes of such recorded talks are now available and the talk can be easily reproduced in the class room. These talks provide an inspiration to the students and such a talk once recorded can be used again and again. Such recording can either be used to introduce a topic or to develop a topic. Even the voice of different birds and animals can be recorded and reproduced in the class while teaching about such animals or birds.

III. Audio-Visual Aids

In this catagory those teaching aids are included which involve the use of two of our senses *i.e.* hearing and seeing. These are classified as (*i*) optical aids and (*ii*) Television.

Optical Aids

Some such aids are discussed here. *Magic Lantern (or Glass slide projector).*

Psychologists have now confirmed that a child grasps abstract facts slowly and can only remember a name which recalls some definite reality. Thus he should be confronted with visual teaching aids to broaden his experience.

A *magic lantern* is a simple device used to project pictures from a glass slide on a screen or wall. Teacher can make use of this device when he intends to show some small figure or illustration to whole class. Many a schools have a *magic lantern* in their laboratories as it is not very costly slides are readily available in the market on various science topics. These can also be got prepared on demand and the cost of such a slide is quite reasonable. Such slides can even be prepared by science teacher himself after some practical training which can be provided by extension service department of training colleges.

Epidiascope

Epidiascope is a more costly instrument but it can project opaque objects as well as transparent objects. The pictures projected by epidiascope are much brighten and needs a less powerful light so that room need not be absolutely dark. Epidiascope can be used to project any picture, map, diagram, photograph or small object. No slide is needed for projection with an epidiascope.

The name *epidiascope* is given to this machine because of the fact that it works, as an *episcope* when it is used to throw the image of an opaque object. This machine can be used to project slides and this is possible just by moving a lower provided for the purpose. When it is used to project a slide then at serves as a *diascope*. Thus *epidiascope* is a combination of these two *i.e. episcope* and *diascope*.

Advantages of Epidiascope. In comparison to other projection machines *epidiascope* has some advantages. Some of these are as follows:

(*i*) It can be operated in a room which may not be absolutely dark.

(*ii*) With the help of this machine original colours of the picture or photograph can be projected.

(*iii*) The projection on the screen can be kept for some time during which teacher can explain and discuss it in the class.

(*iv*) It provides teacher an option to handle the lesson according to himself.

Following points provide useful hints for the proper handling of an epidiascope.

(*i*) The apparatus works well in a dark room.

(*ii*) While projecting with an epidiascope an effort be made to keep exposed to the head of the lamp for minimum time delicate pictures, photographs or other such objects.

(*iii*) The person handling the apparatus must be given some practical training before he is allowed to handle the machine.

Film Projector, Micro-Projector, Film-Strip Projector

There are further improvements on the teaching aids discussed so far. These have brought about a revolution in teaching of science. Science films are shown to the students to illustrate various applications and uses of science as also to supplement the class room teaching. Both type of films have some basic objectives to serve.

Film Strip-Projector

It is an improvement on magic lantern and this machine can be used to project many a topics on a single strip. One such strip generally consists of 40-100 separate pictures and such film strips are available on loan from Central Film Library, NCERT, New Delhi. On such a film strip pictures concerning one topic are arranged in a definite order.

This machine can be easily handled by the science teacher. The machine is operated by hand and thus can be stopped at the discretion of the teacher whenever he wants to explain some aspect of a topic being shown on machine.

Micro-Projector

This is most commonly used in biology teaching for showing microscopic slides, small living specimen and growth or crystals. This projector is generally operated in a dark room. The projection can be taken on vertical screen if whole class is expected to see it. However such a film cannot be distinctly seen by a student if he is sitting at a distance more than 12 feet from the screen.

Film Projector

This machine is used for showing science films. Some good science films on various topics are available and these can be had on loan some times even free of charge from the source, given below:

(*i*) Central Film Library, NCERT, New Delhi.

(*ii*) U.S. Information Service, New Delhi.

(*iii*) British High Commissions Office, New Delhi.

(*iv*) Some Other Embassies, New Delhi.

For projecting this films in school generally 16 mm projector ('RCA', 'Bell and Havell') are used. These 16 mm projectors are less costly and easier to transport as compared to a 35 mm projector.

Advantages of Motion Pictures. There are some definite advantages of motion pictures to be used as teaching aids, some of these are as follows:

(*i*) They draw attention of the students.

(*ii*) They help to bring past to the class room.

(*iii*) It is possible to reduce or enlarge the size of the object by using the machine.

(*iv*) They can be used to show a process which a naked human eye cannot see without its aid.

(*v*) They can be used to show a record of an event.

(*vi*) They can serve a large class at a time.

(*vii*) They provide a good aesthetic experience.

(*viii*) They help in understanding relationship between things, ideas and events.

Some Important Motion Pictures

Following motion pictures are very useful as teaching aids in life science.

(*i*) An animal life cycle – AIBS films, No. 13269.

(*ii*) Behaviour – AIBS films, No. 13266

(*iii*) The Blood – Encyclopaedia Britanica, film No. 1819.

(*iv*) The cell structure – Unit of life, Coronef films.

(*v*) Bacteria – Laboratory study – Indian University films.

(*vi*) Beach and sea animal – Encyclopedia Britanica films, No. 1534.

Precautions. The teacher should take the following precautions whenever he wants to use a film projection as a teaching aid:

(*i*) He should satisfy himself about the lighting management and seating arrangement in the room where such a film show is to be given.

(*ii*) He should himself see the film before hand.

(*iii*) He should give a complete background of the film to the students before the actual screening of the film.

(*iv*) He should see that complete calm and peace is maintained during the screening of the film.

(*v*) Immediately after the film show, he should invite comments, questions etc. from the students and try to answer all the quarries of the students.

(*vi*) He should encourage some of his students to write articles etc. based on the film show and such articles etc., may be shown on well magazine, may be printed in school magazine.

Television

The role of television in the present day world is becoming more and more important and it is one of the most important teaching aids. It combines the advantages of a radio (broad cast) and of a film. This can be used for mass education and now U.G.C. programmes are a regular feature on "Door Darshan". The topics of discussion are announced in advance and lesson from well qualified persons and specialists in their fields are shown on TV. Teacher can easily plan his work accordingly and in this way he can make use of TV as a teaching aid.

IV. Activity Aids

Activity aids include

(*i*) Science museum.

(*ii*) Nature study garden.

(*iii*) Science fairs.

Science Museum

A museum ought to be a very valuable part of a science department in school. Nature study and chemistry provide many examples of things which may be kept in such a museum. Though the ideal way to gain knowledge is to observe objects and phenomenon in their natural setting but in the present educational set up there is only a little opportunity for this. A science museum helps in this aspect. Museum not only provides necessary help in teaching but also helps in creating the right type of scientific atmosphere in the school.

A good museum should be scholar built. An effort be made to avoid exhibiting readymade articles. Change is the law of nature and it is always good to replace with better objects those exhibits which have become unsatisfactory either because of their age of because of their use. The teacher should make all efforts to enrich the science museum and should encourage his students to make new additions to the school museum. The museum should consist of:

(*i*) Dry exhibits such as leaves, roots, weeds, specimen of ores and minerals etc.

(*ii*) Fish, snakes, water-weeds, etc.

(*iii*) Butterflies, insects and shell-fish are exhibited in boxes having cork bottom. Silver plated pins should be used for fixing these objects to avoid rusting. It is always advisable to place some naphthalene balls in the boxes to avoid danger from moths.

In addition to these a science museum may exhibit models of various mechanical devices, specimens of some local industrial products, various stages in the manufacture of items such as a match box, pencil etc. can also be depicted. Some of the preparations done by the students can also be depicted in the science museum.

Some other important points about a science museum are:

(*i*) Systematic arrangement of various exhibits, and

(*ii*) Clear and complete description of various parts of the exhibits.

For this purpose an ideal arrangement will be that a card of suitable size (5′′ x 4′′) be attached to each item exhibited in the museum and the following information be typed on this card or written in a good hand writing on the card.

(*i*) Scientific as also the common name of the exhibit. For biological specimen the family to which the exhibit belongs should also be indicated.

(*ii*) The place where from the exhibit has been obtained and the other relevant information.

(*iii*) Importance of the exhibit.

The language used for providing the above information should be simple and all efforts be made to avoid phrases and technical terms in the description of the exhibit.

Care for Living Things. Provisions must be made for caring for all types of living things in the museum. A variety of suitable containers be made available for housing them. The wise teacher will always have the following containers available insect cages, small animal cages, aquariums, and terrariums.

Insects

For housing we can use small cake pans, coffee cans, or covers from ice cream cartons for cover and base. Roll wire screening into cylinder to fit base and lace together with strand of wire.

Cut windows in paper coffee container, oatmeal box, or shoe box. Glue Saran, cellophane, silk, or nylon stocking over windows.

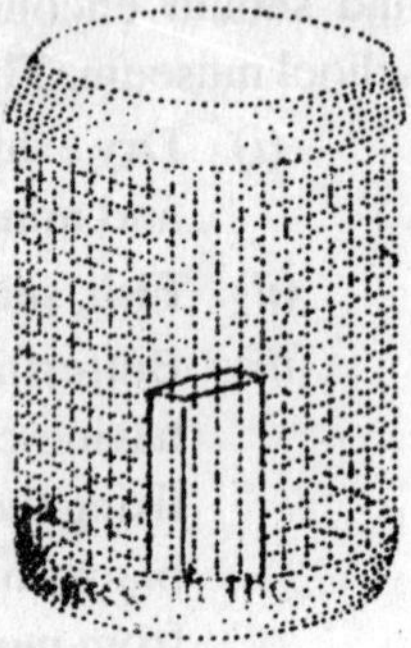

Fig. 10.1

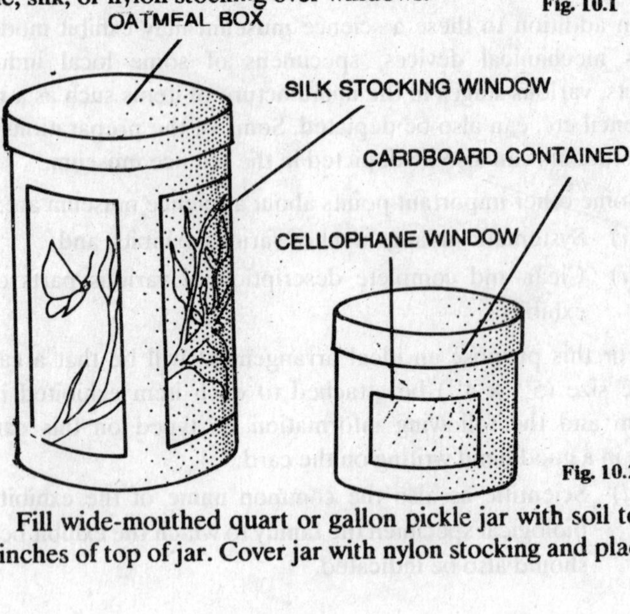

Fig. 10.2

Fill wide-mouthed quart or gallon pickle jar with soil to within two inches of top of jar. Cover jar with nylon stocking and place jar in pan of water. Can be used for ants, termites, worms, etc. Cover jar with black construction paper after putting in insects.

Animals

Some of the insect containers described above can also be used for small animals. For housing larger animals we can easily construct cages.

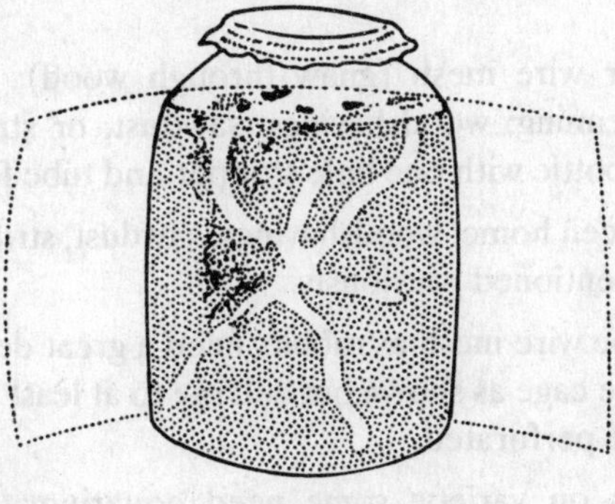

Fig. 10.3

A cage for a larger animal can be made from wire screening. Cut the wire screening as shown. Fold where dotted lines are shown. Tack or staple three sides to a wooden base. Hook one side to enable easy cleaning.

Terrarium

Get six pieces of glass any size and place them as follows: arrange glass according to diagram (Fig. 10.4). Use tape one inch wide

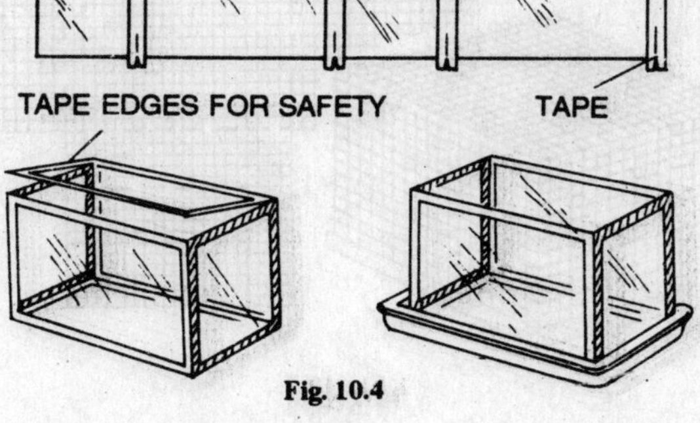

Fig. 10.4

(plastic or adhesive) on joints and rub very hard to make sure of good adhesion. Turn over and put tape on other side in same manner. Place tape on lid according to diagram and another piece for a handle. Place glass terrarium in cookie or cake pan.

Some suggestions for housing some of the more commonly used animals are given below.

Housing. Wooden box or crate of about 24 in. x 16 in. x 12 in. with door.

Metal or wire mesh (gnaw through wood); removable solid bottom for cleaning; woodshavings, sawdust, or strips of paper on floor of cage, bottle with one hole stopper and tube for water.

Wire screen home; woodshavings, sawdust, strips of newspaper; water bottle mentioned previously.

Should be wire mesh as rabbits need a great deal of ventilation; use type of wire cage as shown but enlarge to at least 3 ft. x 2 ft. x 2 ft.; floor should be perforated.

Depends on variety; some need aquarium; some woodland terrarium; some combination of two; escape easily so place tight cover on them.

Wire mesh; wooden branch for support; must be solid with tight cover as snakes escape easily.

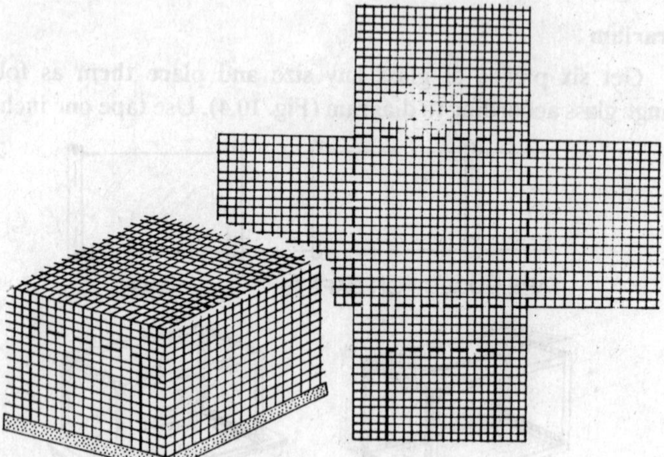

Fig. 10.5

Terrarium is thus miniature replica of terrestial habitat containing specimen plants and animals representing that habitat.

Types of Terrarium

Terrarium is of four types as under:

(*i*) Desert terrarium.

(*ii*) Wood land terrarium.

(*iii*) Swamp terrarium or Bog terrarium and

(*iv*) Semi-aquatic terrarium.

Uses of Terrarium

The terrarium is useful as a teaching aid in the following ways.

(*i*) It helps students in studying various kinds of plants and animals.

(*ii*) It helps students in understanding the inter-relationship of factors affecting the life of animals and plants.

(*iii*) It helps students in understanding the living and feeding habits of animals.

Aquarium

It is one of the most important teaching aids for teaching of life sciences.

Following *guide lines* be followed for forming and maintaining an aquarium:

1. Clean an keep the aquarium tank dust free.
2. Place one or two inches (3-5 cm) of sand to cover the bottom of the aquarium tank.
3. Always pour clean pond water into the aquarium tank.
4. Keep the aquarium exposed to strong diffused sunlight.
5. Use plants springly at the first instance.
6. Use animals which can get along together.
7. Keep a constant watch on the aquarium tank and remove any dead animals at once.
8. Feed the animals sparingly.

Precautions for maintaining aquarium

Following precautions be observed in maintaining an aquarium:

1. Aquarium should have a permanent place in the laboratory.
2. Water in it should not be frequently and unnecessarily changed.
3. Use only healthy specimen and any contaminated specimen be given a potassium permangnate bath for about half an hour.

Uses of Aquarium

Some of the important uses of aquarium as a teaching aid are as follows:

1. It is very helpful in teaching concepts relating to ecology.
2. Students can directly observe the locomotion of aquatic animals.
3. It helps to develop a love, for animals, in students.

Vivarium. It is the term which denotes aquarium, terrarium, wormery and aviary etc.

Nature Study Garden

Nature study garden is a must for every school involved in nature study. Such a garden should have a pond as well. Teacher should encourage his students to maintain the nature study garden of

Fig. 10.6

the school and to maintain as many varieties, of plants and animals in this garden, as is possible. These plants and animals can then be shown to the students while actually discussing about them in the class.

Hence school garden is essential for providing an opportunity to the pupil for studying the living things in their natural setting.

Nature Calender

It is simply a record of events that occurred in nature over a period of time in a specific region or location. Students may maintain Nature Calender of flowers, birds, insects, vegetables etc. For example nature calender, on insects tells us about the events relating to the life of insects in a particular locality during different seasons. This calender require and develop keen observation. The principle such as unity in diversity and principle of co-existence are well understood by students simply by observing the inter-relationship of events that take place over a period in a locality. Thus in teaching and learning biology the Nature Calender becomes much more important.

10.5 SCIENCE FAIRS AND EXHIBITIONS IN SCHOOLS

We find that functions such as prize distribution, parents day, sports day etc. form a regular feature of most schools. Just like these functions an effort should be made to hold an annual science fair or exhibition may be along with any of these days. A science fair provides an excellent opportunity for display and dissemination of various activities that are being carried over by the science club. A science fair can also serve the purpose of acquainting the parents in particular and people of locality in general with the diverse nature of scientific work that is undertaken in the school. The organisation of a science fair or a science exhibition can easily be entrusted to the school science club. In recent years various government agencies encourage the organisation of science fairs and science exhibitions. The encouragement is provided in the form of financial and other help. Such fairs are encouraged by NCERT and SCERT of various states.

NCERT (National Council of Educational Research and Training) has outlined the following objectives for organising science fairs.

(*i*) To give impetus and provide encouragement to students to try out their ideas and to apply their knowledge of science into some creative channel.

(*ii*) To provide opportunities to students to see for themselves some achievements of their colleagues and in this way stimulate them to plan their occur projects.

(*iii*) To make science activities more popular amongst the students thereby hoping to improve standards of performance.

(*iv*) To encourage bright and enthusiastic students having special science talent.

(*v*) To identify talented students in science and nurture the future scientists.

(*vi*) To provide an opportunity to the people of area to come in contact with school and to meet the teachers and students.

(*vii*) To provide a competitive forum to various science clubs in the area.

Exhibits. There could be a variety of exhibits in a science fair. For exhibiting in a science fair the science master can select a few interesting experiments, charts, working models of useful appliances specimen collected by students during excursions, applications of scientific principles to daily life, scientific toys etc. For sake of convenience exhibits can be classified as under:

(*i*) Experiments
(*ii*) Models
(*iii*) Specimens
(*iv*) Collections
(*v*) Improvised apparatus
(*vi*) Charts and diagrams
(*vii*) Investigatory projects.

Organisation of a Science Fair. Whenever a science teacher plans to organise a science fair he should inform his students about it well in advance. Then he should start to find a good and suitable location in the school where such fair can be organised. Having located a suitable place he should start planning or arrangements of exhibits. In this planning he should always keep in mind that time consuming exhibits are spread all over the available space and are not accumulated at one place.

He should then train some selected students to act as students guide. Science teacher should see that these students volunteers can guide the visitors and can explain to them various scientific principles involved in any exhibit.

Evaluation. To encourage the participants some prizes in the form of general science books or merit certificates may be instituted and awarded to pupils whose exhibits have been adjudged best by a panel of judges. For purpose of award of prizes various exhibits at a science fair be classified in various categories and prizes be awarded separately for some good entries in each class. While judging an exhibit some criteria on the following lines may be used by the judges. Various aspects be given the following weightage.

1.	Scientific approach	30%
2.	Originality	20%
3.	Technical skill	20%
4.	Thoroughness	10%
5.	Dramatic value	10%
6.	Personal Interview	10%

10.6 PREPARATION OF SPECIMEN AND SKELETONS ETC.

Following points be given due consideration in the preparation of specimen and skeleton etc.

1. Slider should be kept carefully. Labelling be done properly.
2. These should not be handled in rough and careless manner.
3. All efforts be made to keep plants, trees etc. healthy.
4. A careful choice be made to select those specimen's which are to be kept for permanent use.
5. As far as possible, small animals be kept in their proper surroundings.
6. While preserving the specimen in glass jars etc. care should be taken to provide for proper lights inside as also outside.
7. They should not be in multilated form. For those specimen which are to be kept for long the most important thing is that they are in proper shape and use.

10.7 TEMPORARY AND PERMANENT MOUNTS

Temporary Mounts

It is a specimen of slide which is temporary wet mount. Fluid in it evaporates, keeping the mount temporary.

Permanent Mounts

Permanent mounts are as under:

1. Clear tissues in xylol.
2. Fix tissues and harden.
3. Embedded in paraffin.
4. Dissolve paraffin with xylol.
5. Dehydrate through series of alcohols.
6. Fix section to slides.
7. Stain, counter stain and destain if required.
8. Dehydrate through a series of alcohols to xylol.
9. Pass through a series as alcohols to distilled water.

10.8 STUDENTS PROJECTS IN LIFE SCIENCES

1. In higher classes students can be allotted projects of a broad-based study of a similar type in their area.
2. It would help them go on learning from 'simple to complex'.
3. There exists enough scope in life sciences to take of studies of local importance.
4. Students be encouraged to go from 'known to unknown'.
5. Projects should be executed in group situations.
6. When an allotted project has been completed by a group it be allotted another project which may be a bit more difficult.

10.9 CONCLUSION

The life science teacher uses the teaching aids in the modern scientific way. Rather life science cannot be taught without the audio-visual aids. A life science teacher uses the teaching aids at every step in his teaching. Whatever method he may adopt in his teaching be needs more and more aids to quicken the learning process in his class.

10.10 IMPORTANT SOURCES FROM WHERE TEACHING AIDS FOR LIFE SCIENCES ARE AVAILABLE

Some important sources are listed below:

1. C.S.I.R. New Delhi.
2. N.C.E.R.T. Arbindo Marg, New Delhi.
3. School of Science Policy, J.L.N. University, New Delhi.
4. A.I.I.M.S. New Delhi.
5. Indian Agriculture Research Institute, Pusa, New Delhi.

10.11 LIST OF NATURAL SCIENCES LABORATORIES

1. Central Building Institute, Roorkee (U.P.)
2. Central Drug Research Institute, Lucknow (U.P.)
3. Birla Industrial and Technological Museum, Calcutta (W.B.)
4. Central Electro-chemical Research Institute, Pilani (Rajasthan)
5. Central Fuel Research Institute, Jealgora (Bihar)
6. Central Food Technological Research Institute, Mysore (Karnataka)
7. Central Glass and Ceramic Research Institute, Jadavpur (W.B.)
8. Central Indian Medical Plant Organisation, Lucknow (U.P.)
9. Central Leather Research Institute, Madras (Tamil Nadu)
10. Central Mechanical Engineering Research Institute, Durgapur (W.B.)
11. Central Mining Research Station, Dhanbad (Bihar)
12. Central Public Health Engineering Research Institute, Nagpur (Maharastra)
13. Central Road Research Institute, New Delhi
14. National Biological Laboratories, Palampur (H.P.)

15. National Botanical Garden, Lucknow (U.P.)
16. National Environment Engineering Institute, Nagpur.
17. National Institute of Oceanography, Panji (Goa)
18. Meterological observatory, Pune (Maharastra) and Delhi
19. National Archives of India, New Delhi
20. National Dairy development Board, Anand (Gujrat)
21. Indo-Australian Sheep Farm, Hissar (Haryana)
22. National Museum, New Delhi.

Chapter 11

Miscellaneous

11.1 SCIENCE KITS

With introduction of science as a compulsory subject in primary schools, the teaching of science posed a serious challange specially to remote single teacher village schools. To face this challange of teaching of science in such schools the idea of science kits originated. This is based on our age old belief that for teaching of science we need costly, sophisticated apparatus and equipment in addition to spacious and well built laboratories provided with all the essential amenities such as drainage, water supply and gas supply, since such facilities were not available in our village schools so the difficulties were faced even by dedicated science teachers in teaching of science in village schools.

With introduction of science as compulsory subject from class I to class X such facilities were required in more than 5 lakh primary schools, one lakh middle schools, 35 thousand high and higher secondary schools of the country. It was practically impossible to arrange the facilities for science teaching on such a large scale. This tremendous challange was met with by introducing and producing simple, inexpensive, improvised apparatus. Such apparatus is suitably stored in small handy boxes called *science kits*.

Unicef Aid for Project

Realising the importance of science teaching and introduction of science as a compulsory subject in India, UNICEF offered all out assistance to Government of India for achieving the aim of teaching of science as a compulsory subject and in upgrading the teaching of science in Indian Schools.

Utilising the UNESCO aid through NCERT, Government of India developed new curriculum for teaching of science in primary and middle classes and also devised science kits to cover the curriculum so developed.

To start with 50 primary and 30 middle schools were selected from each state to try out new curriculum and science kits. Most of the funds for translating new science books in various regional languages were provided by UNICEF. Funds were also provided by UNICEF to cover the cost of providing science kits to schools. In addition to these enough funds were provided, by UNICEF, for organising inservice training of science teachers. For conduct of such inservice training of science teachers UNICEF provided funds to State Institutes of Science Education and Teachers Training Schools and Colleges. These funds were used by such Institutes and colleges for the purchase of equipments, apparatus, work-shop tools and science kits required by them for the conduct of inservice courses for science teachers. Thus we find that major financial burden for universal science education was born by UNESCO.

Science kits were prepared at Central Science Workshop (NCERT, Delhi) and some other production centres in our country. These are all UNICEF aided and so the whole process is known as UNICEF aided project.

Science Kit

Science kit contains quite simple, inexpensive, improvised apparatus which are stored in a small handy box. This box called *science kit* is simple in shops and is made of wood or iron and is provided with shelves and drawers. It can serve the function of a small movable mini-laboratory. Such kits are found to be very suitable for use in village schools where no facilities exist for science rooms or laboratories. Since the apparatus and equipment stored in such kits are indigenous. So these kits are quite cheap and the items can be easily operated: Majority of the items stored in the kit are quite hard and sturdy and thus there is no fear of these items getting broken so easily.

Separate kits have been developed for physics, chemistry and biology. Further separate kits have been developed for demonstration purposes (*Demonstration kits*) and for use in practicals by students (*Pupil's kits*).

Demonstration Kits

Demonstration kits contain such items which are needed by the science teacher for demonstration in class room. A demonstration kit has enough material for a class of about 40 students. The items stored in these kits are comparatively larger in size so that students sitting on back benches can distinctly see the various details of the apparatus, equipment.

Pupil's Kits

These kits contain sufficient items for various students experiments and one such kit can serve the requirements of a class of 40 students. In addition to apparatus these kits also contain consumable items such as chemicals etc. The store of such consumable items in a kit is expected to last one year.

The kits developed by NCERT are as under

1. *Primary Science Kit.* This kit can serve as a complete science laboratory for a primary school and can serve the purpose of a demonstration kit as of the pupil's kit.

2. *Physics Demonstration Kit No. I* 3. *Physics Pupil's Kit No. I*	Both these are meant for class VI
4. *Physics Demonstration Kit No. II* 5. *Physics Pupil's Kit No. II*	Both these are meant for class VII
6. *Physics Demonstration Kit No. III* 7. *Physics Pupils Kit No. III*	Both these are meant for class VIII

8. *Biology Demonstration Kit.* This kit is meant to cover various topics of biology (Science) for Class VI, VII and VIII.

9. *Chemistry Demonstration Kit* 10. *Chemistry Pupil's Kit*	These are meant for class VI, VII and VIII.

Contents of the Primary Science Kit

Primary Science Kit can serve the purpose of a demonstration kit as also of pupil's kit for classes III, IV and V. The kit box is made of iron and has provision for a chalk board and a demonstration table (collapsable). It is aiso provided with special shelf for hand tools which can be used for carrying out minor repair work if required.

Biology Kit

This can serve as a complete biology laboratory for classes VI, VII and VIII. It contains 99 items for use by teacher for demonstration and for use by students in their practical classes. It covers the items from Plant life (botany), Animal life (zoology) and Human life (physiology). It also contains a set of hand tools which can be used by the teacher for carrying out minor repair work.

The kit opens on both sides and thus all the four sides can be used for demonstration. Zoology articles are stored on side I, side II and III store physiology items and side IV is used to store botanical articles.

For biology this kit also serves as the pupils kit and there is no separate pupils kit in biology.

Advantages of the Kits

Some of the important advantages of the science kits are summarised below:

1. *Low Cost.* These kits are very economical and a primary science kit costs only around rupees one hundred. All the kits for a middle school are not likely to cost more than Rs. 3000/-.
2. *Use of Indigenous Resources.* Majority of items stored in science kits are indigenous and no import or foreign collaboration is required.
3. *Easy Replacement of Items.* Various items stored in science kit can be easily replaced in case of loss or breakage etc.
4. *Easily Portable.* The kits are easily portable and can be easily used for demonstration in classes being met in open or under trees.
5. *Economy of Time.* Being planned in a very systematic way, minimum time is needed for setting up an experiment by using such kits.
6. *Consolidated Material.* All the essential items of apparatus, equipments, chemicals etc. are arranged in such a way that any item can be put to multipurpose use. In this way material is consolidated in a science kit. Moreover all the material needed for an experiment is consolidated in the kit.

7. *Economy in consumption.* In a science kit the items stored are in mini size and so the consumable items such as chemicals etc. are consumed in small amounts.
8. *Teacher's Innovation.* The science kits can serve to motivate and inspire an innovative science teacher to work out new ideas and he can encourage his students to improvise new apparatus and experiments.
9. *Students Involvement.* Since the various items stored in science kits are quite simple so they can be easily handled by the students. It encourages the students and they become active participants in the teaching-learning process.

Conclusion

The challange of imparting universal science education in various schools in India was boldly faced by Government of India. The role of NCERT must be commended as it devised very simple, economical and easy to operate improvised apparatus and suitably arranged and packed them in different boxes named science kits. These kits were found so handy and useful that we the science teachers shall ever be grateful to the NCERT for this innovation science kits have served their purpose so well that it is hoped that diversified efforts will be made by various science institutes and training colleges and schools in the country for furthur improvements and modifications in these science kits. These science kits are a boon to a science teacher and for proper appreciation and enjoyment of these kits science teachers are advised to make through study of kits and kit guides.

11.2 SCIENCE LIBRARY

Introduction

One of the important recommendations made by the Secondary Education Commission was that every school should have subject libraries which are under the charge of subject teachers. It was felt that subject teachers can enrich their teaching making use of small collections of books on their own subjects. The need for subject library is utmost. A science library should be an essential part of each school which undertakes science teaching.

An explosion has occurred in scientific knowledge in the recent past the teachers find it difficult to keep themselves equipped with the newest knowledge in the subject. For acquainting himself with such a knowledge he needs a good science library where from he can find out at latest and new books to update his knowledge. He can then recommend some books to his students and may encourage them to acquire the habit of extending and supplementing their knowledge by making proper use of school library. Science library thus is a wonderful teaching aid. By reading extra books students can get a good deal of general knowledge which he may not get if he depends entirely on class-room teaching.

Thus there is a need for the establishment of really good libraries in schools and the provision of an intelligent and effective library service. The library may well be regarded as an essential instrument for putting progressive method into practice. In the following pages we will take up the organisation of library and other related matter.

Organisation of Library

Though a well equipped subject library under the charge of subject teacher is desirable yet a *science library* under the charge of science teacher can serve the purpose of all science subjects. Such a library be set up preferably in a small room or in a corner of the science laboratory where some shelves or almirahs be reserved for storing the library books. The science teacher can equip the library depending on the availability of funds and accommodation for the purpose. For setting up a rich library with limited funds, it is necessary that science teacher is very thoroughly acquainted with the latest and good books available as the subject. For building up a good science liabrary teacher should select for the liabrary only such books which cover wide range of topics. These should be the books that deal with topics in physics, chemistry, biology, astronomy, geology, nature study, environment, ecology, pollution etc. Books on romance of science, engineering, scientific discoveries and inventions, science quiz, science projects, magic in science, experiments in science, fun in science etc. must also find a place in science library. Science library should also have some books on the lives and achievements of some great scientists and some books dealing with scientific hobbies like photography, motor cycle, radio, television etc. Some standard reference books and books on methods of teaching science be also purchased for school library.

The selection of books is a difficult task and science teachers can solve it by making use of fairly exhaustive list of science books available from various publishers. For list of such books he can also seek guidance and help from N.B.T. (National Book Trust) of India, NCERT and other such organisations as SCERT of their state. Science teacher should also read reviews of books published in some good journals for schools *e.g. School science review, popular science and industry etc.*

Recommendations of All India Seminar

Important recommendations about science library as made by All India Seminar on the Teaching of Science are as under:

(*i*) Each school should have a separate science library.

(*ii*) Science books of general interest be stored in the school library.

(*iii*) A separate section be allocated in science library for reference books. Reference books are for use by teacher as also by students but these should not be ordinarily issued for home use.

(*iv*) Books on methods of teaching science be stored in a separate section in science library and these are meant for use of science teacher.

(*v*) Science teacher be asked to become in incharge of science library. He may be assisted in his library work by a small committee of students.

(*vi*) Teachers should take some measures to encourage love for library books amongst his students. Teacher can ask the students to prepare a brief review of the books read by them and some of these reviews considered good be published in science magazine and science bulletins.

(*vii*) A cross reference index be prepared in which teacher and students should indicate briefly the information contained in the book read by them. Such an information may be provided under the relevant heads and a proper use be made of this index for guiding the students in their reading.

(*viii*) Complete sets of various text books should be available in school library.

(*ix*) A few laboratory manuals must also be available in school library.

Life Science Library

The importance of library is much more felt in case of life sciences. Since life science teaching is a recent phenomenon and books are not easily available, a good library having choicest books and text books is a must for schools offering courses in life sciences.

For the students of life sciences such a library is a big entertainer, full of life and a live workshop. The library should have some good books. Some of the important books as life sciences are:

1. The story of man, earth, sun, moon etc.
2. The Human Machine.
3. Zoologist.
4. Wonders of pond life.
5. Penicillin.
6. Birds, Plants etc.
7. Dictionaries of Botany, Zoology, Biology etc.
8. Encyclopaedia of Science.
9. History of Science.

Library should also contribute to important Science Journals. Some of these are:

1. Science Today
2. Science Reporter
3. Junior Scientist
4. School Science
5. Vigyan Shikshak.

11.3 TEXTBOOKS AS TEACHING AIDS

Text book is a record of racial thinking organised for instructional purpose. It is the most widely used teaching instrument. It is not merely a source of information but a course of study, a set of unit plans and a learning guide. It employs both the "text book" 'recitation method' and 'stimulating ways'. It gives factual information and stimulates self-directed activities.

Advantages of Textbooks

Textbooks as instructional material have the following advantages:

(*i*) They are cheap and economical;

(*ii*) They facilitate individualised instruction;

(*iii*) The organise and provide uniformity for class instruction;

(*iv*) They stimulate active learning;

(*v*) They develop the skills of teachers; and

(*vi*) They stimulate "self-directed activities of the learner".

Criticisms Levelled Against Textbooks

Textbooks are often over used and some times misused. Textbooks are considered to be good servants but bad masters. Textbooks as teaching aid are criticised on the following grounds:

(*i*) Textbooks make reading a matter of 'reading to remember' since they present matters in logical *predigested* forms;

(*ii*) They treat subjects too sketching and they prevent further pursuit and thinking;

(*iii*) The use of textbooks results in deadly routine of assigned reading and recitation; and

(*iv*) They become out dated quickly.

Role of Textbooks

In the present educational set up the role of textbook is of prime importance. However we find that little attention is paid to this important aspect of education. Most of the textbooks in science are not of good standard. They follow the prescribed syllabus too rigidly and no attention is paid to develop the topics according to the need and interest of students. A good textbook is one which is a source of knowledge arranged systematically and it enables the reader to acquire the needed information quickly. It inspires the student to invent, to discover and to inculcate scientific methods. However teacher should not depend solely even on the best of the textbooks because even such a textbook omits many details which teacher wants to tell to his students.

The use of a textbook is made by the students for completing the preparatory part of an assignment. They also use their textbook for doing revision of course. Some students also consult and use their textbooks to study at home, the demonstration lesson given to them by their teacher in school. In this way textbooks are used to supplement the class work. Textbooks also provide a help to students in correct understanding of basic concepts and principles of science.

Bases for selecting a science textbook

Academic considerations have to be taken bases for selecting a science textbook. Vogel F. Louis has enumerated important bases for selecting a science textbook.

Generally a number of books are prescribed by board or university to be used as textbooks. NCERT prepared textbooks are available upto class XII. While recommending a textbook to his students the teacher should consider the following points to assess the worth of the book.

(*i*) Correctness of matter.
(*ii*) Purity of languages.
(*iii*) Simplicity of diagrams.
(*iv*) Quality of printing and binding.

(*i*) *Correctness of Matter*

In this correction the standing of the author and the reputation of publishers should be considered. The books written by well known author having a long teaching experience of teaching the subject and possessing requisite qualifications be recommended. It would be much appreciated if certain minimum qualifications and experience for authors is laid down by authorities.

(*ii*) *Purity of Language*

A textbook that presents the subject matter in a simple, clear and lucid language should be preferred. For textbook in a regional language, the scientific terminology should also be given in English with in brackets. In such books only standard terminology evolved by the Central Ministry of Education and State Governments should be used.

(*iii*) *Simplicity of Diagrams*

Only simple and well labelled diagrams be given in textbooks. Such diagrams are self explanatory and help the student in properly understanding the subject matter.

(*iv*) *Quality of Printing and Binding*

It is desirable that a textbook makes use of a good quality paper and the quality of printing, and type of letters in fine. It should be so bound that its binding is appealing to the student.

In addition to the above a good textbook is expected to select and arrange the subject-matter in a psychological sequence. The book should follow the aims of teaching science and should serve as a guide for demonstration lesson as also for individual experiments. Each chapter should start with a brief introduction and a summary of the subject matter be given at the end of the chapter. Some assignments should also be given at the end of each chapter and the assignments should cover such areas as applications to life situations, numerical questions, suggestions for experimental work and projects, objective type tests etc. Heading and sub-headings be given in bold type. A table of contents be provided at the beginning and a subject-index be provided at the end. Glossary of some important scientific terms be given at the end of the book.

Each text-book should be accompanied by a laboratory manual. However the use of laboratory manual, unless good, should be avoided. The printed laboratory manuals give too many details and thus the work becomes almost mechanical.

Modern Biology Textbook

Due to modern changes in content and education a significant change has been brought about in school textbooks of biology.

Now there is a growing tendency to make textbooks more than just a statement of the content. Most modern textbooks are study-guides also. They help students learn the content. They provide vocabulary lists, summaries, suggestions for further reading, suggestions for activities, ideas for discussion and opportunities for individual evaluation of progress in achievement through questions and tests. Some also include instruction for practical work so that learning activities are smoothly sequenced and integrated.

Modern biology textbooks also lay stress on modern views of science. An effort is also made to introduce the students to achievements of individual scientists, to the role and character of scientific community, to limitations of science and to scientifically based issues of social relevance. An emphasis is placed to high light particular issues like bioethics and the determination of appropriate scientific policy for a community or a nation.

Most of the good textbooks on the above lines have been produced in United Kingdom, Canada, India, Singapore and the United States.

The modern manuals which combine text, study guide and practical work tend to be written in simple, logical and organised way. They are clearly illustrated. Each topic begins with clearly illustrated. Each topic begins with clearly stated objectives. To provide opportunities for creative discovery the suggested activities are left open ended and unstructured.

11.4 IMPROVISED APPARATUS

For teaching of science availability of good apparatus and well equipped laboratories is a must. However it should lead us to a wrong conception that teaching of science cannot be carried out in the absence of expensive apparatus. One of the reports by NCERT observes that from among various factors that stand in the way of science education in our country one is lack of adequate resources for laboratory building, purchase of good and adequate apparatus and equipment. This lack of funds and resources makes improvisation of apparatus almost a necessity in India.

Need for Improvisation

India is a poor country and so we have only limited financial resources. For imparting effective and efficient science education, due to this financial constraint we require the production of improvised and inexpensive learning aids. A teacher with some ingenuity and manual skill can make a number of valuable and serviceable articles from discarded things all around him. For this purpose every science room should be equipped with a work bench and a kit of tools that may be used by students and teacher in making and improvising equipment for science teaching.

Definition of Improvisation

Some of the definitions of improvisations are given below:

It refers to a make shift arrangement for accomplishing the intended learning task.

It refers to contrived situation that is created from reading available material for sake of convenience.

It refers to a stimulating situation for demonstrating and imparting learning is respect of controls and operations making use of low cost materials.

It refers to those learning aids which are prepared from simple and readily available cheap material by students and teacher.

Significance of Improvisation

Improvisation is quite significant and has many values as the process of improvisation needs resourcefulness and ingenuity on the part of the science teacher. It is based on the concept of solving some problem by a make shift or alternate arrangement given below are some significant values attached with the process of improvisation:

(*i*) It splashes the cost of apparatus and is quite helpful in making the school self-reliant.

(*ii*) It has instructional value as well. When we are carrying out any improvisation we do get a proper feeling for the scientific process and designing. Thus we learn by doing.

(*iii*) It help develop the dignity of labour and also satisfies the urge of creative production.

(*iv*) It helps to develop the habit of cooperation and coordination.

(*v*) It provides training in thinking skills through the process of looking for low-cost substitutes or alternatives

Process of Improvisation

It refers to a systematic way of constructing a piece of apparatus or designing an experiment. It involves the following steps:

(*i*) Making a careful study of the conventional apparatus or experiment.

(*ii*) Thinking of some low cost substitute that may be available in the market.

(*iii*) Designing the improvised apparatus or experiment.

(*iv*) Putting the improvised apparatus or experiment to test.

(*v*) Making further improvements in the improvised apparatus keeping the test results in mind.

(*vi*) Making use of the improvised apparatus in the laboratory for demonstration or practical work.

Advantages of Improvised Apparatus

Some of the advantages of improvised apparatus are

(*i*) These are quite cheap and economical.

(*ii*) They have great educational value. While devising such apparatus students gains more familiarity with the underlying principles of the apparatus.

(*iii*) It helps to develop the creative and constructive instructs of the child.

(*iv*) It inspires young students to explore and invent new things.

(*v*) It develops the lower of initiative and resourcefulness in the student.

(*vi*) It helps to develop power of scientific thinking.

(*vii*) It helps to inculcate the habit of diligency in the students.

(*viii*) It galvanises dignity of labour.

(*ix*) It solves problem of leisure time.

Chapter 12

Evaluation

12.1 INTRODUCTION

Once a teacher has a clear idea of what she will teach and how she will teach it, she is concerned with knowing to what extent children learn from her lessons. This chapter will deal with specific procedures for evaluating the effectiveness of life science teaching-learning.

Evaluation is a continuous process which is an integral part of teaching. It is not merely a test at the end of a life science lesson or unit. Instead, evaluation goes on constantly during lessons and units and is clearly related to the teacher's goal and points of view on life science teaching.

Besides being a continuous experience, evaluation is cumulative. A cumulative science record should be kept for all children. If such a record is available then his science exposure can be quickly and easily seen.

The recent trends in learning and evaluation link them to behavioural objectives. According to behaviourist psychology learning is defined as a *change in the behaviour of an individual that can be described in terms of observable and measurable performance*. The changes in behaviour are affected by providing experiences and through teaching.

The test efficiency of teaching, to judge the progress of students and to discover their achievements and evaluate the whole school system, we require some sort of measuring tools. These tools are *tests* or *examinations*. Tests are essential to grade and rank pupils, however, if evaluation is used merely to indicate areas of science to which children have been exposed or for classifying and categorizing students, a great value is lost. The same loss occurs if evaluation is interpreted only as arriving at numerical or alphabetical ratings for report cards. In this way much of the positive use of evaluation as a means of teaching and learning could be destroyed.

Effective instructional planning and evaluation of students performance have always stressed upon the statement of instructional objectives so that they are of great help to the student. According to Muller, an instructionally usable objective must state the intended outcome in terms of the terminal behaviour of students. Terminal behaviour here stands for the behaviour of students after the class-room instruction and evaluation can be made if the learning outcomes are carefully specified. By coupling continuous evaluation with immediate application of what has been learned, the teacher can provide for:

(*i*) The stimulation of students who learn rapidly to greater growth toward goals by application of advanced works.

(*ii*) The identification of specific weaknesses and difficulties in functional understanding (concepts, principles, generalization) and the needed reteaching of varied activities skills or problem solving abilities, and

(*iii*) The clarification, modification or complete alternation of the goals as needed for the unit.

Evaluation, teaching and learning are the three corners of the education system. *Evaluation* is concerned with finding out how far students have learned as a consequence of teaching. There are two kinds of evaluation depending upon whether the comparison of student is made with some absolute performance standard or with other students of a given group. These are known as *criterion referenced evaluation* and *norm referenced evaluation*.

Criterion-Referenced Evaluation

It assesses the students performance in terms of a specified performance standard or criterion without any mention of the performance levels of the other students of the group. This evaluation method is related to mastery and developmental tests.

Norm-Referenced Evaluation

It assesses the students performance relative to other students of the group. Students are awarded marks and relative ranks in this method of evaluation.

12.2 PURPOSE OF EVALUATION

Evaluation fulfils the following purposes:

(*i*) It assesses the extent of learning by students and gives them the feed-back about their performance.

(*ii*) It gives feed-back to the teacher about the learning gaps of the students. It also provides the teacher a feed-back about the quality of his class room instructions.

(*iii*) It provides the student an opportunity to show his worth.

(*iv*) It serves as a screening tool for selecting students for special purposes.

Our evaluation has another goal besides assisting the teacher in assessing and modifying her teaching procedures. This goal *self-evaluation* is not solely for the students. As teacher and students actively engage in all levels of a study such as initial planning, organizing and carrying out activities they can be guided in developing ability to evaluate themselves. Knowing the general and specific goals can aid the pupil in checking himself all along the way. This makes the learner an active participant in class room activities. It also places some of the responsibility on him for learning and assessing what and how much he has learned. Self guided evaluation stimulates healthy and realistic achievement goals. A logical first step self evaluations is setting up of realistic goals. These goals for science teaching in elementary schools are:

(*i*) *Functional understandings* such as concepts, principles, generalizations, and the facts needed.

(*ii*) *Problem solving skills* such as defining problems, proposing hypotheses and techniques necessary for the solution of the problems, observational techniques, discussion and interpretations skills.

(*iii*) *Scientific attitudes, interests and appreciation* such as open mindedness and humanity.

The easiest area to evaluate is functional understanding because a rich variety of tests are well known and are widely used in elementary schools. Before we proceed to actual discussion of these tests let us consider the criterion of a good examination and pre-requisites of a physical test.

12.3 EVALUATION SYSTEM IN LIFE SCIENCE SUBJECTS

Under the new 10+2+3 system there would be subject-wise grades for the students. They will be graded on a seven point grading system.

Under this new scheme the procedures are:

1. Question-banks.
2. Rationalising evaluation procedures.
3. Internal as well as External Assessment.
4. Standardization of raw-scores.
5. Grading in place of marks-seven point grading system.
6. Improving the question papers.

12.4 OBJECTIVES OF EVALUATION

Kothari Commission has given the following objectives of evaluation.

1. Classification of objectives.
2. Changes in curriculum.
3. Promotion of learning.
4. Improvements in instructions.
5. Provision for guidance.

12.5 STEPS OF EVALUATION IN LIFE SCIENCE SUBJECTS

1. Decision about objectives be made.
2. The evaluation of results is done quickly.
3. Definition in terms of behaviour changes be completed according to schedule.
4. Learning experiences are taken into account.
5. Assessment procedure is fully deviced.

There are a large number of procedures for applying the tests. Following is a suggestive list of such tests.

1. Achievement Test.
2. Aptitude Test.
3. Interview.
4. Interest Inventory.

5. Inquiry Forms.
6. Intelligence Tests.
7. Pupils Products.
8. Personality Tests.
9. Records in Schools.
10. Sociometic Records.
11. Teacher's observation.

12.6 CRITERIA OF A GOOD EXAMINATION

Though a variety of tests are available to test the functional understanding of the child but for true assessment of such aspects of growth as the elements of reflective thinking, scientific attitudes, resourcefulness, creativeness or such other objectives or interests we require more precise and accurate instruments of evaluation. According to most of the psychologists and educationalists the following are essential criteria of satisfactory evaluation.

1. *Validity.* Any good test should measure what it claims to measure.
2. *Reliability.* A good test is one that is reliable *i.e.* it gives same rating to a candidate even if he is examined by different examines and even at different times.
3. *Objectivity.* A test can be considered objective if the scoring of the test is not affected in any way by the examiner's personal judgment. Thus the opinion, bias or judgment of the examiner can have no influence on the results of an objective test.
4. *Comprehensiveness.* By comprehensiveness of a test we mean that it covers the whole or nearly the whole course content and the questions are uniformly distributed to cover the course content.
5. *Practicability.* A test is called practicable if it can be easily administered and is acceptable to average examines. While preparing such a test, the time and cost of administration must be taken into consideration. The test should be usable and should serve a definite need in the situation in which it is used.

6. *Interpretibility.* A test can be considered as interpretable if its scores can be used and interpreted in terms of a common base having natural or accepted meaning.
7. *Easy to Administer.* A good test should be easy to administer so definite provision be made for collection and preparation of test material. It should give simple, clear and precise instructions.

Pre-requisites of a Good Test

There are certain pre-requisites for preparing a science test. These are as under.

Aspects	*Description*
Aims	– Acquisition of knowledge of various science concepts and skills.
	– Development of scientific attitude and interest.
	– Development of laboratory skills.
	– Highlighting the application of science in everyday life and technology.
	– Development of skills of information processing, observation, enquiry and design
	– Acquisition of problem solving abilities.
Objectives	
(*a*) *Knowledge*:	Recall and recognition of factual information such as
	(*i*) definitions of various terms
	(*ii*) statement of laws, principles, rules, conventions etc.
	(*iii*) Description of construction and working of devices and instruments.
	(*iv*) Description of events, processes and phenomenon
	(*v*) Recognising the parts of devices, instruments, appliances and apparatus

(*vi*) Identifying known physical phenomenon, events and occurrences.

(*b*) *Comprehension*: Understanding facts, laws etc.

(*i*) Company and contrasting various phenomenon

(*ii*) Locating errors, limitations and defects.

(*iii*) Illustrating scientific phenomenon.

(*iv*) Reasoning events on the basis of scientific principles and laws.

(*c*) *Applications:* Using knowledge in new situations.

(*i*) Solving numerical problems

(*ii*) Making use of various scientific laws in various situations and events.

(*iii*) Relating various scientific variables.

(*d*) *Skills*: Using psycho-motor skills.

(*i*) Laying out an experimental set-up.

(*ii*) Drawing diagrams, graphs, histograms, flow charts etc.

(*iii*) Reading various measuring instruments.

(*e*) *Analysis:* Breaking up information into parts to reach conclusions:

(*i*) Interpretation observations

(*ii*) Drawing inferences from observations.

(*iii*) Generalising conclusions.

(*f*) *Synthesis:* Combining parts of information to grasp a concept.

(*i*) Designing an experiment

(*ii*) Improvising and experiment, apparatus or device.

(*iii*) Improving the accuracy of an instrument.

12.7 DESIGNING A SCIENCE TEST

A good science test should be constructed in accordance with a definite design or plan. The steps in designing a science test are as under.

(*i*) Allocation of marks for the different cognitive levels to be tested.

(*ii*) Allocation of marks for different chapters or units.

(*iii*) Blue print for the question paper.

(*iv*) Allocation of marks to various types of questions.

TABLE 12.1: **Allocation of Marks for Abilities to be Tested**

Ability	*Symbol*	*Marks*
Knowledge	K	45
Comprehension	C	26
Application	A	17
Skills	S	6
Analysis and synthesis	An/Sn	6
	Total	100

TABLE 12.2: **Allocation of Marks of the Types of Questions**

Question type	*Symbol*	*No. of questions*	*Marks*
Short Answers	SA	17	44
Structured	ST	4	56
	Total	21	100

Similarly allocation of marks for content areas is also made.

After the blue-print is ready the actual question paper is set. Some of the commonly used tests in science are fill-ins, true-false, multiple-choice, short-answer or essay type etc.

Now we shall take up the discussion of some of these tests.

12.8 TECHNIQUE OF UNIT TESTS

The unit now is not only a block of content, but also is a concept of validity in the sphere of recent methods of evaluation. It is a procedural method. Unit test consist of the following:

1. Oral Test
2. Self-evaluation
3. Written Test
4. Interview
5. Self-check test
6. Performance test
7. Puzzles
8. Final test.

12.9 NEW TYPE TESTS OF BIOLOGY

Following type of tests are included in these.

1. Sentence completion type.
2. Objective type tests.
3. True and false type tests.
4. Matching test.
5. Multiple-choice test.

Some of these are discussed in the following pages.

OBJECTIVE TYPE TESTS

This type of tests include the following.

1. Preparation.
2. Evaluation.
3. Planning.
4. Administration.
5. Scoring.

Preparation

Following points be kept in mind while preparing objective type tests.

1. Language and phrases should be clear.
2. Similar items be kept side by side.
3. Multiple-choice type is better for items.
4. Items should be in ascending order of difficulty.

5. More than one type of items be included.
6. Instructions should be complete.
7. There should be 50% difficulty level.

Administration

1. Sufficient time be allowed for the test.
2. Clear instructions be given for the test.
3. Lighting and other physical fecilities be properly provided.
4. Questions be easy, short and to the point.

Evaluation

Following aspects be given due consideration in evaluation.

1. Quality of teaching
2. Test and its significance.
3. Quality of students achievement.
4. Curriculum and syllabi.
5. Achievement of a specific objective.

Scoring

Scoring be done in grading and point awards. This is the most important part of the test both for teacher and students.

12.10 EVALUATION IN LIFE SCIENCES

A good test for evaluation in life sciences should leave the following:

1. Variety
2. Grading
3. Reflectiveness
4. Comprehensiveness
5. Reliability
6. Scoreability
7. Interesting
8. Clarity
9. Validity
10. Objectivity
11. Practicability.

For grading in life-sciences the following symbols are in use.

A	Distinction	or	outstanding	75%
B	Credit	or	very good	60%
C	Pass	or	good	50%
D	Average	or	Fair	40%
E	Poor	or	Fail	30%

12.11 EVALUATION OF FUNCTIONAL SKILLS

Concepts, Generalization and Principles

The need of written tests becomes increasingly important as children progresses through the elementary school grades. This is so because of the following reasons.

(*i*) In upper grades pressures for more "objective evaluation" in science are greater as children are exposed to greater emphasis upon "subject matter grades".

(*ii*) As children's use of language increases, there can reasonably be greater emphasis upon meaningful written and verbal concept development.

(*iii*) As the child builds a background of science concepts, facts, understandings and inter-relationships, a greater need is presented for accurately assessing the child's knowledge.

(*iv*) With larger classes, as is generally the rule for the intermediate and upper grades, teachers require evaluation techniques that are fast, accurate, and easy to apply, score and interpret.

One of the types of written testing devices is the *short answer tests*. One major disadvantage is the superficiality and isolation of factual materials asked for rather than a breath and depth of understanding. They do however offer the teacher:

(*i*) opportunities for including wide ranges of items to be tested.

(*ii*) an ease of writing questions because of the shortness of each.

(*iii*) a minimum of time and effort is needed for scoring because of the shortness of answers expected, and (*iv*) opportunities for involvement of pupils in the self-evaluation because of the ease of scoring and following up incorporate responses.

Basically there are two types of short answer testing devices recall and recognition examinations.

Recall Tests

As the term implies, recall questions ask the student to bring back to mind information that the student was exposed to in the past. Psychologists have indicated that the people usually associate items to be recalled with other items and information and rarely, if ever, completely isolate them. The way in which individuals associate isolated items is still much of a mystery. Even tests of isolation such as the inkblot design used in *Rorschach test*, evoke widely divergent responses because of unique back grounds and associations of individuals. Recall with children thus becomes a problem of framing questions in such a way as to stimulate the remembrance of the situation in which the intended information occurred. One of the ways in which this can be accomplished on recall tests is formulation of a question so that only one word or a few words in needed to answer the query. This simple question and answer procedure might look like this.

1. Name two organs of human body etc.

Another way of accomplishing recall of information in a life-science content study is by supplying statements with blanks to be filled in.

For example

1. __________ is provided for chicks to serve as teeth to grind their food.
2. Two by-products of the process of photosynthesis are __________ and__________ .

Recognition Tests

True and False tests are probably the most commonly used recognition tests in use today. The basic idea involved is illustrated below.

	True	False
1. Carbon dioxide is a product of photo-synthesis		
2. The crop of a bird is the bag filled with sand and gravel and mixed with digestive juices.		

Such tests encourage guessing and it greatly reduces the validity and reliability of the Tests. Because it is very difficult to frame questions that are neither too obvious nor too ambiguous, this type of examination should be used very sparingly. Whenever possible other types of recognition tests such as multiple choice test should be given.

Multiple Choice Test

In this type of test, several alternatives are presented to the pupil from which he must select the one that makes the statement most correct. Such test items can reduce the subjectivity in marking and inter-examiner variability in marking. These tests are the most popular these days and are most useful because in this way guessing is minimised and intelligent thinking is encouraged. Some examples of this type of tests are:

1. Honey bees gather pollen on their (*a*) wings (*b*) tongues (*c*) legs (*d*) none of these.
2. Mosquitoes lay their eggs (*a*) in food (*b*) in running water (*c*) on the blades of grass (*d*) in still water.
3. A scientist who studies rocks is called (*a*) a geographer (*b*) a geologist (*c*) a geometer (*d*) a geopolitist.

Reasoning power can play a big part in answering this type of questions and so called educated guesses should be encouraged. Actually these educated guesses usually are formulated from vague relationships that are seen or sensed. Very often the person cannot explain his reason for selection of correct choices in this type of questions, he just knows. Because there are so many aspects of learning and teaching that are still mysteries to us, teacher should not stand in the way of children learning. Intuition plays an important part in learning as well as in the scientific way of working.

Guidelines for Constructing Multiple Choice Test Items

While constructing multiple choice test items following guidelines be followed.

1. A test-item should have a single concept to be tested.
2. A test-item should be such that it can be used to discriminate a group of students as low, medium and high achievers.
3. The statement of test-item should be very clear and unambiguous.
4. Be sure that of the plausible answers only one answer is correct.

Parts of Multiple-Choice Item

There are generally two parts of a multiple choice test-item, viz., stem and plausible answers. The stem of the test-item contains the statement of the question or problem. There are some important styles of writing the stem of a multiple choice questions. These are:

1. stating the stem in the form of a question.
2. writing the stem as an incomplete statement.
3. writing the stem as a problem to be solved.

The plausible answers are the options available to the student from which he has to choose the correct answer. These are generally written according to following guide lines.

1. Write the answers in such a way that to a student who has not read the topic thoroughly each answer seems to be plausible.
2. Include common misconceptions which an average student holds about a particular learning segment.
3. Options which are true on their own but defy the statement of the problem given in the stem of the test item.
4. Do not provide clues for the right answers.

Cognitive Levels and Multiple Choice Items

Generally at the school level, the multiple choice questions in life sciences are related to three cognitive levels, viz., knowledge, comprehension and application.

Limitation of Objective Type Tests

Some of the limitations of objective type tests are:

(*i*) They fail to test the ability to organise material.

(*ii*) They cannot test how well a thought is expressed.

(*iii*) They encourage guess work.

(*iv*) They are difficult to design.

Matching Tests

Besides the true and false and the multiple choice tests, there is a third type of recognition test, *the matching test*.

In this type of test items two mismatched columns are given, one working as problem statement and the other working as options. The questions and answers given in two columns are required to be matched or compared by the students. By giving the pupil two columns of items and asking him to match the related items, the teacher can quickly and easily see if his student recognises the relationships that exist between the items. There is less of a stress upon sheer memory or recall of fragmentary information because the materials are presented to the student for his correlation. Here are two columns of words that apply to the science study of our own bodies. Draw a line between the word on the right and the correct one on the left to show the proper relationship.

The word pelvis is correctly matched with the term trunk in the proper way.

	Pelvis
Head	Spine
	Knee joint
Legs	Breast bone
Trunk	Jaw bone
	Spinal Cord
Arms	Elbow joint
	Verbebrae
	Ribs
	Skull
	Collarbone

Because matching tests are focused mainly to measuring subject matter, it is not always indicative of the pupils ability to perceive the deeper meaning or real understanding of the relationship between the items used on the tests. Stress upon mere verbalization and memory of isolated bits of information should be avoided. Teachers will find it necessary to use all types of testing instruments so as to get a broad picture of the formulation of his children's science concepts.

Short Answer Tests

With all the drawbacks of the short answer tests, there is a wide use for these tests in science education for elementary schools. They are becoming quite popular these days. As the name suggests such questions expect brief, to the point, limited short answers. Generally the length of answers is specified. They offer the teacher an ease of construction and scoring not possible with other types of tests. The tests offer a greater degree of objectivity than other evaluating techniques and the results of tests can be helpful to the teacher for evaluating and reporting children's progress in science education to their parents. With the teacher's guidance, the simplicity of tests can be useful for self-evaluative examinations for the children. Children can also be involved in writing examinations of this type as well as in scoring them. Teachers can be assured that the objective tests being discussed warrant the expenditure of time and effort required to construct them in correct way. Correctly made, administered and interpreted, the short answer test offers many advantages to the teacher; however, they should never be used as sole testing device. They should only be used in conjunction with other types of oral and written tests as well as teacher observation.

Advantages of Short Answer Questions

Some of the important advantages of this type of questions are:

(*i*) They are easy to design

(*ii*) Scoring is less subjective and easy.

(*iii*) The question paper becomes comprehensive *i.e.* it covers the entire syllabus. The students lose the chance of spotting questions or topics.

Essay Tests

The essay-type examinations are in use in India since long and these have been greatly appreciated due to the freedom of response allowed. Essay tests aid in evaluating science understanding in the intermediate and upper grade of elementary school. Like all testing devices, essays present many serious disadvantages. At the same time they present many possibilities for gathering information. This type of test directs attention to and places emphasis on a larger segment of the subject or on an integrated total unit. It provides the student a chance to create a new approach to a problem as it requires the student to express his views in writing. He is required to produce some thing and not merely to guess or recognise the answer. These tests can measure verbal fluency, skill of expression, organisation of thoughts and the attitude of examinees towards problems and subjects considered in the class, however it lacks most of the qualities of a good measuring instrument.

Obvious advantages and disadvantages of essay test.

1. Shows how well the student is able to organise and present ideas,

   but

   scoring is very subjective due to a lack of set answers.
2. Varying degrees of correctness since there is not just a right or wrong answer,

   but

   scoring requires excessive time.
3. Tests ability to analayze problems using pertinent information and to arrive at generalization or conclusions,

   but

   Scoring in influenced by spelling, handwriting, sentence structure and other extraneous items.
4. Gets to deeper meanings and inter-relationships rather than isolated bits of factual materials,

   but

   Questions usually are ambiguous or too obvious.

Limitations of Essay Type Tests

These tests have low validity, low reliability and are less comprehensive. Discussing about the weaknesses of this type of tests Ross remarks, "The essay overrates the importance of knowing how to say a thing and under-rates the importance of having some thing to say".

This type of tests are not reliable because there is no agreement between teachers about the marks to be assigned and studies have shown that even the same teachers do not agree with themselves. Sandifoard, in his book on educational psychology refers to a study, "In one department of the University of Toronto, the same subject was set for an essay in different years. The essay which had secured 80 marks in one year, was exactly copied by the students in another year and scored 39 marks".

Ashburn who carried out a study at University of West Virginia concluded that, "the passing or failing of about 40% depends not on what they know or do not know, but on who reads the papers and that the passing or failing of about 10% depends on when the papers are read".

Another general complaint of students about essay type tests is that the questions 'did not suit them'. Certainly nine or ten questions generally set in this type of question paper cannot cover the whole syllabus. Hence this types of test is less comprehensive.

In an effort to offset the disadvantages the teacher must carefully consider the construction of each essay question. The teacher should word the question in such a fashion that the pupil will be limited to a certain degree to the concepts being tested.

To minimise the shortcomings of excessive subjectivity teacher should prepare a scoring guide before hand. Each question be scored separately and a list of important ideas that are expected should be made.

12.12 INSTRUMENTS FOR EVALUATING SCIENTIFIC ATTITUDES, APPRECIATION AND INTERESTS

One of the most important ways of judging the effectiveness of life science teaching is to evaluate the growth of individual children. This is especially true in the areas of scientific attitudes, appreciations and interests. The most suitable techniques for obtaining this information are teacher observation and anecdotal records, tape recordings, rating scales, checklists, interviews, children's work products, essay tests and situation testing.

Teacher Observation and Record Keeping

Following forms have been found as useful aid by the teacher as it helps them in making their observations more accurate, systematic and time saving and also provides them with a permanent record of behaviour. These cards can be used for recording anecdotes of children's scientific or unscientific behaviour. As these records accumulate, the teacher can begin to see the direction of growth in behaviour and attitude. It is unsatisfactory to merely say that a child has improved in scientific thinking. We must have some records to substantiate our claims.

Tape Recordings

Use of tape recorder during life-science discussion period can be made for assessing the attitudes and interests of each student. Such tapes of discussions can be analysed by the teacher at his leisure. In many ways the tape recorded sessions have some important advantages over the written records of teachers observations. By use of tape records greater objectivity is possible. These tape recordings can also be used for self evaluation by students. It is expected that such tapes be used for science teaching and learning.

Checklists and Rating Scales

It is a faster but perhaps less comprehensive way of assessing growth in scientific attitudes and appreciations. A sheet is prepared by the teacher and she can use it for his own evaluation also and for modifying his teaching method.

Interviews

Personal interviews of individual or small groups of children enable the teacher to probe into their scientific attitudes and thinking. Interviews may last only a few mintues and the answers given by students are important primarily for the ways in which children attempt to answer and not the amount of factual material verbalised. A special session be organised for evaluation of skills in which practical situations are presented for assessing children's scientific thinking and attitude with greater elaboration.

Children's Work Products

Children's work in all aspects of the elementary curriculum provide us with much evidence about their scientific thinking and attitudes. Children's writings, particularly in the intermediate and upper grades, provide enough information about their concepts of the world and their thinking processes. Creative writing allows freedom for the child to explore scientifically and to speculate. Projects and reports provide the format for students to present examples of their thinking.

Situation Evaluation

The teacher can set up situations in which the student is required to find the answer to a practical problem. The student should be unable to supply the answer from memory because ideally he would never have encountered the particular situations. This procedure is quite valuable for assessing problem solving skills.

12.13 EVALUATING CHILDREN'S SCIENCE INTERESTS

For success of science teaching programme the children should strengthen and broaden their science interests through the evaluation process. Teacher can also analyse children's interest by their choice of books from the class, school or local library. An overview of life science interests of children can be ascertained from their selection of reading materials. By keeping a record of reading interest inventories over a period of time, a teacher can see if children increase their voluntary selection of science books as a result of his science programme. The following types of reading inventories are popularly used.

Name
Book and Author
Dates read
Comments
Opinions

Chapter 13

National Talent Search in Science

13.1 INTRODUCTION

The discovery and development of the creative genius of our youth is of prime importance in educational process. It is precisely this ability that we must want to develop "catch them young" is a popular slogan. The secondary stage is considered right for identifying such talent.

The NCERT in collaboration with Directorates of education of various states initiated a programme for identifying promising students in science and to provide them with necessary help and encouragement to carry out their higher studies in basic and applied sciences under *Science Talent Search Scheme*. A pilot project was launched in 1963 in territory of Delhi and the scheme was extended to all over the country in 1964. Under the scheme about 350 scholars are selected each year. The scheme was previously open to students of science and mathematics but nor it has been thrown open even to students taking up social science subjects such as History, Geography, Political science, Economics etc.

13.2 NATIONAL TALENT SEARCH SCHEME

The Scheme

Its basic aim is to identify outstanding students at the end of class X, XI and XII (where there is a public examination at the end of each class) and it provide them with financial aid for pursuing best possible education and help them to develop their talent for service of discipline as also of the nation.

The scheme is under the control of NCERT. However since 1985 the scheme has been decentralised and the State Councils of Educational Research and Training (SCERT's) are conducting the examinations. The students selected by the states are then finally screened by the examination conducted by NCERT and only those students who are finally selected by NCERT are awarded the scholarships.

13.3 OBJECTIVES OF THE SCHEME

The scheme aims to identify outstanding students at the close of the secondary stage. It also aims to stimulate scientific talent and help such students in pursuing their higher studies in basic and applied sciences. Scholarships are awarded from B.Sc. to Ph.D. level. Under the scheme some special programmes are provided in science so as to nurture the talent. The scheme also aims at encouraging schools to take an active interest in the search of talented students and in this way help in building up a body of scientists. Such persons (scientists) will then contribute in the scientific advancement of India.

The scheme is also expected to create a consciousness for improvement in science syllabi, methods of teaching science and evaluation techniques in science. It also hopes to provide colleges, universities and other technical institutions with a means of contacting science students of high ability. In this way it aims at mobilising the interest and support of higher education centres for development of science talent in the country.

13.4 SELECTION

For selection under the scheme the following procedure is followed.

(*i*) A written test is conducted to test general mental ability scholastic aptitude test is also given.

(*ii*) General mental ability test consists of test-items on reasoning, analysis, synthesis etc. Class X scholastic aptitude test contains items in Physics, Chemistry, Biology, Mathematics, History, Geography, Economics and Civics. The student has the option to select any four of the light subjects noted above. Class XI and XII scholastic aptitude test has items in various subjects and a student has the option to select any three of the available subjects *i.e.* Physics, Chemistry, Biology, Mathematics, Statistics, History, Geography, Psychology, Economics, Political

Science, Sociology, Elements of Commerce and Accountancy. The student can offer English or any other Indian language as the medium of the test.

Those students who qualify the written test have to appear for an interview held at different places in the country.

13.5 ELIGIBILITY

The test in open to any regular student in Class X, XI and XII (at the end of which he takes a public examination). The blank forms for admission to the examination can be had from (*i*) Head of the Institution where student is enrolled (*ii*) Nearest Centre Superintendent of NTSE (*iii*) Field Advisor of NCERT (*iv*) Section Officer, NTSE Unit, NCERT, New Delhi.

Generally last date for submission of completed forms for the examination is 10th February. The completed form is to be submitted to the Superintendent of the Centre, at which the candidate wishes to take the examination.

Examination is normally held in May every year.

13.6 SCHOLARSHIP

Scholarships are given for studies at +2 stage and higher studies after suitable revalidation at terminal stages upto Ph.D. level in Basic and Social Science including Commerce and upto second degree level in Engineering and Medicines.

Continuance of Award

The continuance of award is subject to the maintenance of high academic standards (prescribed by NCERT from time to time). The scholarship available is subject to the following conditions

(*i*) The awardee must not fail in the class for which he is taking the NTSE or in any other subsequent class and must continue his studies as a regular student.

(*ii*) Scholarship is available for pursuance of higher studies in India upto degree level but is available for studies both in India and abroad for higher studies.

(*iii*) The payment of scholarship is made through the head of the institutions where the awardee is undergoing his studies.

Rates of Scholarship

The existing rates of scholarship are as under:

Name of Examination	*No. of Scholarships*	*Rates*
Class X	250	(*i*) Rs. 150/- p.m. 2 years + Rs. 200/- p.a. for books (*ii*) Rs. 200/- p.m. upto the second degree in Basic and Social Sciences and first degree in Engineering and Medicine + Rs. 300/- p.a. for books.
Class XI	100	(*i*) Rs. 150/- p.m. for one year + Rs. 300/- p.a. for books. (*ii*) Rs. 200/- p.m. upto second degree in Basic and Social Science and first degree in Engineering and Medicines + Rs. 300/- p.a. for books.
Class XII	150	Rs. 200/- p.m. upto second degree in Basic and Social Sciences and first degree in Engineering and Medicines + Rs. 300/- p.a. for books.

13.7 SUMMER SCHOOLS FOR NATIONAL SCIENCE TALENT SEARCH SCHOLARS

To explore and to develop the talents of national science talent search scholars, NSTS, summer schools were started in 1965. These scholars are attached to some renowned Professors of respective subjects in different universities during summer vacations.

Objectives of Summer Schools

The main objectives of these summer schools are as under:

1. To establish an interpersonal relationship between the teacher and the taught.
2. To enable the scholars to develop their intellectual personalities in the best possible way.
3. To motivate the experimental curiosity of students.
4. To stimulate their powers of creativity and research.
5. To enable the students to exchange views amongst themselves and to promote greater appreciation and understanding of each other's views.
6. To encourage the scholars to pinpoint their interests and aptitudes.
7. To accelerate the programme of science education.
8. To design accelerated courses for scholars.
9. To enable scholars to have a better understanding of the basic concepts and recent developments in the subject.
10. To enable scholars to develop new basic concepts in their fields of specialization.
11. To assist the scholars in conducting experiments with simple and improvised apparatus and to encourage them to adopt innovative approaches in their daily life.

13.8 ROLE OF LIFE-SCIENCE TEACHER

The teacher of life-science has a role to play. He can encourage and motivate good students to take up the national science talent search test. He can provide guidance to the students on the subject matter of tests.

Chapter 14

Lesson Planning in Life Sciences

14.1 INTRODUCTION

A proper planning of the lessons is key to effective teaching. The teacher must know in advance the subject matter and mode of its delivery in the class room. This gives the teacher an idea of how to develop the key concepts and how to correlate them to real life situations and how to conclude the lesson. Lesson planning is also essential because effective learning takes place only if the subject matter is presented in an integrated and correlated manner and is related to the pupil's environment. Though lesson planning requires a hard work but it is rewarding too. L.B. Stands conceives a lesson as 'plan of action' implemented by the teacher in the classroom. According to G.H. Green, "The teacher who has planned his lesson wisely related to his topic and to his class room without any anxiety, ready to embark with confidence upon a job he understands and prepared to carry it to a workmanable conclusion. He has foreseen the difficulties that are likely to arise, and prepared himself to deal with them. He knows the aims that his lesson is intended to fulfil, and he has marshalled his own resources for the purpose. And because he is free of anxiety, he will be able coolly to estimate the value of his work as the lesson proceeds, equally aware of failure and success and prepared to learn from both".

Meaning of Lesson Plan

Lesson Planning thus in a true sense, represents the task of theoretical chalking out of the details of the journey which a teacher is going to perform practically alongwith his students for the realisation of some specified instructional objectives in a specified school period. Thus in a lesson plan we have planned that which is to be taught by the teacher. It is planned in a methodical way by writing a less plan related with a particular unit of his subject.

14.2 ADVANTAGES OF LESSON PLANNING

Some of the advantages of planning a lesson are as under:

(*i*) Lesson planning makes the work regular, organised and more systematic.

(*ii*) It induces confidence in the teacher.

(*iii*) It makes teacher quite conscious of the aim which makes him conscious of attitudes he wants to develop in his students.

(*iv*) It saves a lot of time.

(*v*) It helps in making correlation between the concepts with the pupils environment.

(*vi*) It stimulates the teacher to ask striking questions.

(*vii*) It provides more freedom in teaching.

14.3 FEATURES OF A LESSON PLAN

Some Important features of a good lesson plan are as under:

(*i*) *Objectives.* All the congnitive objectives that are intended to be fulfilled should be listed in the lesson plan.

(*ii*) *Content.* The subject matter that is intended to be covered should be limited to prescribed time. The matter must be interesting and it should be related to pupil's previous knowledge. It should also be related to daily life situations.

(*iii*) *Method(s).* The most appropriate method be chosen by the teacher. The method chosen should be suitable to the subject matter to be taught. Suitable teaching aids must also be identified by the teacher. Teacher may also use supplementary aids to make his lesson more effective.

(*iv*) *Evaluation.* Teacher must evaluate his lesson to find the extent to which he has achieved the aim of his lesson. Evaluation can be done even by recapitulation of subject matter through suitable questions.

14.4 STEPS IN LESSON PLANNING (HERBARTIAN STEPS)

Formal steps in lesson planning are:

(*i*) Introduction (or preparation)
(*ii*) Presentation
(*iii*) Association (or comparison)
(*iv*) Generalisation
(*v*) Application
(*vi*) Recapitulation

1. Introduction

It pertains to preparing and motivating children to the lesson content by linking it to the previous knowledge of the student, by arousing curiosity of the children and by making an appeal to their senses. This prepares the child's mind to receive new knowledge. This step though so important must be brief. It may involve testing of previous knowledge of the child. Some times the curiosity of pupil can be aroused by some experiment, chart, model, story or even by some useful discussion.

2. Presentation

It involves the stating of the object of lesson and exposure of students to new information. The actual lesson begins and both teacher and students participate. Teacher should make use of different teaching aids to make his lesson effective. Teacher should draw as much as is possible from the students making use of judicious questions. In science lesson it is desirable that a heuristic atmosphere prevails in the class.

3. Association

It is always desirable that new ideas or knowledge be associated to the daily life situations by citing suitable examples and by drawing comparisons with the related concepts. This step is all the more important when we are establishing principles or generalising definitions.

4. Generalisation

In science lessons generally the learning material leads to certain generalisations leading to establishment of certain formulaes, principles or laws. An effort be made that the students draw the conclusions themselves. Teacher should guide the students only if their generalisation is either incomplete or irrelevant.

5. Application

In this step of lesson plan the knowledge gained is applied to certain situations. This step is in confirmity with the general desire of the students to make use of generalisation in order to see for themselves if the generalisations are valid in certain situations or not? No lesson of science may be considered complete if such rules, principles, formula etc. are not applied to life situations.

6. Recapitulation

In this last step of his lesson plan the teacher tries to ascertain whether his students have understood and grasped the subject matter or not. This is used for assessing the effectiveness of the lesson by asking students questions on the contents of the lesson. Recaptulation can also be done by giving a short objective type test to the class or even by asking the students to label some unlabelled sketch.

One most important point to remember is that the six steps given above for lesson planning are formal Herbartian steps and teacher should not try to follow these very rigidly. These are only guide lines and in many a lessons it is not possible to follow all these steps.

There is another way of lesson planning which is gaining currency these days. It is known as *Glover Plan*. This plan has four steps as follows:

1. *Questioning.* Teacher must introduce and develop his lesson through related and sequential questions. Start the lesson by asking questions about previous knowledge of the students. The questions should then lead to new knowledge under consideration.

Lesson can also be introduced with the help of some teaching aid like a picture, chart or model etc. the introduction can also to made by describing a situation or by telling a short story.

However teacher should hear in mind that the introduction is brief and interesting.

2. *Discussion.* For discussion the class be divided into smaller groups and in such groups students be encouraged to express their

ideas and opinions freely. This helps the students in removal of their difficulties.

3. *Investigation.* The students are encouraged to do a project or investigation on the lesson topic either individually or in small groups by processing information or by laboratory work.

4. *Expression.* It concerns the strategy in which the student's and teacher's communication of ideas through observation and listening (passive expression) or through doing (active expression) or through fine and performing arts (artistic expression) or by arranging learning situations (organisational expression).

In developing a lesson a teachers must keep in mind the following psychological principles.

(*i*) *Principle of Selection and Division.* The teacher should wisely select and divide the learning material into smaller segments. It is also for the teacher to decide about the quantum of subject matter to be covered by him and that which has to be illicited from the students.

(*ii*) *Principle of Successive Clarity.* It is for the teacher to see that the different learning segments of lesson are well structured, sequenced and connected. Teacher must ensure, at each segment, that students have grasped the subject matter given to them.

(*iii*) *Principle of Integration.* Teacher should conclude his lesson only after combining various learning segments to produce some generalisation.

Design for Writing a Lesson Plan

Lecture-Cum-Demonstration Method

The style given below is generally followed for writing a lesson plan.

Class:	Date:
Subject:	Duration
Topic:	of period:

Instructional Material

General Objectives

Specific objectives

Previous Knowledge

Questions

1. ?
2. ?
3. ?

Introduction

Questions

1. ?
2. ?

Announcement of Aim

Presentation

Matter	*Method*	*B. B. Summary*

Generalisations

Applications

Recapitulation

Questions

1. ____?
2. ____?
3. ____?

Home Task ____

____

14.5 SPECIMEN LESSON PLAN

Class: X– Date:

Subject: Biology Duration

Topic: Structure of human heart of period: 40 minutes

Instructional Material (Teaching Aids)

1. Black board, duster, coloured chalks.
2. A model of human heart
3. A few actual specimens of heart some of which are dissected and at least two are in original state, dissection material such as dish, slide, pin, spirit, scissors, forceps, needle, cotton etc.

General Objectives

1. To develop scientific attitude amongst the pupil.
2. To develop power of observation and sense of enquiry amongst the pupil.
3. To develop reflective thinking in pupils.

Specific Objectives

To make students understand the structure and functioning of human heart.

Previous Knowledge

It is presumed that the students know about the various internal organs of human body.

Introduction

For introducing the lesson teacher will prick the pin in the finger of one of the students (while doing so the teacher will not say anything and he would also see that the pin he uses for pricking should be first dipped in spirit). When the pin is pricked some blood on a slide and then he will put the following questions:

1. Can you tell me from where has this blood come?
2. Can you tell me the position of heart in human body?
3. Can you tell me something about the structure of human heart?

Announcement of Aim

When no satisfactory answer is given by students to question 3 above, the teacher will announce the topic by saying that, "Today we will learn about the structure and working of human heart"

Presentation

To present the lesson teacher will use the actual specimen and model of human heart. He will also instruct the students to note him what they are told and what they observe.

Matter	*Method*	*B. B. Summary*
1. The heart is situated on the left side of body below the bones of chest.	Question will be asked from students. 1. Do you observe any throbbing on the left side of your body below the chest? 2. What is it due to?	Heart
2. It is like a closed first or the shape of a *pan* leaf.		
3. It is covered from outside by their membrane called *pericardium*.	Pericardium will be shown by the teacher from actual specimen of human heart.	*Pericardium*
4. *Pericardium* protects the heart from any external shock.		

Matter	*Method*	*B. B. Summary*
5. Heart is divided into two by thick muscular partition. (*i*) right side (*ii*) left side. These two halves don't communicate with each other.	Teacher will show these parts by removing wall of heart in the model. Then he will ask, how many chambers do you see?	
6. The anterior chambers are two *auricles* and posterior are two *ventricles*.		*Auricle* *Ventricle*
7. The auricles are communicated by ventricles through aperture called *valves*.	What is a valve?	
8. Valve acts as a watchman because it helps to check the entry of blood from ventricles back to auricles.	What is the functions of a valve?	
9. In the right auricle we find two large *vena cavae.* One of these bring blood from anterior portion of body (superior vena cavae) and the other from lower portion (inferior vena cavae)	How many tubes enter the right auricle?	(1) Superior vena cavae (2) Inferior vena cavae
10. From right ventricle a pulmonary artery takes away impure blood towards the lungs for purification.	Pulmonary artery will be shown by the teacher from actual specimen.	Pulmonary artery.
11. Pure blood from left ventricle (by pulmonary vein in left auricle) through *dorsal aorta* goes to the various parts of the body.	Dorsal Aorta will be shown to the students from the actual model of heart.	Dorsal Aorta.
12. *Working* The impure blood from various parts of human body first of all comes in right auricle through veins. The blood goes to right ventricle by contraction of	What do you see in between the auricle and ventricle? How does the blood goes from the auricle to the ventricle? How is blood supplied	

auricles. On getting blood ventricles relaxes and simultaneously it contracts and blood is pumped. The pure blood from lungs comes in the left auricle through pulmonary veins. The auricle starts contraction and blood is forced into the ventricle through valve. At this stage the ventricle starts contraction which forces the blood into dorsal aorta and through it to different parts of human body. Thus we find that functioning of heart involves alternate contraction and relaxation.

parts of our body? What do you understand by alternate contraction and relaxation?

Black Board Summary

A labelled diagram of human heart will be drawn on the black board. In this students will be actively involved. The diagram will show all the parts of human heart and it will not include any other part of our body.

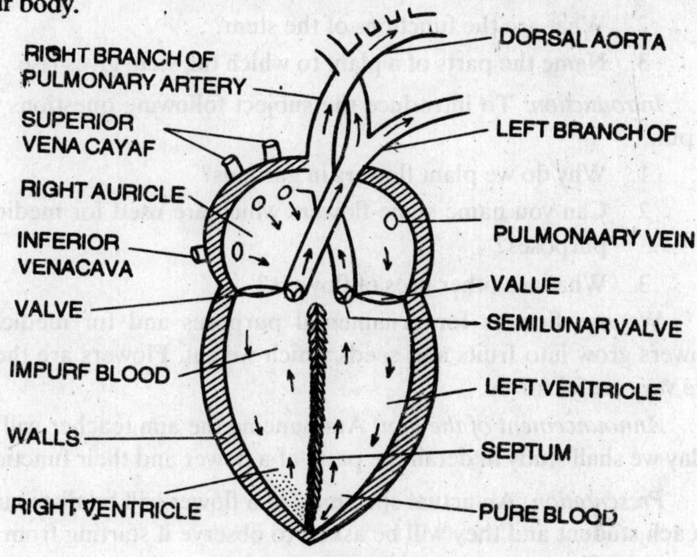

Fig. 14.1. Structure of Heart.

Recapitulation

For recaptulation students will be asked to draw a well labelled diagram of the human heart.

Home Task

Students will be asked to make a model of human heart.

14.6 LESSON NOTES OF SOME PLANS

Parts of a Flower and their Functions

Aim: To tell the pupils about the various parts of a flower and their functions.

Aids:
1. Chart showing the various parts of a flower.
2. The model of a flower.
3. Actual specimens of flowers and buds.

Previous knowledge: Students have already studied the different parts of a plant and familiar with their functions. They have also seen different kinds of flowers.

Testing previous knowledge: P.K. will be tested by putting the following questions,

1. Name the various parts of a plant.
2. What are the functions of the stem?
3. Name the parts of a plant to which the stem gives rise.

Introduction: To introduce the subject following questions will be put.

1. Why do we plant flowers in gardens?
2. Can you name some flowers which are used for medicine purposes?
3. What are other uses of flowers?

We use flowers for ornamental purposes and for medicine. Flowers grow into fruits and seeds which we eat. Flowers are therefore very useful for us.

Announcement of the aim. Announcing the aim teacher will say today we shall study in detail the parts of a flower and their functions.

Presentation. An actual specimen of a flower will be distributed to each student and they will be asked to observe it starting from the base of the flower.

Matter	*Method (Questions)*	*Blackboard Summary*
1. The lowest part of the flower by means of which it is attached to the branch is known as the pedicel. It is green in colour. It keeps the flower exposed to air and sunshine and carries food from the branch to the flower.	1. What do you see at the base of the flower? 2. What is the colour of the stalk? 3. What is the medium through which food is transported from the branch to the flower?	1. The green stalk is known as the pedicel. It helps to carry food to the flower.
2. The outermost whorl of the leaves is green in colour. Each leaf of this whorl is known as a sepal. Sepals serve to protect the flower in its bud condition.	1. What is the colour of the outer whorl of leaves? What is the function of the sepals?	2. The green outermost leaves known as the sepals serve to protect the flower in bud condition.
3. Next to sepals are a number of brightly coloured leaves in a whorl. These leaves are known as petals. They give a pleasant smell. Because of the colour and smell of petals, flowers attract insects.	The teacher will instruct pupils to remove the sepals and note that inside these are brightly coloured leaves. They are known as the petals. Pupils will also be asked to discover whether the petals give any smell.	3. Next to the sepals are the brightly coloured and scented petals. They serve to attract insects.
4. Inside the petals there are stamens. These are made up of anther lobes and filaments. The anther lobes possess yellow pollen. This is the male part of the flower.	The teacher will ask pupils to remove the petals and note the threadlike filament with the bag like anther-cap at the top. They will be instructed to touch the anther with their finger and to see what happens to the finger.	4. Stamens is made up of anther and filament. They serve as the male part of the flower.
5. In the centre of the flower there is the carpel or pistil. It has three parts: (a) Ovary (b) Style (c) Stigma This is the female part of the flower.	The teacher will instruct pupils to remove the stamens and see the carpel or pistil. He will draw attention to the difference in its shape at the base, middle and the top. The lower swollen	5. The carpel: It has three parts: i. Ovary ii. Style iii. Stigma It serves as the female part of the flower.

Matter	*Method (Questions)*	*Blackboard Summary*
Recapitulation: For recapitulation of he lesson, following questions will be asked while by showing the model of a flower, and by the explaining the diagram on a chart. 1. What are the parts of a flower? 2. Enumerate the functions of each part. *Blackboard Summary:* As above. *Application and home-work:* Students will be asked to collect flowers of different colours, note their various parts, and preserve them in an album.	portion is the ovary, the middle is the style and the head is the stigma.	

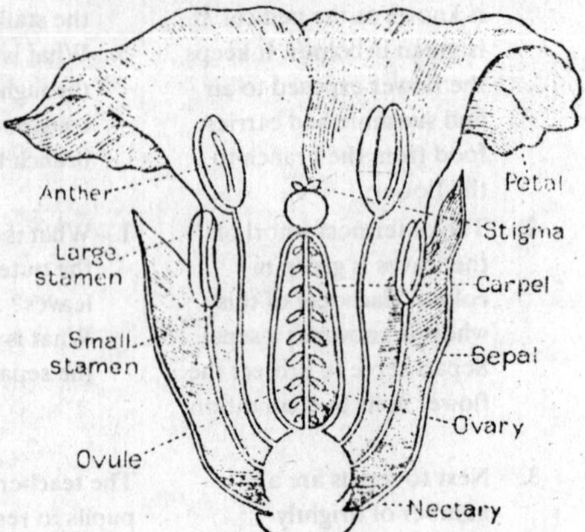

2. Mosquitoes

Aim: To teach the students the four stages in the life-history of a mosquito, to tell them how to get rid of mosquitoes, and hence to teach the means of fighting malaria.

Aids:

1. Charts showing the different stages in the life of a mosquito.
2. A model showing egg, larva, pupa, and adult mosquito.
3. Actual specimens of life stages of the mosquito contained in bottles.
4. D.D.T., quinine, paludrine, mosquito-cream.

Previous knowledge. Students already know the names of some common insects, harmful as well as useful and they are also familiar with the name of malaria fever.

Testing previous knowledge. To test P.K. following questions will be asked:

1. Name some common insects.
2. Name insects which are harmful and cause diseases?
3. Name the insect that troubles you most at night?

Introduction. To introduce the topic following questions will be asked.

1. In which season does malaria generally occur?
2. Do you know how malaria is caused?

Statement of the aim. When the students fail to give a correct answer to question 2 above. The teacher will tell them that the mosquito is responsible for spreading malaria. He will then announce the aim saying today we shall study the life-history of a mosquito, how to get rid of mosquitoes and how to get rid of malaria.

Presentation. I. Mosquitoes take a heavy toll of human life every year by spreading malaria. The disease spreads during the rainy season when mosquitoes abound. Mosquitoes breed in dark dingy places under shelves and furniture, in marshy places and on standing water.

II. The students will be told that there are two kinds of mosquito-Anopheles and Culex. Their characteristics will be taught by reference to models and the chart showing diagrams of the two kinds. The characteristics taught will be summarised on the balck board.

III. Destruction of mosquitoes: In this connextion the following points will be educive from the students by suitable questions and will be put on the balckboard.

(*i*) To prevent mosquitoes breeding we should not allow water stagnant or to stand near our houses.

(*ii*) Always sprinkel kerosene oil on stagnant or standing water to kill the larvae.

(*iii*) Always spray D.D.T. or Flit in rooms so as to kill mosquitoes.

IV. How to save ourselves from malaria? The following points will be educed and put on the balck board:

(*i*) For guarding ourselves from mosquitoes use mosquito nets at night is essential. Apply mosquito oil or cream and do

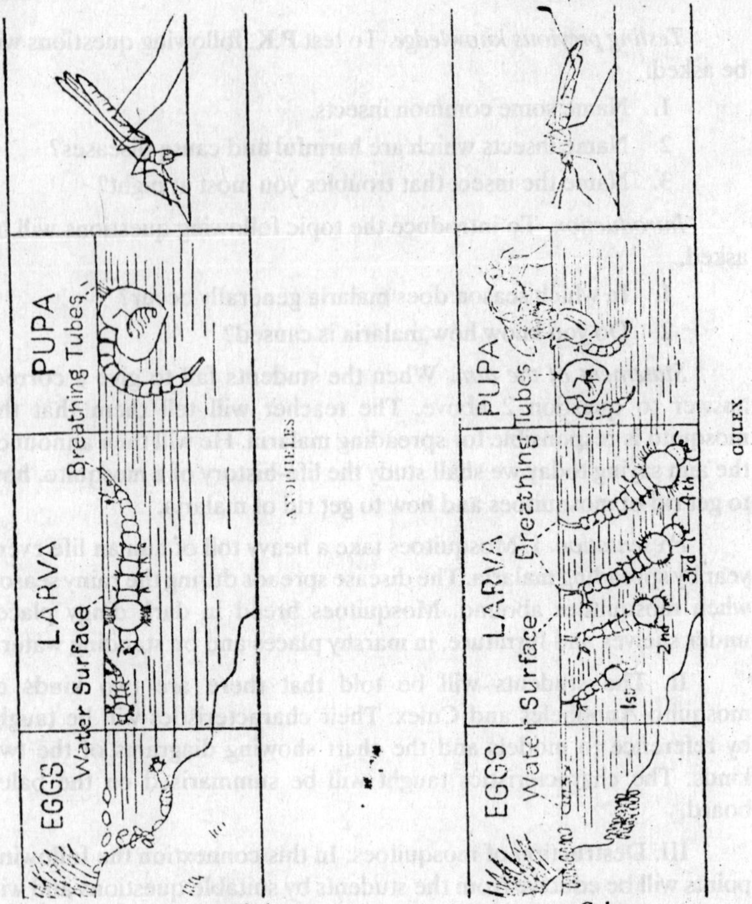

Anopheles *Culex*

Anopheles	Culex
1. Eggs are laid in water. They float signly or in groups.	1. Eggs are laid in water. They float as one compact mass.
2. The larva lies parallel to and just beneath the surface of water.	2. The larva lies with head downwards in water.
3. The pupa has a shape like a letter C.	3. The pupa has a shape like a letter C.
4. The mosquito lies in a position slanting to the surface.	4. The mosquito lies in a position parallel to the surface.
5. The adult has spotted wings.	5. The wings of the adult are not spotted.
6. The female anopheles is responsible for the spread of malaria.	6. It does not spread malaria.

not allow any part of the body to be exposed to the bites of mosquitoes.

As a precaution against malaria, take quinine during the malaria season. Two tablets of 5 grains each per week taken regularly is considered effective for this purpose.

Application. Some question will be asked to educe the following:

(*i*) We should not live in dirty, dingy and dark places and should avoid living near marshy places, ponds, stagnant and standing water.

(*ii*) We should fill any pits in our neighbourhood with earth, we should use mosquito nets at night, and mosquito oil or cream on the exposed parts of the body.

(*iii*) We should sprinkel D.D.T. or Flit in our houses regularly.

(*iv*) We should take quinine or paludrine during the malaria season as a precautionary measure.

Recapitulation. For the recapitulating the lesson following questions will be asked while explaining the diagrams of mosquitoes on a chart. Suitable questions will also be put to ensure that the points taught have been grasped by pupils.

Black board Summary

(*i*) Characteristics of the two kinds of mosquitoes.

(*ii*) Destruction of mosquitoes.

(*iii*) Precautions to save ourselves from malaria.

Home Task The students will be asked to observe for themselves the precuations which have been taught to protect ourselves from malaria, and also actively put them into practice in their own homes.

Chapter 15

Contributions of Biologist and Naturalist to the Teaching of Science

15.1 INTRODUCTION

The teaching of science has developed step by step to reach its present day shape. Various educationists, psychologists, and scientists have contributed a lot in the process. In this chapter an attempt will be made to discuss the contributions of some of these.

15.2 JEAN PIAGET'S CONTRIBUTION TO TEACHING OF SCIENCE

Jean Piaget is a biologist and naturalist who served psychology over 40 years. He is much more interested in epistemology as compared to psychology. He makes a choice of his problems from the area of cognition and leaves other variables such as intelligence, socio-economic conditions etc.

He inherited his ideas from Gestalt a famous psychologist. However his approach is different from that of Gestalt's approach. Unlike Gestalt's approach, Piaget's approach is elastic and flexible Piaget tries to discuss the properties of thinking using symbolic logic and attempts the formulation of a psychological theory of operations which links psychology to logic.

Operation is a means of transferring data mentally. Operations are reversible and coordinated into a system. They evolve gradually. Piaget distinguishes four main stages in the development of operations. The four stages of interaction between organism and environment suggested by Piaget do not take into consideration the individual differences at a particular stage. The succeeding stage grows over the gains of preceding stage. Piagets four stages of interaction are:

(*i*) Sensory motor period (upto 2 years)

(*ii*) Pre-operational stage or Representation stage (2 – 7 years)
(*iii*) Concrete period (7 – 11 years)
(*iv*) Formal period (11 – 15 years)

Gains of Sensory-Motor Period

The gains of Sensory Motor period are as under:

(*i*) reacting to distant objects;
(*ii*) scope for qualitative and quantitative evaluation;
(*iii*) responses are used into single action sequence;
(*iv*) co-ordinates different experiences into one scheme;
(*v*) awareness of time;
(*vi*) recognition of a particular stimulus as a part of an entire action sequence, and
(*vii*) stresses the internal aspects of the prospective behaviour of the child.

Various phases of pre-operational stage

The pre-operational stage is the second stage of interaction between organism and environment. The pre-operational stage has two phases. They are: (*i*) Pre-conceptual (2 – 4 years) and (*ii*) Intuitive (4 – 7 years). To Piaget these years constitute a transitory period. It involves a transformation from self-satisfying to a socialised behaviour. The preconceptual phase of the pre-operational stage is one of continuous exploration and investigation, The second phase of the pre-operational stage visualises widening of social interest and the child becomes less self-centred.

Characteristics of intuitive thinking in pre-operational stage

Intuitive thinking finds a place in the second phase (4 – 7 years) of the second stage (2 – 7 years) of the Sensory-Motor period. In this stage social interest begins widening. The child becomes less self-centred. He begins to think. He finds it difficult to distinguish new ideas from old ones. This type of intuitive thinking needs four important features. They are as under:

(*i*) the child feels difficulty in expressing his thoughts;
(*ii*) He can imagine his past actions and plans his future action;

(*iii*) He becomes less self-centred and even fails to communicate and understand; and

(*iv*) Perceptual consideration of the situation governs his thinking.

The Educational Implications of Piaget Ideas

Piagets idea relevant to science teaching has the following four educational implications:

(*i*) At the pre-operational stage the child should be offered with more corrective experiences so as to clarify and develop concepts.

(*ii*) The obstract ideas in a science should be offered very concretely to the child at the concrete operational stage (7 – 11 years). Science teaching should be self-motivated and self-instructional. The child may be free to learn with experiments independently. Science club, field trips, and such other community sources should be the base for science at this stage.

(*iii*) In the formal stage (11 – 15 years) the child is capable of reasoning and hypothesising. The child can do controlled experimentation. They may master the elements of scientific methods. At this stage education showed aim at not only developing problem solving attitude but to build a variety of anticipatory chemata based upon sensory events. It makes the child active, inquiring and experimenting.

(*iv*) Self activity and self experience and not more teaching are advocated by him. He insists the process of science by doing and not by teaching.

Jean Piaget explained two basic ideas relevant to science teaching. They are: (*i*) Intellectual structures are outcome of the constant interaction between the organism and the environment. Piaget introduced two inseparable and contemporary variants of a single mechanism. They are organisation and adaptation. Organisation is an internal aspect and adaptation is an external aspect. Adaptation involves two interrelated concepts namely assimilation and accomodation. Assimilation and accommodation are drawn from adaptation which is unitary event. Assimilation and accommodation act together. They are interlocked and involves simultaneous conflict. They provide complementary opposing pulls. They result in cognitive change. His idea is built upon the biological models of homeostasis, (*ii*) It is difficult to specify the actual beginning of the interaction between the organism and environment and the actual cultivation of such interaction in terms of cognitive development. Individual differences are not considered in the four stages of operation explained by Piaget. Each succeeding stage grows over the gains of preceding stage. Each stage grows horizontally and vertically. The specified age range for different stages may differ from among different cultures.

15.3 BRUNER'S CONTRIBUTION

Bruner's Scanning Strategy

Bruner's stratagies attempt to explain how adults and adolescents expand the already well formed concepts so as to acquire more elaborate concepts. These strategies try to discover the routes used by pupils attempting to expand. Modify and adopt old concepts to new concepts. Bruner's model includes two strategies; (*i*) Scanning and (*ii*) Focussing. In scanning strategy a person works out hypothesis from the information given. He adopts a completely logical approach known as simultaneous scanning by holding in mind all the combination in setting up new hypothesis. In 'successive scanning' a person takes one step at a time. Simultaneous scanning includes only positive instances where as successive scanning includes negative instances also.

Bruner's Focussing Strategy

Bruner's Focussing strategy does not involve hypothesis testing. The individual proceeds by changing one attribute value at a time or more than one attribute at a time Focussing is of two types: namely conservative focussing and focus gambling. In conservative focussing the individual proceeds by changing the value of a single attribute. On the contrary, in the focus gambling, the individual proceeds by changing the value of more than one attributes.

15.4 CONTRIBUTION OF BENJAMIN BLOOM

Benjamin Bloom explored the idea for the classification of educational objectives at the convention of American Psychologists held at Bostan in 1948. Bostan convention decided to classify educational objectives Under, Cognitive. Affective and psycho motor domains. To Bloom, the cognitive domain included six educational objectives such as; Knowledge, Comprehension, Application, Analysis, Synthesis and Evaluation. Bloom has proposed a hierarchy of objectives under Affective domain. It is (*i*) Receiving, the lowest in the hierarchy of Affective domain; (*ii*) Responding, second from the bottom; (*iii*) valuing above responding; (*iv*) Organisation, the fourth from the bottom; and (*v*) characterisation, the highest level of affective domain. No objective has been classified under Psychomotor domain so for.

15.5 CONTRIBUTION OF AUSUBEL

Ausubel contributed the theory of 'cognitive subsumption'. It is a theory of meaningful verbal learning based on a concept of cognitive subsumption. Meaningful learning is an outcome of relating the new ideas to the ideas already known. Thus previous learning decides subsequent learning. He arranged a congnitive structure. In this structure the general principles and concepts were placed at the top. The specific knowledge was placed at the lower level. To explain his theory of cognitive subsumption, he introduced the concept of "advance organiser". It is only a generalised statement which is to be followed by presentation of specific facts related to a general statement. Thus the advance organiser is an introductory statement attempting to establish an overview of the main concepts. Teaching should commence with units of most general ideas and subsequently subconcepts have to be introduce. The relation between the old and the new concepts has also to be explored and explained. The advance organiser achieves following functions. (*i*) it increases the meaningfulness of reception learning; and (*ii*) it strengthens retention by offering association of facts.

15.6 GAGNE'S CONTRIBUTIONS

Gagne proposed eight types of learning in a sequence. To him, simple and concrete things are to be learnt first. Subsequently abstract and complex learning should be introduced. Gagne's model of specifies to generalities is useful when the purpose of a lesson is to introduce the pupils to a set of principles or problem-solving skills. Ausubel's cognitive subsumption is to be used for introducing the students to many specific facts. Ausubel's model is concerned with reception learning where as Gagne's model is concerned with optimisation of initial learning obstruction and problem solving.

Gagne's book, "the conditions of Learning" was published in 1965. A complete description of his classes of behaviour appeared in this book. Here he explained and distinguished light types of learning involving observable behaviour and performance. His eight types of behaviour are as under:

(*i*) signal learning involving a conditioned response to signals;

(*ii*) stimulus response learning which involves precise movements of the skeletal muscles in response to specific stimuli;

(*iii*) chaining or skill learning which links two or more, units of stimulus response;

(*iv*) verbal association which links verbal units;

(*v*) multiple discrimination in which students learn different confused stimuli;

(*vi*) concept learning where the students respond to stimuli; in terms of abstract characteristics;

(*vii*) Principle learning where two or more concepts are related.

(*viii*) Problem-solving in which the goals are achieved with the use of principles.

15.7 CONTRIBUTIONS OF DR. HARGOBIND KHURANA

Dr. Hargobind Khurana an Indian born scientist was awarded the Nobel Prize for medicines and the science of genetics in 1968. The other two Indians, prior to Dr. Hargobind Khurana, to be awarded Nobel Prize are Dr. Rabinder Nath Tagore (1913, for Gitanjali) and Dr. C.V. Raman (1930, for 'Raman Effect'). Now Dr. Hargobind Khurana has adopted American citizenship and has settled in America with his Swiss wife and two daughters (Amila and Julie).

Dr. Hargobind Khurana went to England on Indian Government Scholarship and got the chance to work under Dr. Todd, a Nobel laureate on 'Constitution of nucleride'. He returned to India in 1949 after obtaining his Ph.D. from the University of Liverpool. In the absence of proper service avenues in India he went back to England where he worked for two years on 'nucleoids' in the National

Research Institute. Then he went to Canada where he worked hard for seven years. He migrated to America in 1960 where he got an opportunity to work with the Institute of Engime Chemistry in the University of Wisconsin. He continued his research on 'Genetics' and was awarded Nobel Prize for the discovery of 'genetic code'. He shared the Nobel Prize with two American Scientists Dr. Marshen Neren Berg and Dr. Holly.

Gregory Mendel was the first to propound that the unit of heredity was *'gene'*. Since then scientists were attempting to separate the 'nucleus' of this small unit 'gene' and were also making efforts to separate nucleic acids. In about 1940 it became clear that nucleic acid was mainly responsible for transmission of the traits from one generation to other.

Dr. Watson and Dr. Krik (1953) found that the unit containing traits of personality resembles the formation of a twisted two staircases and contains nucleorides. The gene is made up of DNA and RNA. Dr. Khurana's work was mainly directed to discover how protein or the amino acid and nucleic acid, responsible for the formation of gene, can be made chemically.

Speaking on the occassion of investiture ceremony of Nobel Prize to Dr. Hargobind Khurana it was remarked that the scientists of the world have now learnt the secret of genetics. This research will help the scientists to check control and cure certain heredity diseases. Now we will be able to control the physical aspects and also mental faculties of our future generations.

The research work of Dr. Khurana will be a boon to humanity. It will help not only to overcome the dreaded disease but will also help to produce artificial life in the laboratory. It may also fulfil the dream of producing future generation with certain predetermined traits of character personality and specific qualities of head and heart.

Chapter 16

Content Enrichment

16.1 INTRODUCTION

Since pupils have to learn 'life sciences' which is a regular study of life so a content enrichment is essential because man's knowledge of life sciences is as old as man's own history of life. The latest research work in the field of life science and some new aspects of life sciences if given to the students will be good. It is with this in mind that content portion is assigned to the syllabus for teaching of life sciences. In the following few pages some concept of life sciences will be taken up for discussion.

16.2 CELL STRUCTURE AND CELL THEORY

Definition

Cell is a unit of biological activity. It consists of an organised mass of protoplasm surrounded by a protective and selectively permeable covering.

It is a unit of both structure and function of living beings which is represented by a small mass of protoplasm having a nucleus and delimited from its surroundings by a selectively permeable membrane.

It is the smallest unit of living organism that can exhibit all properties of life (growth, metabolism, reproduction) in a medium free of other living systems and is made up of colloidal complex known as *protoplasm* surrounded by selectively permeable membrane.

Cell biology is that branch of biology which deals with the study of morphological, biochemical, physiological, genetical, developmental and evolutionary aspects of cell and its components.

History of Discovery of cell

The term cell was introduced by an English scientist Robert Hooke in 1665. Robert Hooke found that a thin slice of cork contained a large number of little boxes or compartments which he named as cells (Latin *Cella*–hollow spaces or compartments). The credit for observing unicellular organism and other small structure goes to Dutch scientist Antone' van Leeuwenhock (1672). He was also the first to observe *nucleus.* Malpighi (1675) gave an account of internal structure of plants. In 1831 Robert Brown described and named *nucleus.* Purkinie (1839) and Von Mohl (1846) gave the name of *protoplasm* to the semifluid contents of the cells. In 1839 Schleiden and Schwann postulated the famour *cell theory.* Bowman (1840) coined the term *nucleolus* for the deeply staining rounded portion of the nucleus. In 1862, Kolliker introduced the term *cytoplasm* for protoplasm outside the nucleus.

Many other scientists studied and discovered the 'division' and 'multiplication' of the cell in detail.

Cell theory

Cell theory was proposed by Schleiden and Schwann. M.J. Schleiden from his studies of plant anatomy found that all plant parts are formed of cells which function as independent units. They contribute to the life of the whole organism. Schwann studied the development of animal embryo and found that growth of the animal consisted of growth and multiplication of cells.

According to cell theory *the bodies of all organism are made up of cells and their products so that cells are units of both structure and function of living organism.*

Some important and fundamental observations of this theory are:

1. Organism are made up of cells and their products.
2. New cells arise from pre-existing cells.
3. Cells are units of both structure and function of living organism.

Cell theory has since been modified and the *modern cell theory, cell doctrine* or *cell principle* believe as under:

1. The bodies of all living beings are made up of the cells and their products. Cells are, therefore, units of structure in the body of living organism.

2. Every cell is made up of a small mass of protoplasm having a nucleus, a number of organelles and a covering membrane.
3. The cells belonging to diverse organism and different regions of the same organism have a fundamental similarity of structure, chemical composition and metabolism.
4. Growth of an organism involves the growth and multiplication of its cells.
5. Genetic information is stored and expressed inside cells.
6. Life passes from one generation to next in the form of a living cell.
7. All present day cells have a common ancestry.
8. Basically the cells are totipotent (*i.e.* a single cell can give rise to the whole organism).

According to *protoplasmic theory* given by Max Schultze (1861), the living matter of organism is not cell but protoplasm.

According to *organismal theory* given by Sachs (1874), the body of a living being is made up of a continuous mass of living matter which is incompletely divided into compartments called cells. The whole organism functions as a single entity.

There are many a similarities in plant cells and animal cells.

Similarities

1. Both contain a substance called *protoplasm*. Life functions are carried out by protoplasm.
2. Both contain *cytoplasm* which is surrounded on all sides by a thin membrane known as 'plasmalemma'.
3. Both contain *nucleus* which is the central part of the cell and is surrounded by cytoplasm. It is the most vital part of the cell.

There are many a differences in the plant cells and animal cells. Some parts are found only in plant cells and some parts are found only in animal cells.

Structures found only in plant cells

1. **Cell wall.** It is present in plant cells only. It is made of cellulose and protects the cell membrane and plasma. It also gives shape to the

cell. It is permeable to liquids and allows them to pass from one cell to another. Its function can be compared to that of the backbone of some animals.

2. **Plastids** are found only in plant cells. However their certain exceptions. They grow with cell. They can be further classified as (*i*) Leucoplasts (*ii*) Chloroplasts and (*iii*) Chromoplasts.

3. In some plants are find some solid or liquid substances which are peculiar to those plants and give them their identity. *e.g.* starch in potatoes.

Structure found only in animal cells

1. **Golgi bodies** which appear as pile of plates. Each cell contains one such golgi bodies. These plates are made up of double membranes and in lower plants these are referred to as *dictosox.*

2. **Centosomes** are found only in the cells of Thelephyta. Only one Thelephyta is found in each cell near the nucleus. It is sound and transparent. Its central part which is dense is known as 'centriole'. They play an important role in the division of cells.

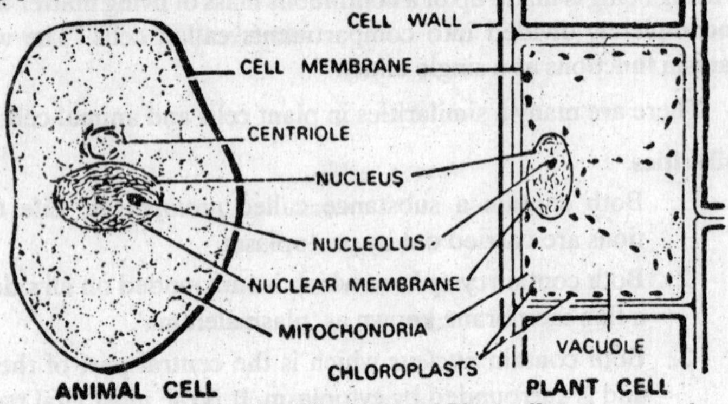

Fig. 16.1. Animal cell and Plant cell.

Cell Division

Fleming (1880) studied the details of division of *somatic cells* and called it *mitosis.* Strasburger (1888) and Winiwater (1890) studied the details of double division that occurs prior to the formation of **gametes.** They found the reduction of chromosome number in *gametes* as compared to parent cells. Farmer and Moore (1905) named this division as **meiosis.**

Cell cycle

The series of changes which involve the growth and division of a cell is called *cell cycle.*

16.3 SPACE BIOLOGY

Present age is called the space age. Man is acquiring more and more knowledge about the moon and planets etc. He has already landed on moon and planning similar projects for other planets. Projects have already been undertaken by some countries to land on mars. Space rockets are commonly used in all such projects. These rockets are fitted with apparatus and equipment which help us to get information about life as these planets, environment of there planets and other relevant data. It is hoped that man will be able to establish a communication to and fro the planet of his choice with the help of space-stations. Man also hopes to establish colonies on planets.

In this type of projects the space-stations shall have to be established for transportation of necessities of life and instruments of communications. These space-stations will have to be provided with work-shops for carrying out repair work for any defects in space-station. To man these work-shops scientists and other crew members are to be seat to there space-stations.

Some of the important problems which astronauts face during launching of space-rocket are as under:

1. During firing of rockets, astronauts are subjected to two opposing forces (gravitational pull of the earth and the upward thrust) and there is a danger of their bones being crushed. To save themselve, they are advised to lie down in perpendicular position to the direction of motion during upward flight.

2. When the space-ship is put in its orbit it no more feels gravitational pull of earth and the astronauts experience weightlessness. They simply float in their cabin. It becomes difficult for them even to drink water. They are therefore required to press the bottle of water to push the water through a tube in their throats.

3. In space-craft in weightlessness condition there is a danger of arteries getting burst. Since brain is not provided with its proper quantum of blood astronauts feel a "black out". To overcome these

some physical exercises have been desired which astronauts are required to perform for about four hours a day.

4. Disposal of human waste in space in another important problem. If not disposed properly it is likely to create pollution and man will not be able to stay for long in space.

However our knowledge of life sciences has helped us to find solutions for these problems and to make it possible for man to stay for long periods in space.

The problem of pollution in the absence of proper disposal of waste has been solved. Because of researches in life sciences now it is possible to purify the waste and convert it into useful products without polluting the atmosphere of space-craft.

Space-laboratories have been installed and from researches in these laboratories new medicines for curing incurable diseases, such as cancer, have been developed.

Now we are pretty sure that man can survive and function in space. Space-medicine which is a branch of biological and medical sciences makes assessment of health risks of astronauts. Scopolamine, a drug, is used to overcome space sickness.

The most serious problem because of weightlessness appears in the form of bone degeneration and muscle wasting. A three months stay in space is likely to cause a loss of about 20% of bones (by volume). It is about the same degree of degeneration as is observed in a 95 years old on earth. The cause of this degeneration has been traced to the calcium loss from bones. Some rigorous exercises have now been framed to check this loss and degeneration of bones.

Radiation problem is another major problem. Special shields are provided on space-craft to protect astronauts from radiations. Powerful medicines and drugs are also being developed to counteract the effect of radiations.

It is hoped that due to various researches in life sciences astronauts will be able to lead a healthy and enduring life free from all diseases. They will be provided with enough energy and resources to carry out the tedious tasks assigned to them. This will ultimately lead to the fulfilment of man's dream to live and work in space safely and comfortably.

16.4 BIOLOGY AND HEALTHY ENVIRONMENT

Physical science help us in understanding the material aspects of life, the life sciences help us to understand the life in all its aspects. The study of life science is found quite useful for healthy living in healthy environment.

1. *Knowledge of body structure systems and their functions* help us in leading a healthy life.

2. *Knowledge about balanced diet and hygenic principles* also help us to lead a healthy life. The balanced diet provides us with all important constituents of food required by our body. The knowledge of all body systems help us in regulating our life routine and adjust it in such a way so as to keep all the systems in proper order.

3. *Safety from diseases.* The 'germ theory' propounded by Luis Posteur have helped diseases like T.B., small-pox, cholera, plague etc.

Diseases, caused by virus, such as dephtheria, piles etc. can be prevented and cured because of sufficient knowledge about them.

4. *Solutions to food problem.* There has been a tremendous increase in food crops production which has helped us to solve our food problem. All this has become possible because of study of life sciences which provided us the means to save our crops from destruction by locust, white-ants, harmful insects etc.

The increase in crop yield has been possible because of study of soil, study of plant physiology etc. The use of chemical fertilizers has been an important source in the increase in production of foodgrains various hybrid varieties have been discovered which resist various plant diseases, nature in lesser time and are high yielding varieties. Another important factor contributing in increase of foodgrain production is the significant imporovement in the sources and methods of irrigation.

The knowledge of life sciences has also helped us in developing a large number of quality paultry farms. From such farms we get a large quantity of eggs and meat.

Fisheries have also been developed in large numbers. All these have helped us to solve our food problem.

5. *Population control.* In this century we face the problem of population explosion and controlling population is the crying need of

the hour. A knowledge of human physiology and reproductive system has been used to devise artificial means of checking this population explosion. Government of India has also taken other measures for checking the population growth. These are as under:

(*i*) Providing population education.

(*ii*) Increase in marriage age for both sexes.

(*iii*) Proper and timely use of various birth control methods.

6. *Solving Environmental Pollution Problem*. The population of environment in general and air and water pollution in particular are very serious problems of the day. To check the pollution we have taken various measures and adopted various methods. Some of these are as under.

(*i*) Replacement of coal by liquid petroleum gas and electricity for running factories.

(*ii*) Devising better combustion engines which produce less harmful gases.

(*iii*) Converting surface drains into underground sewerage.

(*iv*) Production of bio-gas from sewage waste.

(*v*) Sinking more and more deep wells in villages to provide drinking water.

7. *Preservations of Plants, Birds and Animals.* We know that plant life and animal life are inter-dependent. They help us to maintain oxygen cycle and carbon dioxide cycle in nature. These cycles will be disturbed if proper balance is not maintained between plants and animals. For their we should protect the forests and wild animals. Birds are useful in dispersing seeds and thus growth of plants. Some wild carnivorous animals are useful to agriculturists as they decrease the population of those animals and birds which are harmful to plants. All these help us in maintaining a delicate balance in nature.

8. *Preservation of Food Products.* The study of life sciences have now provided us knowledge of how to protect our food from germs and bacteria of various diseases. It has helped us in storage of food for longer time without their being spoiled.

APPENDICES

Appendix I

Suggested Books for Biological Sciences

1. Allen, L.R. Investigations in biology for tropical schools Oxford U.P.
2. Association for Science Education: Science master's book. Edited by B.S. Beaumont and others, Murray.
3. Belfield, W. Models and methods in practical biology for secondary schools. (Common Wealth and International Library). Pergamon Press.
4. Tricker, R.A.R. The contribution of science to education. Mills and Boon.
5. Bryant, J.J., ed. Biology teaching in schools involving experiment or demonstration with animals or with pupils. Associatiaon for Science Education.
6. Crossan, C.J.A. Teachear's guide to biology in the primary school. Collins.
7. Devon Trust for Nature Conservation. School projects in natural history, Devon Trust for Conservation.
8. Greensill. T.M. Handbook for rural science teachers in tropical areas. Evans.
9. Hurry, S.W. and Mackean, D.G. Enquiries in biology. Teachera's guide. Murray.
10. Hutchinson, M.M. Children as naturalists. 1966. Allen and Unwin.
11. Mahoney, R. Laboratory techniques in zoology. Butterworths.

12. Nuffield Foundation Science Teaching Project: Biology. Teacher's guide 1. Introducing living things.
13. Purvis, M.J. and others. Laboratory techniques in Botany. 2nd edition. Butterworth.
14. UNESCO. New trends in biology teaching. Vol. I. Prepared by R. Heller.

Appendix II

Kurukshetra University

B.Ed. Syllabus of
Teaching of Life Science for 1986 and Onwards

Note: Students will be required to attempt five questions out of ten, selecting one from each Section and not more than two from any Section.

SECTION A

(*i*) Place of Life Science in school curriculum.

(*ii*) Modern developments in Life Science and its impact on the school. Life science curriculum.

(*iii*) Professional growth of Life Science Teacher. Life Science journals, instructional materials, etc.

(*iv*) Role of Life Science in our lives.

(*v*) Aims and objectives of teaching Life Science.

SECTION B

(*i*) Syllabus of Life Science in a school. Its analytical study.

(*ii*) Major units of secondary Life Science syllabus and development of experiments involved therein.

(*iii*) Major concepts in Life Science. Significant development in the field of their relationship with school Life Science.

(*iv*) Developing a Life Science Programme. Experiments in India (NCERT) and other countries towards improving Life Science Programme.

SECTION C

(*i*) Training in scientific method through teaching of Life Science. Demonstrating experiments and individual practicals.

(*ii*) Student's projects-setting and mainatenance of an aquarium.

(*iii*) Problem-Solving.

(*iv*) Life Science laboratory; developing a museum; Life science equipment and materials connected with middle, high and training institutions.

(*v*) Problems connected with Life Science learning.

(*vi*) Lesson plan.

(*vii*) Teaching aids.

(*viii*) Evaluataion.

Practical Work (Not to be included in the theory paper)

(*i*) Setting and maintenance of acquarium.

(*ii*) Collection, culturing and preservation techniques for:

(*a*) Plants

(*b*) Animals.

(*iii*) Preparation of laboratory stains.

(*iv*) Preparation of temporary and permanent mounts-atleast 10 permanent specimens, 10 slides and 1 skeleton.

(*v*) Arranging at least 5 demonstration experiments.

(*vi*) Carrying out an investigatory project. Submission of its report with all the data.

Appendix III

Maharishi Dayanand University, Rohtak

B.Ed. Syllabus of
Teaching of Life Sciences for 1986 and onwards

Unit 1. Place of Life Sciences: Inclusion of life sciences and present position of life sciences in the school curriculum.

Unit 2. Aims and Objectives of teaching of Life Sciences:

2.1. General aims of teaching of life Sciences:

2.2. Formulation of instructional objectives of life sciences.

Unit 3. Methodology of life sciences and methods of teaching life sciences.

3.1. Lecture-cum-demonstration Method:
Pre-demonstration preparations. Setting up of the demonstration, post demonstration activities. Illustration with suitable content (Actual demonstration of the above method).

3.2. Project method:
Selection of suitable project of life sciences, planning of the selected project. Execution, evaluation and recording of the selected project.

3.3 Heuristic approach with pertinent example from contents related to particular class.

3.4. Lesson planning based on the above methods.

3.5. Problem solving approach.

Note: Every specific method of teaching of life sciences is to be demonstrated by selecting some appropriate content.

Unit 4. Evaluation in life sciences:

Nature, purpose and technique, preparation of objective based and objective type tests, evaluation of practical experiments in Biology. Assessment of projects and sessional work

Unit 5. Co-curricular Activities in Life Sciences:

5.1. Importance and organisation of science club, Hobbies and fairs.

5.2. Biological Excursions and visits to places of scientific interest.

Unit 6. Teaching aids in Life Sciences:

Charts, diagrams, models, specimens, their use and importance.

Unit 7. Problems connected with teaching of life sciences:

7.1. Identification of the problems.

7.2. Remedial teaching and enrichment programme, preparing a diagnostic test in life sciences.

Unit 8. Professional growth of life science teacher:

8.1. New trends and experiments in life sciences, Programmes with special reference to projects in India and abroad.

8.2. Life Science journals and instructional material.

8.3. National Talent Search Scheme (N.T.S.S.)

8.4. Biology work-shops, seminars, Teacher associations,

8.5. National and state level institutions of science.

Unit 9. CONTENT PORTION.

9.1. Biology and Healthy environment.

9.2. Space Biology

9.3. Cell structure and cell theory

9.4. Life history and scientific contribution of Dr. Hargobind Khurana.

Practical Work: Any two of the following:

(*i*) Preparation of objective-based tests on a topic IX or X class.

(*ii*) Collection of material such as cutting of science articles and pictures from news-papers and science magazines.

(*iii*) Arranging atleast five demonstrations of Biological experiments.

(*iv*) One group project by students.

(*v*) Improvisation of four items related to topics of school stage and using them in the discussion lessons.

Appendix IV

Delhi/All India Senior School Certficate Class XII Examination

SYLLABUS FOR BIOLOGY

Unit 1. Multicellulariaty: Structure & Function Plant Life

Introduction: Multicellular way of life in plants and animals. The basic philosophy of form and function in plants and animals. Tissue system in flowering plants: meristematic and permanent Mineral nutrition-essential elements, major functions of different elements, passive and active uptake of mineral. Modes of nutrition, transport of solutes and water in plants. Photosynthesis: photochemical and bio-synthetic phases, diversity in photosynthetic pathways, photosynthetic electron transport and photophosphorylation, photorespiration Transpiration and exchange of gases stomatal mechanism. Osmo-regulation in plants: water relations in plant cells, Water potential Reproduction and development in plants: major forms of plant reproduction asexual and sexual, brief account of mode of sexual reproduction in multicellular. Lower plants with emphasis on antheridia and archegonia. Structure and functions of flower: development of male and female gametophytes in angiosperms; pollination, fertilization and development of endosperm, embryo, seed and fruit. Differentiation and organ formation. Plant hormones and growth regulation: action of plant hormones in relation to seed dormancy and germination, apical dominance, senesesoence and absi-cission. Applications of synthetic growth regulators. A brief account of growth and movement in plants. Photomorophogenesis in plants including a brief account of phytochrome.

Note: 'Read' – Introduction .....in plants and animals as 'Form and function'.

Unit-2. Multicellularity: Structure and Function-Animal: Life

Animal tissues, epithelial, connective, muscular, nerve. Animal nutrition; organs of digestion and digestive processes, nutritional requirements for carbohydrates, proteins, fats, minerals and vitamins; nutritional imbalances and deficiency diseases: Gas exchange and transport; Pulmonary gas exchange and organs involved, transport of gases in blood, gas exchange in aqueous media. Circulation; closed and open vascular systems. Structure and pumping action of heart, arterial blood pressure, lymph. Excretion and osmoregulation; aminotelism, ureotelism, uricotelism excretion of water and urea with special reference to man. Role of kidney in regulation of plasma, osmolarity on the basis of nephron structure, skin and lungs in excretion. Hormonal co-ordination; hormones of mammals, role of hormones as messengers, and regulators. Nervous coordination: central autonomic and physiology peripheral nervous systems, receptors effectors, reflex action, basic physiology of special senses, integrative control by neuroendocrinal systems. Locomotion: Joints, muscle movements, types of skeletal muscles according to types of movement, basic aspects of human skeleton. Reproduction; human reproduction, female reproductive cycles. Embryonic development in mammals (upto three germ layers). Growth, repair and ageing.

Unit 3. Continuity of life

Heredity and variation: Introduction, Mendel's experiments with peas and idea of factors. Mendel's laws of inheritance. Genes: packaging of hereditary material in prokaryotes-bacterial chromosome; plasmid and eukaryote chromosomes. Cell division. Extra-nuclear genes viral genes. Linkage and genetic maps. Sex determination and sex linkage. Genetic material an its replication. Gene manipulation. Gene expression; genetic code, transcription. Translation gene regulation. Molecular basis of differntiation.

Unit 4. Origin and Evaluation of life

Origin of life: Living and non-living. Chemical evolution organic evolution; oparin Medel's ideas. Miller-Urey eperiments Interrelationship among living organisms and evidences; Common features of life processes-energy transformation, genetic code Protein synthetic machinery. Fossil record including geological time scale.

Morphological evidence-homology vestigeal organs embryological similarities.

Darwin's two major contributors. Common origin of living organisms and recombination as sources and variability, selection acts upon variation, adaptation (Lederberg's replica plating experiment for indirect selection of bacterial mutants) reproductive violation, speciation. Role of selection change and drift in determining gametic composition of a population. Selected examples industrial melanism: drug resistance, mimicry, malaria in relation to G-6 PD dificiency and sickle cell disease. Human evolution: paleontological evidence, man's place among mammals. Brief idea of Dryopitheous. Australopitheous, Homo erectus, H. neanderalensis. Cromagnon man and Homo sapiens, Human chromosomes similarity in different racial groups. Comparison with cromosomes of non-human Primates to indicate common origin, cultural biological evolution.

Unit 5. Application of Biology

Introduction. Role of biology in the amelioration of human problems. Domestication of plant's historical account improvement of crop plants: Principles of plant breeding an plant breeding and plant introduction. Use of fertilizers, economic and ecological aspects.

Use of pesticides: advantages and hazards. Biological methods of pest control. Crops today, Current concerns, gene pools and genetic conservation. Under-utilized crops with potential uses for oil seeds, medicines, beverages, spices, fodder. New crops-Leucaena (subabul) Jojobe, Guayule winged bean etc. Bio fertilisers-green manure. Crop residues and nitrogen fixation (symbiotic, non-symbiotic). Applications of tissue culture and genetic engineering in crops. Domestication and introduction of animals. Livestock, poultry, fisheries (fresh water, marine-aqua-culture) Improvement of animals: principles of animal breeding. Major animals disease an their control Insects and their Products (silk, honey, wax and Lac). Bioenergy-biomass, wood (combustion gasification, ethanol) Cow dung cakes, gobar gas, plants and sources of hydrocarbons for Producing petroleum, ethanol from starch and lignocellulose. Biotechnology, a brief historical account-manufacture of cheese. Yoghurt, alcohal, Yeast, vitamins, organic acids anti-biotics, steroids, destrins. Scaling up laboratory findings to industrial production. Role of genetic engineering and tissue culture: production of insulin, human growth hormones, interferon. Communicable diseases including STD and diseases spread through blood transfusion (hepatitis AIDS etc.). Immune response, vaccines and antisera. Allergies and inflammations. Degenerative disease symptoms and control. Inherited diseases and dysfunctions, sex linked diseases, genetic incompatibilities and genetic councelling. Cancer-major types, causes, diagnosis and treatment. Tissue and organ transplantation. Community health serivices and measure blood banks. Mental health, smoking alcoholism and drug addiction-Physiological symptoms and control measures. Industries wastes toxicology, pollution-related diseases. Biomedical engineering spare parts for man, instruments for diagnosis of diseases and care. Human population growth, problems and control inequalities between sexes-Control measures, test-tube babies, amniocentesis. Future of Biology.

Note: Unit-Application

Only the following portions of this unit are to be evaluated:

(*i*) Biofertilizers ... nitrogen fixation (sympiotic, non-sympiotic).

(*ii*) Communicable diseases ... blood transfusion (hepatitis AIDS etc.)

(*iii*) "Immune response ... antisera – Allergies & inflammations".

(*iv*) Inherited diseases ... and genetic counselling. Cancer major types, causes, diagnosis & treatment.

(*v*) 'Mental health ... and control measure'.

(*vi*) 'Human population ... test tube babies eminocentesis'.